CORNELL STUDIES IN CLASSICAL PHILOLOGY

EDITED BY

JAMES HUTTON * G. M. KIRKWOOD
GORDON M. MESSING * PIERO PUCCI

VOLUME XXXVIII

Poetry and Poetics from
Ancient Greece to the Renaissance
Studies in Honor of James Hutton

Early Greek Monody
by G. M. Kirkwood

The Attalids of Pergamon
by Esther V. Hansen

Sophrosyne
by Helen North

St. Jerome as a Satirist
by David S. Wiesen

JAMES HUTTON

POETRY AND POETICS FROM ANCIENT GREECE TO THE RENAISSANCE

Studies in Honor of James Hutton

Edited by G. M. KIRKWOOD

CORNELL UNIVERSITY PRESS

ITHACA AND LONDON

International Standard Book Number 0-8014-0847-4
Library of Congress Catalog Card Number 74-10410

Printed in the United States of America

Preface

Volumes in this series have in the past consisted of single monographs on subjects related to the field of classical philology. The present volume is not an indication that the editors mean to change this long tradition henceforth. On the contrary, this book is intended as a unique departure from tradition, to pay a tribute of recognition to James Hutton, Kappa Alpha Professor Emeritus of Classics at Cornell University. Among James Hutton's contributions to scholarship has been his uniquely generous service as an editorial counselor of remarkable powers of discrimination and breadth of knowledge. Many studies in this series have benefited from this generosity of learning, as have countless volumes of the scholarly work of his friends and colleagues at Cornell and throughout the world of humanistic literary study. Dedication of a special volume of *Cornell Studies* seems therefore particularly appropriate. The range of the articles in this volume corresponds in some measure to the breadth and variety of James Hutton's range in literary studies.

The editorial committee for this volume consists of the present senior members of the Cornell Department of Classics: Gordon M. Messing, Piero Pucci, Michael C. Stokes, and the undersigned. To keep the length of the book within the normal limits of the series we invited contributions only from present or past Cornell Classics colleagues of long standing and a few other friends whose work and interests have brought them close to James Hutton. From the uniformly enthusiastic responses of those who were invited to participate we are aware of how much more broadly inclusive our list of contributors could have been.

G. M. KIRKWOOD

Ithaca, New York
June 1974

Contents

Abbreviations

Abhd. Sächs. Ak.	*Abhandlungen der sächsischen Akademie der Wissenschaften*
AJP	*American Journal of Philology*
CCL	*Corpus Christianorum, Series Latina*
CR	*Classical Review*
CSEL	*Corpus Scriptorum Ecclesiasticorum Latinorum*
GRBS	*Greek, Roman and Byzantine Studies*
HSCP	*Harvard Studies in Classical Philology*
MGH	*Monumenta Germaniae Historica*
Mus. Helv.	*Museum Helveticum*
PL	*Patrologia Latina*
RE	*Revue d'esthétique*
REG	*Revue des études grecques*
RFIC	*Rivista di Filologia e di Istruzione Classica*
Rh. Mus.	*Rheinisches Museum*
SB Heid. Ak.	*Sitzungsberichte der Heidelberger Akademie*
SIFC	*Studi Italiani di Filologia Classica*
TAPA	*Transactions of the American Philological Association*

POETRY AND POETICS
FROM ANCIENT GREECE
TO THE RENAISSANCE

The Conclusion of the *Odyssey*

FRIEDRICH SOLMSEN

The modest tribute of gratitude offered here to James Hutton, a testimony of friendship rather than of scholarship, makes no secret of its experimental character. It owes much to B. A. van Groningen, James's dear friend, whose book *La composition littéraire archaïque grecque*[1] has led us to recognize and appreciate some characteristics of the early Greek epic. Dealing with Hesiod, van Groningen shows by a careful analysis that the *Theogony* was "extensible" and that of the *Works and Days*, a collection of wise counsels and practical instructions, the same should be true "à plus forte raison."[2] Some of the "extensions" or expansions are Hesiod's own, others are due to rhapsodes who probably often composed them to satisfy an audience asking for fuller information. Van Groningen, while finding additions by other hands at the end of the *Theogony*, considers most of the "Days" (*Op.* 765-821) as genuine and assigns to another poet only the last seven lines of the poem (vv. 822-828) as well as the *Ornithomanteia* announced in *Opera* 828.[3] Here I regret to dissent, since in my view not only the "Days" but a good deal that precedes them offer excellent illus-

---

[1] *Verhandelingen der Koninklijke Nederlandse Akademie*, n.r. 65 (1958), 2.

[2] Pages 302 f.; see the entire chs. xi and xii, esp. pp. 275 ff., 286 ff.

[3] *Ibid.*, pp. 291 ff.; see also his remarks in *Gnomon* 37 (1965), 332. For different views on what is and what is not "authentic" see esp. F. Jacoby's (Berlin, 1930) and M. L. West's (Oxford, 1966) editions of the *Theogony*; Wilamowitz's (Berlin, 1928) and A. Colonna's (Milan and Varese, 1969) of the *Opera* (*et Dies*); A. Rzach's (Berlin, 1902 and 1913), P. Mazon's (Paris, 1928) and my own (Oxford, 1970) edition of both works; and, besides many other special studies, *Entretiens sur l'antiquité*, VII (Fondation Hardt, Vandœuvre, Geneva, 1962). The new *RE* article "Hesiod" (Suppl. XII, [1970], s.v.) is unfortunately vitiated by an extremely onesided conservatism; cf. West's critique of this method in *CR* 18 (1968), 27 ff.

trations of van Groningen's approach. In any case, his approach is firmly established.

How far is it possible to adopt the same point of view toward Homer? Prudence may warn us to stay out of the labyrinth of the Homeric question or to be content with the thought that Homeric scholars, as far as they are not out-and-out unitarians (and even some of these),[4] recognize additions within the body of the epics. The voice of prudence is wise and true. We do not mean to ignore it and shall in this essay confine ourselves as strictly as we can to concluding sections where special conditions prevail and facilitate "a growth through accretion." Thus, to go back to Hesiod, we believe that in the *Theogony* to a stock of genuine divine marriages there were added first some more of these (vv. 930 ff.), and then some unions between goddesses and mortals (vv. 963-1018), and, when these in turn were followed by unions between gods and mortal women, this subject continued to grow at a rate which made necessary the development of the *Catalogues* as a separate epic. Correspondingly the *Works* grew by the addition first of a variety of taboos (vv. 724-759), unworthy of Hesiod in content as well as language, then of the "Days" (vv. 765-825 or 828), and finally of the *Ornithomanteia*, which need not have moved on a lower level of superstition than the preceding two sections; yet again for some reason—perhaps of length—it was treated as a separate poem.[5] Homeric scholars do not seem aware of such favorable conditions for growth at the end of an epic.

Surely there are great differences between the two kinds of epics; we must not expect to find close parallels, and to say it at once, our chances in the *Iliad* are nil. For no matter what modern analysts may think of Ω, how "late" they hold it to be, and whether or not another large scale composition, the "true" or "great Iliad,"

---

[4] K. Reinhardt, *Von Werken und Formen* (Godesberg, 1948), p. 137, admits additions in λ, and in *Die Ilias und ihr Dichter* (Göttingen, 1961), pp. 293 ff., treats the 'Doloneia' as unique. So do others, e.g., W. Schadewaldt, *Iliasstudien* (*Abh. Sächs. Ak.* 43.6 [1938]) 142, n. 4.

[5] I do not mean to exclude its origin as a separate poem; the link at v. 828 is probably secondary. For the "Days" see my fuller discussion in *TAPA* 94 (1963), 293 ff., reprinted in *Kleine Schriften* (Hildesheim, 1968), I, 22 ff.

carried the story to the death of Achilles,[6] the fact is that once Ω had become the conclusion, it was accepted as such. Evidently rhapsodes and public appreciated—more than some recent scholarly critics—the ethos of this Book and were happy to have the *Iliad* end with the reconciliation of Priam and Achilles and the return of Hector's body.[7] If the narrative had to continue, it had to do so where Ω ended, and the continuation probably would be another epic. The *Aethiopis* which included the death of Achilles began with the line: ὡς οἵ γ' ἀμφίεπον τάφον Ἕκτορος · ἦλθε δ' Ἀμαζών, that is, the last line of Ω appropriately changed.

In the *Odyssey* the auspices are far better. The ancient critics show us the way. Aristophanes of Byzantium and Aristarchus were agreed on the "end" of the *Odyssey*; ψ 296, where Odysseus and Penelope ἀσπάσιοι λέκτροιο παλαιοῦ θέσμον ἵκοντο, was the πέρας or τέλος τῆς Ὀδυσσείας.[8] The meaning of these statements is however far from certain.[9] Was ψ 296 for them the actual, "physical" end of the *Odyssey* or does the action attain its goal and reach its destination there? Perhaps the ancient critics meant the one as well as the other; realizing that the action was completed, they may have inferred that this verse should be or had once been the physical ending. Even if they never had seen or heard of a copy that did not go beyond this verse, they may still have found in the copies at their disposal unusually large divergences after it. Such

[6] Wilamowitz, *Die Ilias und Homer* (Berlin, 1916), p. 71, recognized the merits of "das schöne Gedicht" but felt a sentimental tinge in its beauty and was sure "wie der Dichter, ein grosser Dichter, dem man nachfühlen und vorfühlen darf, weiter erzählt hat" (pp. 78 f. "unendlich schöner") from Hector's death to Achilles' own. See p. 321, where he speaks incidentally of the conclusion as inviting "*Umarbeitung und Erweiterung.*"

[7] Achilles' death αὐτίκα μεθ' Ἕκτορα (Σ 96, 98; cf. X 359 f.) is known to the hearer or reader of Ω, adding pathos and depth.

[8] See *schol. ad loc.* (several versions in the edition of W. Dindorf [Oxford, 1855]). μέν *solitarium* after pronouns (in ψ 295 οἳ μὲν ἔπειτα), though not listed for Homer by Denniston, occurs e.g. A 421, K 442, passages indicated by W. Theiler, *Untersuchungen zur antiken Literatur* (Berlin, 1970), p. 126. This should allay some worries.

[9] Cf. the disquisition by Denys Page, *The Homeric Odyssey* (Oxford, 1955), p. 101 and n. 2, where further references will be found.

possibilities need not be ruled out;[10] yet we may as well credit the
Alexandrian scholars with a sound critical perception and admit
that modern analysis confirms their judgment. Most scholars who
are not committed to the unitarian creed agree on the presence of
later additions in the *Odyssey* and do not consider ω as a part of the
"real" or "original" *Odyssey*—we venture to call it the *Odyssey* of
a great poet.[11] In the following pages we shall concentrate on ω,
and then briefly discuss the bearing which the analysis of ω has on
the preceding Book, ψ.

The analysts of the last two or three generations have made
many valuable observations. Evidently ω consists of several quite
different episodes. Denys Page distinguishes three such episodes,
each of which he examines from the linguistic as well as the artistic
point of view.[12] However he does not decide, in fact he barely
raises the question, whether the three sections have different
authors.[13] This attitude is shared by other Homeric scholars. Once
the continuation after ψ 296 is separated from the main body of
the epic and its artistic shortcomings are castigated, no interest is
shown about the number of authors at work in ω. Moreover there

---

[10] The Peisistratean *recensio* has been rehabilitated by R. Merkelbach,
Rh. Mus. 95 (1952), 23 ff., with whom Page, von der Mühll, and others agree.
Recensio is a treacherous word. If even the edition of Aristarchus did not monop-
olize the transmission, a text adopted in sixth century Athens is a potiori
unlikely to have ousted all others.

[11] Perhaps even "*the* great poet"; for I cannot share the conviction of Eduard
Schwartz (*Die Odyssee* [Munich, 1924], esp. pp. 292 ff.), von der Mühll, and
others that the last poet of the Odyssey compares poorly with his precursor(s)
whose work he again and again corrupts by changes and additions. I do not
minimize problems like those presented by σ 158-303, an episode not intended
for "our" *Odyssey*. Here, as often, the difficulty is to find the right standard of
"unity."

[12] Page (see n. 5, pp. 101 ff.) actually distinguishes four episodes in the
"continuation." The first of these is ψ 297-372. See below pp. 27 f.

[13] "Our poet" (p. 112); "a later poet or poets" (p. 116 in a hypothetical
context). And yet Page notices in the second episode of ω more departures
from normal Homeric usage than in any other. ω was declared "einheitlich"
by many analysts from A. Kirchhoff in his fundamental *Die Homerische Odyssee*
(Berlin, 1879), p. 557 n., to W. Theiler, *Mus. Helv.* 7 (1950), 108, = *Untersuchungen* (see above n. 8), p. 73, and W. Schadewaldt, *SB Heid. Ak.* (1959) 2,
20, 25.

is a tendency to find in ω the same poets who have been active in the main body of the *Odyssey*. This tendency is not confined to analysts like von der Mühll who are content to divide the *Odyssey*[14] between two poets and are understandably reluctant to change this economic procedure at the end; it is shared by scholars who generously identify a larger number of authors. There are a few exceptions,[15] but it has not been realized how easy and tempting it was for talented rhapsodes to add something new after ψ 296. Our hypothesis that ω embodies additions composed by *three* different poets requires a fresh consideration of the Book.

The first episode is known as the "second Nekyia." Its author was probably inspired by the Nekyia in λ, and if we believe with Wilamowitz that poetic visits to the Underworld had come into fashion, it should not surprise us to find some new ideas about the behavior of the dead.[16] The dead cannot again and again go through the ceremony of drinking blood; in ω their φρένες are ἔμπεδοι. After vv. 1 ff. we would expect the arrival of the dead suitors to be the dominating theme, but the poet is actually preoccupied with something different.[17] Time does not seem to exist in the Underworld; at the very moment when the dead suitors arrive, the ψυχή of Agamemnon meets for the first time those of Achilles and his friends. Agamemnon calls Achilles happy (v. 36) because after he had been killed and his body saved, extraordinary tributes of honor and lament were paid to him by men and by

---

[14] See the apparatus of his edition on ψ 296, his article "Odysee," *RE*, Suppl. VII (1940), 76 ff., as well as his lecture, *Die Dichter der Odyssee* (Aarau, 1941), pp. 22 f. I have left the 'Telemachy' out of account.

[15] Wilamowitz, *Die Heimkehr des Odysseus* (Berlin, 1927), p. 81, recognizes the later insertion of the "second Nekyia"; G. S. Kirk, *The Songs of Homer* (Cambridge, 1962), pp. 249 ff., regards ω as a "patchwork" that shows in language, taste, and poetic capacity the decadence of the epic. I share Kirk's skepticism (pp. 238 f.) concerning the large influence of the *Telegony* on these accretions; however see below n. 41.

[16] Wilamowitz, *Heimkehr*, p. 81. For an impresive list of new features see pp. 117 ff.

[17] I find at most a slight awkwardness in εὖρον (v. 15). The grammatical subject is clearly the same as in v. 13, i.e., the suitors, although the poet forthwith turns to other matters. Page (p. 119) greatly exaggerates the difficulty.

gods.[18] On his own disgraceful death Agamemnon touches briefly
at the close of his speech (vv. 95-97). For eighty lines (vv. 15-97)
we have lost sight of the new arrivals; finally (in vv. 105 ff.) one
of the suitors, Amphimedon, is given an opportunity to report
what happened when Odysseus unexpectedly returned to his
home. Not everything in this report tallies with the second half of
the *Odyssey*, but it is easy to see that the only larger divergence is
in maiorem Penelopes gloriam. According to Amphimedon's version
she arranged the contest with Odysseus' bow not because she was
ready for a new marriage but because she had a secret understanding with her husband (whom she therefore must have
recognized beforehand).[19] This gives Agamemnon once more a
reason to call one of his fellow warriors happy—ὄλβιε Λαέρταο παῖ
(v. 192; cf. v. 36)—this time on account of his wife whose μεγάλη
ἀρετή (v. 193) contrasts sharply with the conduct of his own wife.
The one will become a "song of delight" (vv. 187 f.), the other a
"hateful song" (v. 200).

The author of this episode clearly composed it as a sequel to the
events in the two preceding Books, especially in χ. Nothing in χ
or ψ points ahead to this episode; nothing in the subsequent
sections presupposes it.

The second episode, Odysseus' meeting with his father, corresponds to our expectation; for at the end of ψ (vv. 359 f.) Odysseus
has announced his intention of going to his farm to "see" his
father. When he arrives at the farmhouse (vv. 205 ff.), he immediately takes control and gives instructions. Next he looks for
Laertes. On finding him, Odysseus is moved to tears by the sight
of the old man dirty and hard at work in self-inflicted suffering.
He wonders whether he should at once embrace his father and tell
him about his return or whether he first ἐξερέοιτο ἕκαστά τε

---

[18] On these the poet dwells with obvious delight, and it is here (esp. vv. 47 ff.)
that he finds the best opportunity to display his (epic? dramatic? perhaps
after all, melodramatic) talent.

[19] It might also be argued that Amphimedon, who could not know what had
passed between Penelope and Odysseus, reconstructed a "likely" sequence of
events; yet psychological explanations of the kind, if at all admissable, are less
convincing than a poetic purpose. I cannot follow Page (pp. 121 ff.) or Kirk
(pp. 245 ff.) in the large inferences they draw from the discrepancies.

πειρήσαιτο (v. 238), slightly cryptic words whose meaning does not become much clearer when Odysseus decides for the course now described as κερτομίοις ἔπεσιν διαπειρηθῆναι (v. 240). Actually we may as well consider the alternatives as pondered by the poet and the choice as made by him. The motif of trying out a person's reaction by a teasing, fictitious story, belongs to the inventory of the *Odyssey*.[20] It usually takes the form of Odysseus pretending to be another person, yet in some way connected with Odysseus; in this role he reports that he has met Odysseus, who is on his way home and likely to be back soon. In the epic inventory we should include also the technique of suspense, greatly advanced by the *Odyssey* and this time carried to the point where Laertes breaks down in an agony of sorrow and despair (vv. 315-319). Here finally Odysseus' own emotions respond. He reveals himself to his father, adding at once that on the preceding day he has killed the suitors. Laertes, again in accordance with established practice, asks for "proof" (σῆμα, v. 329), and only when Odysseus has satisfied this demand and removed the last doubt about his identity does Laertes accept him as his son. He is again on the point of breaking down, this time not from sorrow but from joy and happiness (vv. 345-350). Odysseus barely keeps him on his feet, and both return to the farm house (v. 362), where in the meantime a meal has been prepared and where soon some old friends appear, who are delighted at Odysseus' return and whom he welcomes—although not as warmly as we might think natural (vv. 387-411).

We shall speculate later[21] about the reason for this rather casual reception of old and faithful friends and consider in particular the possibility that another poet has changed or shortened parts of the original text. For the present, we refrain from holding the poet of the second episode responsible for such flaws. In fact he even deserves credit for his treatment of suspense and of emotions,

---

[20] Wilamowitz (*Heimkehr*, p. 82), admitting that there is no need for Odysseus' "testing" of his father, explains simply and truly: "Da wollte der Verfasser ein Gegenbild zu den Lügenreden des Odysseus in ξ ρ τ liefern."

[21] See below p. 26.

particularly of juxtaposed and contrasting emotions.[22] In his handling of Laertes' crisis of despair he shows a certain originality (about his success with the other crisis it is again necessary to suspend judgment).[23] Quite clearly, had our poet chosen the alternative course of producing the recognition, he would have deprived himself of opportunities for displaying his peculiar talent. Even in that case however it would be hard to imagine Odysseus simply walking up to his father and introducing himself without the barest minimum of psychological preparation.

The third episode, somewhat shorter than the other two, has difficulties in getting off the ground, and almost everything that happens in the course of it looks like a miniature edition—if not like a caricature—of normal epic action. As soon as "Fama" (v. 413) spreads the news of the great slaughter, the kinsmen fetch the bodies of the suitors and carry or send them home. Then Eupeithes, father of Antinoos, with some show of grief and indignation, declares it a matter of honor not to let Odysseus go unpunished, but to avenge both the men whom he took to Troy and failed to bring home and those whom he killed on his return (vv. 425-438). His appeal is close to success when advocates of caution appear. Two men who were present at the killing are sure that Odysseus slew the suitors with divine help (vv. 439-449), and of the kinsmen themselves one is old and wise enough to realize that the suitors by their own ἀτασθαλίαι caused their death and that the kinsmen who did not restrain them share the responsibility (vv. 454-463). These prudent opinions cause a division in the group; still the majority[24] follow Eupeithes to a place outside the city (v. 469).

---

[22] See vv. 305-317; 315-320 (vv. 323 f.); note also v. 345. Cf. Theiler (above, n. 13), p. 73 (108). It may be surprising that at vv. 351 ff. Laertes without a word of joy at Odysseus' presence turns at once to the punishment of the suitors, first in its satisfactory, then (v. 353) in its ominous aspect. As indicated, we suspect here some tampering with the original version.

[23] See the last note.

[24] W. W. Merry (in his commentary [Oxford, 1896] ad loc.) interprets vv. 463-466 thus, and it seems to me natural to find this meaning, although the poet's idiom suffers here from obscurity; others understand that the majority remained behind.

In the meantime Zeus and Athena deliberate what is to happen and decide on a peaceful settlement (vv. 472-488).[25] Both have a hand in effecting this decision but only after a good deal of fighting has taken place, in which Odysseus and his son strike at their foes right and left and "would have killed all of them and deprived them of their way home" (v. 528), if Athena had not stopped the bloodshed. However before she acts as peacemaker, she plays a very different role. The great event in the fighting is the ἀριστεία (vv. 516-525)—again, to be sure, a miniature ἀριστεία—which old Laertes is by Athena enabled and encouraged to perform. With youthful vigor he kills Eupeithes, the moving spirit of the rebellion. This turns the battle in favor of Odysseus.

There is no denying that this section looks like a parody of normal epic techniques. The great poet of the *Odyssey* is not likely to have lost his creative powers at the end and produced such a stumbling and stuttering conclusion.[26] We may ask why this episode was conceived and worked out. Yet the major question is not this—for third rate poets may conceive and work out anything —but rather why this accretion was accepted and why consider- able alterations in ψ meant to prepare us for it were tolerated.[27] The main impulse behind the first episode of ω may be found in the vogue of νεκυῖαι; the raison d'être for the second is very probably that Laertes and his withdrawal to the farm and hard life there have been mentioned repeatedly (α 189 ff.; λ 187 ff.; ο 353), so that audiences would be curious to hear about Odysseus' meeting with him.[28] The motive for the third accretion is less

[25] There is to be love, peace, and plenty, Zeus says in effect at the end of his speech (vv. 485 f.), a generous yet curiously utopian promise which, as far as I can see, is unparalleled in Homer.

[26] Nothing seems impossible in Homeric studies. I learn (after writing the sentence in the text) that even this explanation figures in the armament of the unitarians (cf. n. 44). It is difficult to dissent from Page's harsh and scathing description of the last section.

[27] See below passim, esp. the last paragraph.

[28] This means that a rhapsode *may* have composed the episode in response to questions asked after his recital. In the design of the *Odyssey* the meeting with Laertes is (despite the frequent references to him) superfluous and point- less. Odysseus' desire is ἣν πατρίδα γαῖαν ἱκέσθαι (α 57 ff.; cf. the καπνός motif θ 15, 151 ff. al.) and to be reunited with Penelope (see esp. ε 209 ff.). No doubt

obvious; but as we have referred to passages in ψ which prepare the ground for it, we may ponder one of them, vv. 118-122. Odysseus suddenly reminds his son of the precautions the slayer of even one man considers necessary and how much more reason they have to reckon with avengers (v. 119), after they have killed so many members of the best families. This is good common sense, and if the author of a heroic epic is normally guided by loftier inspirations and moves on higher level, we realize why an addition prompted by common sense is apt to look mock-heroic.

Our account of these three sections has been brief, involving even simplification and omissions. We have not mentioned yet that our second and third episodes coalesce at the end. In the last 60 verses (489-548) two actions become one, and this leads us to consider whether the recognition scene and the revolt are not after all the work of one and the same poet. Closer study does not bear out this suspicion; nor does it suggest that a later poet has cut off the end of one episode—sc. the second—and made two developments converge. To me the evidence recommends another solution. Since the second episode is substantially complete before it converges with the third, whereas the third needs the second to move beyond its initial stages, it seems likely that the author of the third has composed the last 60 verses of ω, thereby giving his own section a περιπετεία and conclusion—and the second a sequel not germane to its ethos. Our arguments will show why other explanations of the coalescence are less probable and will confirm our thesis regarding three different poets.

The author of the final section not only has manipulated the preceding one, but he or somebody else (quite probably he), wishing to announce his subject and emphasize its importance ahead of time, has interfered with the events in ψ.[29] One instance

---

in real life a man returning after twenty years and finding his father alive would be anxious to see him too, but we are not dealing with real life and even the question whether or not Odysseus is attached to his father is irrelevant and unjustified.

[29] Wilamowitz (*Heimkehr*, pp. 83 ff.) treats also passages in υ and χ as pointing ahead to the revolt of the kinsmen and as inserted by the author of this section. Actually υ 41-55 is self-contained and does not point ahead, and χ 205 ff., if used in ω (vv. 443 ff.), need not therefore be composed for use in it.

of this has been mentioned, though from a somewhat different point of view. In early sections of ψ Penelope is so overcome by the sudden news of Odysseus' return, so utterly surprised, that she remains unable to collect her thoughts and to recognize her husband. For a long time she sits opposite him, speechless, unsure, and wavering (vv. 89-95). Telemachus, impatient and too young to understand his mother's struggle, upbraids her for what he considers an unfeeling heartlessness (vv. 96-103). His outburst causes her first utterance, in which she refers to σήματα (vv. 109 f.) known only to herself and Odysseus. Now Odysseus himself speaks, and it is a curious speech. Addressing his son he (a) asks "let the mother . . . put me to the test";[30] (b) mentions his dirty appearance and clothing as an obstacle (which indeed they are, cf. v. 95); (c) suggests ἡμεῖς δὲ φραζώμεθα ὅπως ὄχ' ἄριστα γένηται (v. 117). If, following our natural inclination, we refer this line to his bath and other measures of improving his appearance, we are mistaken, for Odysseus continues:

καὶ γάρ τίς θ' ἕνα φῶτα κατακτείνας ἐνὶ δήμῳ
ᾧ μὴ πολλοὶ ἔωσιν ἀοσσητῆρες ὀπίσσω
φεύγει κτλ.

Thus the worry about avengers of the slain suitors is introduced, and if we ask which poet introduced it and went on to describe the first precautions taken (vv. 117-152), the likely answer is the author of the last section of ω.[31] In vv. 130 ff. Odysseus decides how to act. For the time being the fate of the suitors must remain unknown in Ithaca; on the next day Odysseus and Telemachus will go to their farm and see what counsel Zeus may put in their

---

[30] πειράζειν in v. 113 (= πειράομαι v. 181, where the motif is taken up) relates to the σήματα mentioned by Penelope, v. 110. It differs in meaning from πειρήσαιτο in the second episode of ω, on which we have commented.

[31] Would it not be natural for Odysseus πολύτροπος and πολύμητις to consider the inevitable consequences of his deeds? And would Penelope's indecision not allow a break in the action and thus offer the opportunity for such thoughts? The answer in both cases might be yes, but the new topic is brought up in so abrupt and awkward a fashion that we are bound to agree with Kirchhoff (above, n. 13), pp. 556 ff., and all others who, following him, assign vv. 117 ff. to a different poet. Actually Kirchhoff's decision is related to vv. 111-170; see below.

minds. Obeying Odysseus' directions, the servants and others in
the house begin to celebrate with dance and music, which creates
the impression that Penelope has finally consented to a new
marriage (vv. 141-152).[32]

At v. 152 this interruption comes to an end. We return to
Odysseus' bath and other preparations for a new meeting with
Penelope, which after further hesitation on her part and his
passing of the bedstead "test" leads to the recognition and to their
reunion (vv. 205-240).[33]

At ψ 138 the purpose of going to the farm was to devise plans
against the threatening revenge. In the last 20 lines of ψ we find
Odysseus at daybreak ready to go to his πολυδένδρεος ἀγρός, but
he now indicates a different purpose. He is anxious to see his
father. However, immediately after this announcement which fills
only two lines (vv. 359 f.), he turns to measures of precaution
necessary because news about the slaying of the suitors will spread
at once (vv. 362 f.). He tells Penelope how to look after her safety
and orders not only Telemachus but also the shepherd and swine-
herd to accompany him with their arms ready at hand. Thanks to
Athena, their departure takes place unnoticed (vv. 371 f.). Since
the author of the third section of ω uses Odysseus' presence on the
farm and meeting with Laertes, he may have composed this entire
passage (ψ 350-372). Alternatively the author of the second episode
in ω may have written vv. 350-360 (and perhaps a few more lines
which fell by the wayside), while the concluding passage (vv.
361-372) would be due to the "third" poet. As it stands the passage
does not arouse suspicion that more than one hand was at work.[34]

If the author of the final episode knew the "second Nekyia," he
had no reason to tamper with it. By contrast, the scene on the
farm was of major interest for him since he meant to give it a

[32] Vv. 297-299 were in all probability composed by the same author as
vv. 141-152.

[33] On some of the subsequent sections see below p. 27.

[34] I cannot help thinking vv. 350-353 (or even 350-358) somewhat strange
in their particular place; do they not lead us to expect a sequel more germane
to their thought than vv. 359 ff.? Perhaps my feeling is subjective, and the
only section sharply conflicting with them is vv. 248-287. On this subject, we
shall presently say more.

continuation which suited his own ends. To us Odysseus' and Telemachus' arrival on the farm is the sequel of the brief final scene in ψ; in fact, if we had not read in ψ 367 that Eumaius and Philoetius accompany them, we would not gather it from the passage which describes the arrival at the farm house (ω 205). There are δμῶες on the farm, as we learn in vv. 209 f., and when a few lines later (v. 213) Odysseus bids Telemachus and the δμῶες to prepare a meal, we cannot help referring this word[35] to the men who serve on the farm and know their way about it. Some 150 lines later however, when the recognition with Laertes has come about, it is the two herdsmen who have helped Telemachus with the preparation of the meal (vv. 359, 363 f.).

On our hypothesis the δμῶες would belong to the original conception of this episode, whose poet did not need Eumaius and Philoetius, and these would be introduced in vv. 359 ff. by the author of the final section. Do we detect his hand also in the developments leading to Odysseus' recognition by Laertes? In a few places this seems to be the case. One is v. 324 where Odysseus, having finally revealed his identity, at once adds a statement about the vengeance he has taken on the suitors. The statement is brief and cannot be delayed: "there is much need for hurrying." Truly, this is a surprise; so far everything moved at a leisurely pace. Odysseus told his stories unhurriedly as usual, and we never felt that he was under pressure. Moreover when he had two alternative ways of identifying himself to his father (vv. 235-238), he chose the way which was bound to take more time.

Laertes, unimpressed by the need for hurry, insists on a "proof," and several proofs are given, not with a maximum display of epic detail nor with careful avoidance of every unnecessary word either (vv. 331-344).[36] As soon as Laertes has recovered from the physical effects of his joy, he at once expresses a "terrible" fear (αἰνῶς δέδοικα, v. 353) that the entire population of Ithaca and even people of Cephallene might come, sc. to avenge the suitors. With

[35] It is the context, not the word δμῶες which accounts for this. Elsewhere δμῶες is used of the herdsmen (e.g. ξ 80, φ 244, χ 114).

[36] Of the first "proof," the οὐλή (v. 331), the full story has been told in τ 393-466. A brief summary is all we need here.

a few words Odysseus allays this apprehension, and for a while the narrative moves on without hurry or indications of worry about a threatening attack. Laertes has time to take a bath and to appear rejuvenated, in standard fashion with Athena's help (vv. 365 ff.); there is some reminiscing, some meeting with old friends. Still a possibility remains that the "last poet," whom I hold responsible for the sudden hurry in v. 324 as well as for Laertes' astonishingly prompt adjustment to an unexpected situation (v. 353),[37] has reduced some passages and has been rather unsentimental, not to say cruel in his handling of the joy and worries shown by old friends after their long separation from Odysseus.[38]

We leave the company "at work" on their meal (v. 412). At v. 413 the "last poet" definitely takes over, starts the revolt and in spite of some setbacks and defections makes the rioters assemble πρὸ ἄστεος εὐρυχόροιο (v. 468). After the interlude on Olympus, where Zeus and Athena (as we know) deliberate, we are back on the farm, where in the meantime the meal has been finished. Odysseus bids one of his men to go out and look "lest being on their way they are near" (no grammatical subject is specified in this clause, and the next sentences offer only a τούς, v. 493, and a οἶδε, v. 495). The report is that "they" are arriving. The poet has not found a very elegant way to take us back to Odysseus.[39] We remember that as an artist we ranked him below the two other poets of ω,[40] and the remaining developments, the dialogue of Zeus and Athena, Laertes' ἀριστεία, and the peaceful settlement

---

[37] Note especially the absence of any verbal expression of his joy at Odysseus' return. Odysseus' reply too (vv. 357-360) could hardly be shorter and show less emotion.

[38] Odysseus himself, I should add, is rather impatient at vv. 394-396 and almost rude at v. 407. For explanations see W. B. Stanford, *The Odyssey of Homer* (London, 1948), *ad* ω 222 and 387 f. I am not sure that they are appropriate.

[39] Nor has he informed the entire group on the farm of the threatening action.

[40] His place at the very end of the younger epic seems almost symbolic. We should however not look too confidently at his section as a sample of the declining epic. Very probably there were inferior poets in every generation, and his peculiar fate was to survive.

are all equally undistinguished and may be confidently left to the same poet.

Thus there seems to be considerable support for our hypothesis, and whoever remains adamantly opposed to it at least should face the weaknesses and difficulties in these final sections and come forward with alternative explanations. The hypothesis, to be sure, has its own weaknesses and difficulties. It would not be fair to conceal that in ψ we have stayed at a safe distance from some thorny questions. Vv. 117-152, which we have assigned to the "last poet," because they lay the groundwork for the revenge of the kinsmen, form part of a slightly larger unit in the *anagnorisis*; yet this entire unit, vv. 115-170 and not only vv. 117-152, is under suspicion. So are two other sections in ψ, vv. 247-288, where Odysseus, immediately after Penelope has accepted him with great joy, informs her of one more huge labor he must perform to reconcile Poseidon, and vv. 310 (or 306)-343, where Odysseus gives a fairly complete summary in indirect speech of his adventures to Penelope, who cannot go to sleep before she has heard the entire story of his experiences. To me the announcement of the "immense" remaining πόνος at this particular juncture seems the hardest to justify,[41] whereas Telemachus' outburst and Odysseus' bath and more beautiful reappearance seem relatively easy to explain.[42] Whether v. 296, the τέλος of Aristophanes and Aristarchus, or v. 343, where the summary of Odysseus' adventures ends, is a better conclusion remains essentially a matter of

[41] "Gefühllos" is von der Mühll's verdict, *Die Dichter* (see above, n. 14), p. 22. For this section I should more readily than elsewhere admit relations to the *Telegony*, an idea favored and excessively brought into play by Schwartz (see above, n. 11), pp. 134 ff., esp. p. 137, and R. Merkelbach, *Untersuchungen zur Odyssee* (*Zetemata* 2 [1951]), 142 ff.

[42] Is it for us to say when Odysseus should take his bath? And are we to blame him if at χ 481 ff. his desire to see Penelope is stronger than his concern about his own looks? The repetition of ψ 100-102 in ψ 168-170 would probably be thought perfectly in order by the formula school, and we might acquiesce in their verdict. Far more serious is Schadewaldt's argument (see above, n. 13, pp. 11 ff.) for understanding ψ 174 ff. as an immediate reply to ψ 113-116. My only difficulties with his brilliant interpretation are that Odysseus remains to the end in his dirty condition and that he does not at once recognize vv. 177-180 as the expected πειράζειν. Aristarchus athetized ψ 310-343 (cf. the *Scholia*).

subjective taste. I for one am happy to acquiesce in the opinion of
the great Alexandrian critics[43] and accept ψ 296 as a solemn and
dignified conclusion for the "plot" of the *Odyssey*. Surely Penelope
would wish to know all that Odysseus had experienced (and he all
that she had suffered); surely too he would be anxious to see his
father, and surely the killing of so many of the "best" young men
would not pass without some violent reaction in the community.
These and other subjects would prompt lesser poets to compose
their additions. Besides the three whom we necessarily distinguish
in ω[44] and those—far less easy to recognize and distinguish—who
changed the original content of ψ, there were probably others
venturing a continuation. Popularity would be one but not
necessarily the only reason why the work of some survived while
that of others did not. Even accident may have played a part. We
know far too little about the early stages of the transmission to
advance a confident opinion.

[43] For a defense of ψ 310-343, see Schadewaldt (above, n. 13), pp. 24 f. The
problems of ψ are far more complex than those of ω, and if it is at all possible to
unravel them, I make no pretense of achieving it.

[44] By the reasons collected in Stanford's commentary (see above, n. 38) *ad*
ψ 296 ff., any text, however poor and pointless, may be defended.

True and False Discourse in Hesiod

PIERO PUCCI

Among the striking novelties of Hesiod's work are his literary self-awareness as a poet and, more specifically, his elaboration of puzzling and odd views about his art, his poetic song or discourse.[1] The purpose of this essay is to investigate Hesiod's text as it explores the complex, puzzling nature of poetic discourse. As is well known, the Muses, the patron goddesses of poetry, utter in the *Theogony* (26 ff.) one of the most enigmatic statements about poetry to be found in Greek literature.[2]

The Logos as Imitation and Difference

We begin our analysis with a discussion of Zeus and the Muses, who make so forceful an appearance at the beginning of both the *Erga* and the *Theogony*. In the *Erga* passage, Hesiod maintains that

---

[1] Hesiod describes poetic song in various ways: ἀοιδή (*Th.* 22 ff.) ὑμνεῖν (*Th.* 34), but also λέγειν (*Th.* 27) and *logos* (*Erga* 106).

[2] Material concerning Hesiod's views on truth and falsehood has been collected and analyzed extensively. Important recent studies include Lain Entralgo, *The Therapy of the Word* (New Haven, 1970); M. Detienne, *Les maîtres de vérité dans la Grèce archaïque* (Paris, 1967); G. Lanata, *Poetica pre-platonica* (Florence, 1963); and W. Luther, "Wahrheit, Licht und Erkenntnis in der griechischen Philosophie bis Demokrit," *Archiv für Begriffsgeschichte* X (1966), 1-240. My analysis is somewhat parallel to that of Detienne, but our classifications of evidence and our interpretations are different. In particular he is concerned with the mythical and sociological structure that frames and provides connotations for these various notions of truth and falsehood. My analysis tries to show the structure of these notions as operative in the text, and as depending on the text.

I quote the text of the *Theogony* from *Hesiod Theogony*, ed. with Prolegomena and Commentary by M. L. West (Oxford, 1966), hereafter referred to as West. For the text of the *Erga* I quote from *Hesiodi Opera et Dies*, A. Colonna (Milan, 1959). All translations, unless otherwise indicated, are mine.

the right time for sowing is the fall and that if grain is sown at the winter solstice, it will suffer from the dry weather. Yet there are exceptional cases when late sowing might be good, for the mind of Zeus is inscrutable and it changes at every moment (483-484):

> ἄλλοτε δ'ἀλλοῖος Ζηνὸς νόος αἰγιόχοιο,
> ἀργαλέος δ'ἄνδρεσσι καταθνητοῖσι νοῆσαι.

Though Zeus' inscrutability is a conventional trait,[3] his inconsistency ("sometimes he is of one mind, sometimes of another"[4]) reveals a less familiar characteristic. To be sure, Zeus' changes of mind are evident not in his words, but only in the events of nature. Yet his ambiguousness parallels that of the Muses, his daughters (Δί' ἐννέπετε σφέτερον πατέρ' Erga 2) and the teachers of Hesiod.[5]

When the Muses meet Hesiod on Mount Helikon, they tell him (26 ff.):

> Ποιμένες ἄγραυλοι, κάκ' ἐλέγχεα, γαστέρες οἶον
> ἴδμεν ψεύδεα πολλὰ λέγειν ἐτύμοισι ὁμοῖα
> ἴδμεν δ'εὖτ' ἐθέλωμεν ἀληθέα γηρύσασθαι.

> (Shepherds of the fields, poor fools, mere bellies! We know how to say many lies similar [or identical] to true things, but, if we want, we know how to sing the truth.)

The strong assonance—almost an anagram or a reverse reading—of *ethelo(men)* (we consent) and *alethea* (truth) emphasizes the explicit statement that truth depends only on the wishes of the Muses, for they often tell lies that look like truths.[6] To be sure,

---

[3] Hom. *Il.* 18. 328; Aesch. *Supp.* 86.

[4] Ἄλλοτε ἀλλοῖος is a *hapax* in Hesiod and the expression is unprecedented.

[5] To describe the mind of Zeus (*Erga* 658-662), even after the teaching of the Muses, implies a song that not even a god could sing, ἀθέσφατος ὕμνος. This epithet is used for rain in the *Iliad*; it extends its range in the *Odyssey*. For the meaning of the epithet see Apoll. Soph., quoted by Wilamowitz in *Hesiodos Erga* (3d ed., Dublin and Zurich, 1970), p. 117. See also H. Fraenkel, *Antidoron*, Festschrift Wackernagel (1921), pp. 281-282.

[6] Line 27 repeats with small variations *Od.* 19. 203: ἴσκε ψεύδεα πολλὰ λέγων ἐτύμοισιν ὁμοῖα. West finds Hesiod's ἴδμεν . . . λέγειν to be a happier expression than the Homeric one. In fact ἴσκε must be a present of ἔοικα, in the factitive sense of "making similar," and therefore it repeats the notion of ὁμοῖα.

On the priority of Hesiod's or Homer's text, see F. Solmsen, "The 'Gift' of Speech in Homer and Hesiod," *TAPA* 85 (1954), 11 ff., and G. P. Edwards, *The Language of Hesiod in its Traditional Context* (Oxford, 1971), pp. 16 ff.

there is a distinction in the way lies and truth are expressed; the lies that look like truth are prosaically and simply "said" (λέγειν), while the truth that is really truth is qualified by a verb from religious language (γηρύσασθαι) and seems to merit a higher tone. Yet this distinction is only a matter of emphasis. This whole passage, in fact, is complex and deserves close attention. Leaving aside the religious significance of the Muses' statement (see Detienne, pp. 75 ff.), I should like to discuss its linguistic significance.

It is remarkable that Hesiod, that supposedly mythical thinker, should first deny "the Homeric belief in the identity of truth and poetry" (Luther, p. 42) and second present the relationship between truth and falsehood in rationalistic terms. For, by saying that the untrue statements of the Muses look like truth, Hesiod implies the very concept of imitation that is fundamental to Greek thought on language. The precise meaning of this text has never— as far as I know—been elucidated; what is imitated by the false statements of the Muses (ψεύδεα—from ψεῦδος—λέγειν)? What precise relationship is established between the true and the untrue? For ὁμοῖος can suggest both similarity and identity.[7] The word ἔτυμα, i.e., the truth that the false statements of the Muses imitate, might mean both what actually *exists* and what is thought or said to be true.[8] But since ἔτυμος has a positive formation and is possibly connected with εἶναι, one might wish here to stress this meaning and "what actually exists as true."[9] The text of line 27

---

[7] Ὁμοῖος, "similar," "same," "equal," from ὁμός connected with a large IE group of words Pers. *hama* "similar" "same"; Got. *sama* "similar" "same" (see H. Frisk, *Griechisches Etymologisches Worterbuch* s.v. ὁμός).

In Hesiod the word indicates "similarity" as between father and sons (*Erga* 182) or "sameness" (*Erga* 114). Luther (*Archiv*, p. 100, n. 131) maintains that, in the concept ὁμοῖος, the early Greek mind does not distinguish between "similarity" and "equality."

[8] Luther (pp. 30 ff.) states that the archaic Greek language and mind do not distinguish between "real" (*wirklich*) and "truthful" (*wahr*). Thus for instance the "real" "actual" return of Odysseus is ἐτήτυμος νόστος (*Od.* 3. 241), exactly as the truthful words of Eurycleia μῦθος ἐτήτυμος (*Od.* 23. 62 ff.).

[9] Ἔτυμος means something that has truly happened (see Tilman Krischer, "ΕΤΥΜΟΣ und ΑΛΗΞΗΣ," *Philologus* 109 [1965], 166-167). See also H. Hommel in *Antike und Abendland* XV (1969), 174: "Daneben stehet in älterer

would then imply that the Muses' false *logos* (ψεύδεα λέγειν) resembles real things, things that exist or have happened. Since line 27 echoes *Odyssey* 19. 203, where the author comments on Odysseus' ability to invent fictitious, false events about himself, the passage of the *Theogony* might suggest that the Muses *invent* stories similar or even identical to actual things or events. But we should not ignore the different implications of the two passages; whereas the inventions of Odysseus are merely expedient tactical moves typical of everyday language, the *logos* of the Muses constitutes the divine "gift" of poetry. Their definition of it as something tricky applies to the language of all poetry. The poor shepherds whom the Muses address are deceived by the plausibility of the Muses' words, just as Penelope was deceived by the words of Odysseus; however, the poor shepherds represent all the poets and the audiences of poets before Hesiod.

We should explore now the implications of the general principle stating that words are similar / identical to true things. From the view expressed in line 27, it follows that the *logos* has some similarity to true things and, at the same time, some difference from true things. The *logos* imitates things, but with some distortion, or obliqueness. This point can be supported by an analysis of the expressions in Homeric epic meaning lie and truth; they always imply some relation of imitation or closeness between words and real things, events, ideas. In *Odyssey* 4. 347 f. Menelaos assures Telemachos that he is speaking the truth:

> ταῦτα δ', ἅ μ'εἰρωτᾷς καὶ λίσσεαι, οὐκ ἂν ἐγώ γε
> ἄλλα παρὲξ εἴποιμι παρακλιδόν, οὐδ' ἀπατήσω.—

L. S. J. (s. v. παρακλιδόν) translates "I would not tell you another tale beside the mark and swerving *from the truth*," but the words "mark" and "truth" are not in the original. More precisely one should understand "I would not say other things beside (what I heard from the truthful old man) and askance (or obliquely, i.e., deviating from what the same person told me)." Menelaos means

Zeit das ἐτεόν auch ἔτυμον oder ἐτήτυμον das 'Seinsmässige, Echte, Wirchliche'." Ἀληθής instead is the account of something the speaker himself has experienced, an account that does not leave anything unnoticed (Krischer, pp. 163 and 167.)

therefore that he will *repeat* the words he heard, *mirror* them,[10] without distortion or difference. As we have already seen in *Odyssey* 19. 203, Odysseus invents a false story, but its credibility lies in the fact that it is identical or similar to true events; indeed his story is a mixture of half truths.

These interpretations are confirmed when we analyze the Greek expressions meaning "truth," for they aim to designate the things themselves as they are. Thus the expression ἀτρεκέως καταλέγειν, for instance, implies a *logos* without the distortion or deflection that the second term of the compound ἀ-*τρεκος indicates (compare Latin *torqueo*). Moreover, νημερτής, meaning "who does not miss the goal," implies a *logos* hitting the things, going straight to them. The case of ἀλήθεια is well known.[11]

Given these premises and the text of *Theogony* 27, we reach the conclusion that the Muses sing a discourse similar or identical to the true thing, but with some distortion, obliquity, or deflection, in a word with some *difference*. This similarity vouches for the credibility of the discourse as truthful, while its distortion, deflection, and difference make it false. Moreover, this difference is of such a nature that only the Muses can see it or read it. In fact the Muses reveal now for the first time this difference, and by declaring what *had escaped* from men in their song, they really say the *a-letheia* (28). This explains why ὁμοῖα could mean "identical," for, from the point of view of the shepherds, there was really no difference at all between the song of the Muses and the ἔτυμα.[12]

[10] In *Od.* 4. 348 there is no explicit mention of falsehood, though the idea is clearly implicit in *Od.* 4. 331.

[11] See W. Luther, *Wahrheit und Luge* (Leipzig, 1935), pp. 33-50, and below, notes 40 and 41.

[12] The statement of the Muses has sometimes been taken to mean *only* that Homeric epic is false, even though inspired by the Muses (see Luther, *Archiv*, pp. 41 f.). This interpretation is correct, but restrictive; it does not explain the entire sentence of the Muses. They do *not* say: "We know how to say false things, though if we want, we can sing true ones." The Muses make a more complicated assertion: "We know how to say false things which look like true ones." This "paradox" has sense *only* if language imitates true things and yet remains different from them.

One might be tempted to paraphrase the Greek text with a proposition such as "lies similar to truths" and to rely on the common sense plausibility of it,

The shepherds—and with them all of epic culture—saw, in the
logos of the Muses, no distortion, no difference from true things.
They could not have seen it; had they sensed the difference, the
logos would not have been identical to true things.

Human weakness in the face of the surreptitious power of the
logos is demonstrated clearly; only the Muses can see beyond its
magic mirror. (I disregard the question of whether the *logos* is in
rapport with things themselves or with their image in our mind,[13]
a question which we cannot ask of our text and which later will
trouble Aristotle.)[14]

We reach the same conclusions if we interpret the text of
Theogony 27 to mean "we know how to say an untrue *logos* similar /
identical to a true one." With this reading, the relationship
between words and things is replaced by a relationship between
two meanings of the same *logos*. This proposition is supported by
analogy to various words in the *Erga*, each of which evokes
different or even opposite connotations for persons or entities. The
word Eris, for instance, means both a good and a bad Eris (*Erga*,
11 ff.). The text implies that the word Eris evokes two persons at
once: one, Competition, to be praised and the other, Discord, to be
blamed. The word Eris functions as the word for a "double."
Analogously, when Hesiod speaks of a bad *Aidos* (*Erga*, 315 ff.), he
implies the existence of a good one; similarly, he speaks of a day
(*Hemere*, *Erga* 825) viewed either as a mother or a step-mother.
Again the same word conjures up a "double" and includes two

---

without further questioning. But if the phrase, "lies similar to truth," is
seriously analyzed, it will lead to the very problems that concern us in this
essay. Thus the assertion can hardly be made blandly.

[13] K. Latte (*Antike und Abendland* II [1946], 160) maintains that the meaning
of ἐτήτυμα in *Erga* 10 is the content of a representation or of a statement con-
gruent to the actual (real, *wirklich*) facts (*Sachverhalt*). Luther (see above, n. 8)
maintains that the archaic mind does not distinguish between "wirklich" and
"wahr."

The question is complicated by the fact that the *logos* itself, for the Greeks,
is not a "form" or a "tool," but a real *being* (Luther, *Archiv*, p. 32).

[14] Aristotle's definition of language as a conventional symbol (σύμβολα) of
conceptual impressions (παθήματα τῆς ψυχῆς *De Interpret.* 16 a 5 ff.) parallels that
of language as a symbol (σύμβολα) of things (*Soph. El.* 1. 165 a 7: τοῖς ὀνόμασιν
ἀντὶ τῶν πραγμάτων χρώμεθα συμβόλοις.

opposite persons or qualities. Although it is not easy to be precise about a relationship between naming and *logos*, we might be tempted to extend to the paradox of line 27 the notion that one name means two different, yet related entities. The same *logos* of the Muses, in this case, would indicate not a good and a bad person, but would express a true and a false statement. Unlike the case of the word Eris, the Muses claim that their *logos*, though it looks like a true one, *is* untrue and *not* vice versa. Though they establish a relationship of similarity / identity between the two meanings, they seem able to distinguish the original, truth, from its copy, falsehood. This proposition raises some hair-splitting questions, for it implies the difficult problems of assessing the relationship between copy and model and of discerning what marks the model or original. In particular, if we assume ὁμοῖα to mean "identical," the result is the paradox of a lie identical to truth and yet falsely recognizable as a truth. But in this case, one of a perfect homonymy, not even the Muses would be able to read the difference, and moreover a language formed by total homonymy, i.e., without any difference at all, would not even be a language, because it would lack the distinctive and differential marks which generate meaning. If we allow that some distinctive and differential marks exist, only the Muses would be able to read them. The distinctive marks of the *logos* do not reveal to men any sufficient difference between truth and falsehood.

The conclusion of the preceding argument is that the *logos* signifies things or ideas by imitating them with a difference. In the one case, the *logos* displaces things in such a way that they become false; the Muses can always recognize this difference, but the operation is so surreptitious that men fail to see the falsity. In the other case, the *logos* presents itself as having in equal or almost equal force different, even opposite meanings. Again, only the Muses can see that certain marks of truth are in reality the marks of falsehood. For men these marks are simply not readable in their true implications.

The Muses, the donors of the *logos*, alone know how to distinguish the false *logos* from the true one. The insults that the Muses address to the shepherds should be understood as a strong indict-

ment of the weakness and ignorance of men before the *logos*. No
wonder the *logos* is so mysterious; it is a gift of the gods. Not all
song—simply because it comes from the Muses' voice—is true; yet
because it comes from that voice, it always looks like truth. This
disheartening message leaves the poet facing the precariousness of
the *logos* alone. As Hesiod, so often considered to be on the
threshold of mythical thinking, begins a new type of song, he
boldly accepts his individual responsibility for truth and with
great energy denies the general demonstrability of truth.

Hesiod's responsibility for truth, however, implies his faith in
the Muses' intention to tell the truth to him. With a bold movement, the text of line 28 ("we know, when we want, how to sing
true things") sets against the preceding line a series of opposite
premises. They are only implicitly assumed and therefore do not
seem to clash with the previous line. Yet by placing in the Muses'
will the whole power of saying or representing truth, Hesiod
implies (1) that true and untrue things are definable and distin-
guishable prior to all language, (2) that the distortion or displacement of true things does not depend on the mysterious nature of
logos but rather on the volition of the Muses. Thus the structure of
intentions and desires—precisely what is at the origin of the *logos*
—is posited instead as the criterion of true discourse.

Finally, Hesiod asserts that the relationship of similarity /
identity exists and is effective between words *and* things. The
bewildering and hidden difference of language from what it
evokes, the total or partial undemonstrability of the truth of
language, is replaced by the more comfortable conviction that the
truthful *logos*—which the Muses can sing if they wish—will not
distort things and will represent them as they are.[15] For, though
the Muses do not say that their true *logos* is *similar / identical* to true
things, Hesiod's text—as we shall see—provides ample proof that
the poet conceives of himself as singing a *straight* discourse after
his encounter with the Muses: a discourse without difference.

The passage we have been analyzing (*Th.* 26-28) forces us to
recognize two opposite moves of a complex strategy. The first

[15] I have dealt with this at greater length in my forthcoming book, *The
Poetic Language and Hesiod*.

one—which seems to foreshadow the sophistic view of language— suggests that language is something similar to and different from the things it evokes and, consequently, interferes with them. As language deflects, distorts, and displaces, so the "meaning" is realized through deferment, displacement and distortion.

The second move, on the contrary, hints at language as identity (copy) of words with things / notions. This move is made possible by the Muses' / author's desire to control the nature of language.

At this juncture it is easy to see that Hesiod's view of language is by no means less complex and complete than what develops later in Greek thought. On the contrary, Hesiod's conception seems to assume rigorously the contradiction existing in later Greek thought between two different views of language: as *difference*, i.e., as an entity independent of external reality, and as a truthful imitation of things / notions. While the first can be identified approximately with the sophistic theory of language, the second represents the goal toward which both Plato and Aristotle tend, each in their different ways. Even a cursory outline of these theories shows that the contradiction—unnoticed in later Greek thought as in Hesiod's text—is never really resolved and that it still haunts all thinkers and poets.

In the *Hippolytus* (385-386) of Euripides, Phaedra remarks that the same word *aidos* can be used to imply a good or a bad attitude of respect and deduces that the ambiguity of the meaning must mirror some ambiguity in the notions themselves; had *aidos* been two different and distinctive entities, there would be two different words.[16] Here Euripides implies that language ought to, and

---

[16] "If the right occasion were clear there would not be two of them spelt with the same letters" (386-387). The text becomes clear as soon as we explain the philosophical meaning of καιρός. The notion of καιρός in this context derives from sophistic and probably Gorgianic philosophy. Some sophistic philosophers used to say of moral ideas that two opposite *logoi* are possible. It is only καιρός, i.e., the full set of the contextual meanings, that can make the case clear. A fragment of a tragedy (Nauck, 2d ed., adesp. 26) sometimes attributed to Euripides helps us to recognize both the sophistic sense of καιρός and the precise use in *Hipp*. 385-386: "Nothing is absolutely beautiful or bad, but καιρός picks up the same thing and makes it bad and then, by changing it, beautiful" (see A. Rostagni, *SIFC* N.S. 11 [1922], 172 f.). In this passage "beautiful" and "bad" are two different words. *Καιρός*, therefore, causes the replacement of one

normally does, mirror the world of things and notions. On the other hand, the difference of language, the undemonstrability of language as truth and falsehood, haunts other Euripidean characters. In the same play (925 ff.), Theseus expresses the utopian dream that all men should have two voices, a just and honest one added to the usual voice "so that the dishonest voice might be refuted by the honest one and we might escape deception." Obviously Theseus is painfully aware that language does not carry any evidence of truth; trapped between two contradictory statements he then misunderstands both and follows the direction of his own desire. The whole *Hippolytus* could be defined as the sacrifice offered to the Muses in order to assert and recapture the truth for the language of an absolute self. In the *Phoenissae* (499 ff.), Euripides repeats this point in an elaborate passage: words are the same but they mean different things or notions and this is the object of dispute and discussion.

The independence of language from the external world, its inability to mirror the world, its conventional quality, its constituting a trap for logic and truth are the themes of the sophists' theory of language.[17] But a radical application of these themes would imply—as Aristotle saw (*Met.* 1006 A 12 ff.)—the non-sense of talking.

To assess the force of Plato's reaction against the sophists, it is sufficient to recall the thesis he expounded in the *Cratylus*: words are naturally right since there is absolute identity between things and words. Yet the clash between language as distortion and language as the mirror of things haunts Plato too. By a complex

---

word with the other as it changes the interpretation of the same thing or event. But in *Hipp.* 385-386 the *same* word αἰδώς is both good and bad. This fact, Phaedra thinks, must imply that the circumstantial and contextual elements, those that define the good or bad *aidos* are not clear but ambiguous, i.e., easily confused and misunderstood.

[17] See A. Momigliano, "Prodico di Ceo e le dottrine sul linguaggio da Democrito ai cinici," *Atti R. Accademia delle Scienze di Torino* 65 (1929-1930), 95-107. Not all sophists hold the same view; I am thinking here especially of Gorgias, Protagoras and the influential Democritus. On Gorgias—as far as we know the most radical thinker about the self-contained quality of language— see C. P. Segal, *HSCP* 66 (1962), 99-155.

strategy in the *Phaedrus*, Plato ascribes the sophistic attributes of the *logos* to the "written" *logos*; thus he is able to preserve for the spoken *logos* the power of mirroring truth.[18] This strategy, which allows Plato to dispose of the difference and deflection of the *logos* as a sophistic sort of language, emphasizes the permanence and seriousness of the problem. These few hints are sufficient to show that Hesiod's posture is by no means primitive; rather, it reflects a problem that can be found in an equally harsh form in later thinkers. And though the question receives more and more elaborate and complex answers, it continues to haunt Aristotle and the whole of Western philosophy.[19]

As modern linguistic and philosophical thought has made clear, the linguistic sign is arbitrary, i.e., it does not mirror or *re-present* things or concepts. On the contrary, the very nature of the sign as signifier consists in a structure of differences and articulations which deeply affect the signified, the meaning. For the meaning occurs and is realized just within the space opened by those differences and articulations and therefore by a movement of deferment. By "difference" we imply both this spatial protraction and the rôle of vicariousness of language since the signifiers stand for something else. By "deferment" we imply not only a movement away from things but also a dimension of temporality, i.e., the delaying quality of language. The signifiers come always after the

---

[18] J. Derrida, "La Pharmacie de Platon," in *Dissemination* (Paris, 1972).

[19] For Aristotle see P. Aubenque, *Le Probleme de l'être chez Aristote* (Paris, 1962) and J. Derrida, *Poétique* 5 (1971), 18 ff. For the problem in Western thought, see again J. Derrida, *De la Grammatologie* (Paris, 1967).
One cannot refrain from quoting a famous passage of F. Nietzsche, one of the first modern philosophers to recognize the connection between language and all metaphysics and therefore to understand the goal of philosophy as a new scrutiny of language:

> Was ist also Wahrheit? Ein bewegliches Heer von Metaphern, Metony-mien, Anthropomorphismen, kurz eine Summe von menschlichen Rela-tionen, die poetisch und rhetorisch gesteigert, übertragen, geschmuckt wurden, und die nach langen Gebrauch einem Volke fest, kanonisch und verbildlich dunken: die Wahrheiten sind Illusionen, von denen man vergessen hat, dass sie welche sind, Metaphern, die abgenutzt und sinn-lich kraftlos geworden sind, Münzen, die ihr Bild verloren haben und nun als Metall, nicht mehr als Münzen, in Betracht kommen [*Das Philosophenbuch*, ed. A. K. Marietti, Paris, 1969, p. 180].

things they signify, since they enact the "re-present-ation" of
things by means of temporal sequences, duration, of the interaction
of sounds, gestures, and facial expressions. This space of differences
and this movement of deferment constitute the ontological status
of all writing and expression.[20]

The very act of articulating a meaning implies the striving for
a presence, an immediacy, an origin, a *hic et nunc*. This striving
itself imperils the status of articulations and meaning. It does not
alter the nature of the expression, but as its goal consists in denying
and effacing all difference and deferment and even the vicarious
status of language, it brings forth a tension or a broken movement.
The desire for a *hic et nunc*, for a present and stable meaning,
encroaches constantly on the attributes of language as difference,
deferment. The meaning is agonizingly shaped out of the labyrinthine movement of language, hinting at immediacy through the
lag of language and indicating a precise place through the
displacement of language.

These modern views about language can help the critic, but
they can by no means be attributed to Hesiod. He considers the
logos as a whole, as something similar to or different from what it
evokes, but he has no notion of signifier, signified, referent,
arbitrary sign, and so forth. Yet his text records at least one aspect
of the troubling logic that controls the notion of imitation, I mean
the interplay between similarity and difference. Thus, as Hesiod
recognizes that the song of the Muses can be false, though appearing to be true, he recognizes the status of language as difference, as
a labyrinthine movement deprived of demonstrable conceptual or
concrete evidences, but as he sings, aiming at a truthful discourse,
Hesiod implicitly rejects that status of language. This rejection is
sustained by repeated statements that his song is a song of truth
(*Th.* 28: ἀληθέα γηρύσασθαι *Erga* 10: ἐτήτυμα μυθησαίμην) or divine
(*Th.* 31-32: αὐδὴν θέσπιν *Erga* 662: ἀθέσφατον ὕμνον). For in such a

---

[20] Philosophers and linguists of many different schools have made
relevant contributions to this view of language. The most comprehensive and
most original systematic treatment of language following these lines is by
Derrida, *De la Grammatologie*. A short but penetrating critical summary of
Derrida's views by A. Gelley appears in *Diacritics* 2 (1972), 9-13.

discourse everything has the same status of truth, and indeed the same necessity or "logic" (if we do not mean here Aristotelian logic but an inner consequentiality and necessity). The first feature of this discourse consists in its declared "metaphysical" posture: it precedes all distinctions between physics and metaphysics, man and god, nature and man. This discourse controls past and present, gods and men, for it is identical to the discourse without difference. But the difference winds its way into the texture of this discourse (just as the *logos* tries more forcefully to present itself as identical to truth) and by this movement confuses all the neat distinctions, the precise tracks outlined by the *logos*.

The Straight Logos

After a rigorous definition of song as a labyrinthine movement in which the difference, the displacement of things, true, untrue, cannot be read, Hesiod's text introduces a series of distinctions or polarities that imply that language is controllable and readable.

The proposition "Truth looks similar / identical to falsehood" is followed in line 28 by the idea that "truth" is opposed to "falsehood"; consistently in the *Theogony* and *Erga*, the *logos* tends to be recognizable and definable as either straight or crooked, just or unjust, unerring or erring. Though the *logos* can hide all distortions from truth, the poet feels that he can recognize the straight and the crooked *logos*. And while the proposition "Truth looks similar / identical to falsehood" implies a labyrinthine movement of the *logos* as difference, the polarities that now describe the *logos* attribute to it a broken movement of neat oppositions.

Our purpose is to analyze now these polarities. First, we shall see that they are to a degree "extensions" of the first polarity, true : false, established by the Muses in *Theogony* 28 and that, consequently, there is a correspondence between each set. Second, we shall see that each of these polarities undergoes the fate of the first one. Though the poet and the Muses aim at establishing a neat distinction between true : false or straight : crooked, the text again presents the tension found in *Theogony* 26-28. As in the case of the polarity true : false, all the other polarities are established from a text that imperils them; they are shaped in defiance of the textual evidence which shows that the *logos* is difference, a winding, labyrinthine movement.

We begin by the most pervasive polarity of Hesiod's *Erga*, straight and crooked. The connection between straight speech and true speech is implicitly made in the *Theogony* (85-86) when the king, reaching a straight decision, is said to speak ἀσφαλέος, literally "[standing] without stumbling" and metaphorically "unerring."[21] Furthermore, this connection with truth is supported by the fact that the Muses themselves inspire the good king who pronounces straight decisions (*Th.* 81 ff.). An identity between the two values is not implied, but simply a correspondence: truth is to straightness as falsehood is to crookedness.[22] Let us add that in Homer the expression παρακλιδόν "obliquely" is also used (*Od.* 4. 348; 7. 139) with the implicit notion of "diverting from truth."

I shall comment briefly on two passages. The first one concerns the good king who is inspired by the Muses[23] and is able to reach good, just, i.e., straight decisions (*Th.* 85-86):

$$\delta\iota\alpha\kappa\rho\acute{\iota}\nu o\nu\tau\alpha\ \theta\acute{\epsilon}\mu\iota\sigma\tau\alpha\varsigma$$
ἰθείῃσι δίκῃσιν.

This good king speaks unerringly, and with his wisdom he stops

---

[21] "Ἀσφαλέως unerringly. The idea of truth is often associated with that of ἀσφάλεια" (West, p. 184, who quotes various passages from Pindar on).

The steadfastness of this *logos* is remarkable, for elsewhere in the *Theogony*, *Erga*, and *Aspis*, only Earth and Uranos deserve that epithet (*Th.* 117 and 128).

[22] Solmsen (see above, n. 6) writes that "truth" and "straight" sentences do not seem for Hesiod to lie on the same plane (p. 6). But in n. 18 he adds, "I am not altogether sure of this; note that at *Theog.* 233 Nereus is extolled as ἀληθής (ἀψευδής, νημερτής) as well as δίκαιος 235 ff. He is also called ἤπιος, which word in turn is very close to μειλίχιος (see the use of both words in the verses on Leto 407 ff.)." On the passage *Th.* 233 see later in Solmsen, pp. 19 ff. On the relationship between ἀλήθεια and δίκη in mythical thought, see Detienne, ch. 3.

[23] On Hesiod's innovation of defining eloquent speech as a precise gift of the Muses, see Solmsen, p. 5: "Effective speech is for Hesiod not one of the two outstanding excellences of man but one of the two gifts of the Muses. Where the poets of the *Iliad* and *Odyssey* say 'Zeus' or 'a god,' or 'The gods have given' and leave it at that without wishing to scrutinize things any further, Hesiod finds himself able to identify the giver precisely." Solmsen notes also that "this seems to be the only instance in which Hesiod expanded the sphere of a deity whom he knew from tradition."

"even a serious quarrel" (*Th.* 87). The reason why "there are good, sensitive kings,"[24] Hesiod goes on to say, is that they are thus able to establish justice (*Th.* 88-90):

οὕνεκα λαοῖς
βλαπτομένοις ἀγορῆφι μετάτροπα ἔργα τελεῦσι
ῥηιδίως, μαλακοῖσι παραιφάμενοι ἐπέεσσιν.

(They obtain easily a restitution[25] for the people who have been wronged in their dealings,[26] speaking gently [or persuading the wrongdoers] with soft words.)[27]

We have translated, following the suggestion of dictionaries and commentators, as Hesiod obviously meant to be understood, but the word for persuade, παραιφάμενοι, means literally "to speak to deflect, to 'de-viate'." The idea of persuasion in Homeric Greek often carries the notions of deflecting, bending the mind or will of others; in *Iliad* 2. 14 it is expressed by a verb which means literally "to bend": ἐπέγναμψεν γὰρ ἅπαντας. The idea of persuasion therefore implies moving the mind from its path and intimates the power of bending and deflecting rather than the concern for truth. In the Hesiodic passage, as we shall see, the pleasantness of the words (μαλακοῖσι . . . ἐπέεσσιν) already hints at some softening of the truth. Moreover the deflecting *logos* of persuasion expressed by παράφημι and πάρφασις implies often in Homer as well the ideas of leading someone astray, of deception and of deviousness.[28] Strange

---

[24] This seems the best interpretation of the Greek. See West for other interpretations.

[25] L. S. J. translates μετάτροπα ἔργα, more literally, with "deeds that turn upon their author."

[26] Ἀγορῆφι probably with βλαπτομένοις "in their dealings" (West).

[27] Solmsen, p. 7: "The Kings whom Hesiod here has in mind do not *impose* judgments but rely on their gifts of gentle persuasion—an appeal to reason—to settle the disputes. Hesiod draws his picture of the kings who give straight verdicts and do so by persuasion in opposition to the Iliad passage from which he borrows the phrase (δια)κρίνειν θέμιστας (*Il.* 16. 387 ff.)."

[28] On the meaning of the preverb παρά- cf. E. Schwyzer, *Griechische Grammatik* II, 493: "vorbei und zu etwas anderen übergehen, eine Veränderung bewirken: π. πείθω, -πλάσσω, -φημι."
Though the active use of the verb παράφημι seems little affected by the preposition παρά- (see Hom. *Il.* 1. 577, where Hephaistos "advises" his mother), the

logos, then, that of the good Basileus! It stands firm and straight, but it constitutes a deflecting speech. The metaphor implicit in παράφημι suggests that, while Hesiod praises the straightness and firmness of the right *logos*, he actually conjures up the notions of deflection and even of deviousness. This contradiction is emphatic enough even if we do not notice the other slight incongruity contained in μετάτροπα ἔργα (89), the words for "restitution": the restitution obtained by a straight *logos* means literally "something which is turning back."

Our second example confirms this point. The Muses, Hesiod continues, give benefit to kings, though it is Zeus who protects them; yet the Muses especially help the poets (*Th.* 94 ff.). Fortunate is the man whom the Muses love; his voice is sweet like honey, for (98-103):

> εἰ γάρ τις καὶ πένθος ἔχων νεοκηδέι θυμῷ
> ἄζηται κραδίην ἀκαχήμενος, αὐτὰρ ἀοιδὸς
> Μουσάων θεράπων κλεῖα προτέρων ἀνθρώπων
> ὑμνήσει μάκαράς τε θεοὺς οἳ Ὄλυμπον ἔχουσιν,
> αἶψ' ὅ γε δυσφροσυνέων ἐπιλήθεται οὐδέ τι κηδέων
> μέμνηται. ταχέως δὲ παρέτραπε δῶρα θεάων.

---

use of the middle shows, in Homer, the notion of "misleading," "passing over" (*Il.* 12. 249):

> ἤ τιν' ἄλλον
> παρφάμενος ἐπέεσσιν ἀποστρέψεις πολέμοιο.

The idea of "persuading someone" parallels in this context that of "leading someone astray," as it is emphasized by ἀποστρέψεις. Other examples follow.

Il. 14. 216, 217:

> ἔνθ' ἔνι μὲν φιλότης ἐν δ'ἵμερος ἐν δ'ὀαριστὺς
> πάρφασις, ἥ τ' ἔκλεψε νόον πύκα περ φρονεόντων.

Πάρφασις is one of the ingredients of Aphrodite's κέστος: it deceives (ἔκλεψε) the mind (Detienne, pp. 67 ff.).

Od. 2. 189:

> παρφάμενος ἐπέεσσιν ἐποτρύνῃς χαλεπαίνειν.

Od. 16. 287 = 19. 6, where the verb, with μαλακοῖς ἐπέεσσιν means "to calm down, to reassure" and implies deception. In *Od.* 18. 178 παραυδάω may have a similar connotation of deception and deviousness. For the meaning "deceive" after Hesiod, see the commentary of West.

(When a man feels a new anguish in his grieving heart and he is dried up inside from griefs, if the poet, servant of the Muses, sings about the glory of the old generations of men and about the blessed gods on Olympus, that man soon forgets his grave thoughts, and he does not remember his griefs at all. And quickly the gifts of the goddesses turn him away from them.)

The Muses know how to say the truth; they inspire the words of the king who speaks unerringly and who reaches straight decisions. They are the daughters of Zeus who straightens what is crooked (*Erga* 7), and they inspire the poets, in particular, Hesiod, whom they taught on Helikon. Yet the poet, singing under their inspiration, diverts (παρέτραπε 103) the minds of his listeners. The word παρέτραπε recalls παραιφάμενοι, the "diversionary" persuasion of the good king (*Th.* 90).[29] The song of the poet, therefore, constitutes a vehicle of diversion or a detour, a movement that turns aside.

The diverting, winding movement of the *logos* is expressed by a material or literal image, but it does not lack rigor. The Muses, who teach Hesiod the true, straight discourse, cannot even be described without the risk of imperiling their very attributes of truthfulness and straightness. For the text of the *Theogony*, immediately after 27-28, defines them κοῦραι . . . ἀρτιέπειαι (*Th.* 29). It looks as if Hesiod (or better his text) takes a sort of revenge on the Muses' glibness of tongue in their previous statement; ἀρτιεπής is a *hapax* in the Epos and is used there by Hektor ἀλλά τις ἀρτιεπὴς καὶ ἐπίκλοπος ἔπλεο μύθων (*Il.* 22. 281), who accuses Achilles of being "glib of tongue" and falsely boasting. In fact, Achilles was neither of these as the action then shows, but this detail simply complicates the structure of reference, if this passage is to be considered a valid reference at all. It is difficult to know what to make of an isolated word like this when it is not incorporated in at least a formula; Hesiod might have created the adjective independently from

---

[29] See West *ad loc.*: "παρά- has the same force as in παραιφάμενος, παραμυθεῖσθαι." On both passages, 90 ff. and 103, see H. Fraenkel (*Dichtung und Philosophie des frühen Griechentums* [New York, 1951], p. 150), who points out the parallelism of expression for "das Tun des Königs und des Sängers." Notice that παρατρέπειν λόγον (Hdt. 3. 2) means to falsify a story.

Homer and attributed to it the meaning "sound in speech" (see ἄρτια βάζειν *Il.* 14. 92; *Od.* 8. 240).[30]

The *logos* not only has a sort of magic power as a gift of the goddesses, but it also is described as honey (see *Th.* 97). Speech is like honey when spoken by either the good king who deflects the wrongdoer or by the poet who turns away men's grief.[31] But if the *logos*—independent of both the speaker and its own meaning—is like honey, it must be something different from what it says. Some of the stories found in the honey-like song of the Muses in the *Theogony* are bitter and ominous for mortals—Pandora's and Prometheus' story, for example—but the sweetness of the *logos* remains, in Hesiod's words, the same. The *logos*, therefore, derives its good qualities—persuasiveness and healing force—from something other than its meaning or content. The vicarious, rhetorical, supplementary nature of the *logos* is clearly suggested here, and it obviously imperils the *logos*' ability to be similar / identical to truth; in fact, "to sweeten" in the *Odyssey* is already a metaphor for the "distortion of truth."[32] And in fact this comforting metaphor by which the logos sweetens, pampers itself, is already contradicted by the

---

[30] While in the speculative realm, let us notice also the oddity of the name Helikon, the mount where the Muses met Hesiod. The toponym Helikon (Ἑλικών) has often been connected by etymologists with *Viminalis* and interpreted as "the mountain of Willows" (Fick, Solmsen, P. Chantraine, *Dictionnaire etymologique de la langue grecque*, s.v. Ἑλικών), but the most recent philologists such as Frisk, *Griechisches Etymologisches Worterbuch*, s.v. Ἑλικών, and Chantraine feel that, if the word is Greek, the proposed etymology, though possible, is far from proven. On the one hand, "the mountain of willows" would be applied correctly only to well-watered valleys; on the other, it would imply a word Ϝελικᾱ for the willow other than *ἑλικᾱ (Chantraine). Whatever the etymology may be, the connection between the word Helikon and ἕλιξ can scarcely be avoided; the general idea of winding and a spiral is certainly evoked by the toponym. This suggestion, however, is not explicit in the text through any use of puns or other stylistic devices.

[31] Sweetness of speech is a common quality which we find in the song of the poet, in the eloquence of the righteous king (*Th.* 83-84), and in the truthful and righteous Nereus (*Th.* 235-236):

νημερτής τε καὶ ἤπιος . . . καὶ ἤπια δήνεα οἶδεν.

See Solmsen, p. 6, n. 18, and Detienne, p. 40.

[32] The verb μειλίσσω implies distortion of truth in *Od.* 3. 96 and elsewhere.

first words that the Muses say to Hesiod (*Th.* 26): "Shepherds of
the fields, poor fools, mere bellies!"

Another polarity is introduced in the same passage. The song
drives away grief from men's minds or hearts. The Muses are
emphatically described as totally carefree in their own hearts and
entirely involved with their singing (*Th.* 60-61):

$$\hat{\eta}\sigma\iota\nu \ \dot{a}οιδ\dot{\eta}$$
$$\mu\acute{\epsilon}\mu\beta\lambda\epsilon\tau\alpha\iota \ \dot{\epsilon}\nu \ \sigma\tau\acute{\eta}\theta\epsilon\sigma\sigma\iota\nu, \ \dot{a}\kappa\eta\delta\acute{\epsilon}a \ \theta\upsilon\mu\dot{o}\nu \ \dot{\epsilon}\chi ο\acute{\upsilon}\sigma\alpha\iota\varsigma.^{33}$$

The Muses "inside themselves" feel concerned only with song;
they are free from cares or griefs. The text emphasizes, rather
forcefully, the *inside*, the inner attitude of the Muses. The situation
of the poet should be similar, though the text does not enlighten
us on this point. This omission has no bearing on our argument,
but, in view of the fact that the Muses teach and inspire the poet
and that the theme of their song is the same (i.e., "the true-
hearted manners of the immortals" *Th.* 66), we may assume that
the Muses' carefree attitude and exclusive concern for their song
constitute the poet's ideal condition. Thus, at least ideally, the
poetic song flows from a heart free of care; but in its path it
confronts men's griefs. The expression ἀκηδέα θυμόν applied to the
Muses (61) is explicitly posited against the locution πένθος ἔχων
νεοκηδέι θυμῷ (98) applied to men. As we will see later, this ideal
posture of the poet meets with some contradictory statements.
But let us assume that the poet wishes to suggest for himself the
same serene attitude of the Muses. If we follow the implications of
this assumption, we meet a polarity concerning the self and the
other. The poet is free from cares and the other (the audience) is
full of griefs. Yet this ideal polarity cannot really exist because the
poet is aware of the power of his own song to divert men from
their griefs; the emergence of pity would immediately blur the
clear separation between a carefree self and the grieving other.[34]

[33] The expression, ἀκηδέα θυμὸν ἐχούσαις, is Hesiodean, i.e., non-Homeric. See
West *ad loc.*
[34] The question about the Muses' and the poet's posture before their song
is complex, for not even the Muses are represented as always serene; *Th.* 26
is sufficient to prove it.
The neat separation between self and other is in any case denied in other
passages, for instance *Erga* 265-266.

Even more interesting is the speculation that the *other* and the desire for the *other* is the focus around which the winding movement of the *logos* shapes its polarities, distinctions, and discontinuities. Only once is a perfectly straight line mentioned in Hesiod; though this occurs in a context unrelated to language, it is nevertheless instructive. A good laborer—says the poet—can plow furrows in perfectly straight lines, but a younger man cannot do the same task as well. The inability of the young man does not depend on his lack of experience or technical knowledge. No, the reason is that he gazes with excitement at his fellow laborers (μεθ' ὁμήλικας ἐπτοίηται *Erga* 447). Mazon defines this last line as a boutade. But the crookedness of the line, of *dike*, of *logos*, must somehow be represented by the same image which implies the same essential conception of straightness. In all these cases the deviation takes place in a relationship with the *other*.[35]

The Song of Memory and of Oblivion

The tension, self : other, is implicit in the polarity ἀκηδέα θυμόν : νεοκηδέι θυμῷ that we have examined; yet Hesiod seems unaware of its importance and far-reaching effects. On the contrary, he insists on the healing effects of the song. In one passage (*Th.* 98-103), poetry results in forgetfulness of the self, for it effaces one's griefs. At *Theogony* 51 the poet has already said that the song of the Muses delights (τέρπουσι) the mind of Zeus. In the case of mortals, the sweet song of the poet effaces griefs and evidently inspires joy or pleasure. Thus Hesiod can write of the paradox, the real paradox of the poetic *logos*, namely that the Muses, daughters of Memory, bring forth forgetfulness (*Th.* 52 ff.):

Μοῦσαι . . .
τὰς ἐν Πιερίῃ Κρονίδῃ τέκε πατρὶ μιγεῖσα
Μνημοσύνη, γουνοῖσιν Ἐλευθῆρος μεδέουσα
λησμοσύνην τε κακῶν ἄμπαυμά τε μερμηράων.

[35] For Aristotle also the fundamental condition of human discourse lies in the fact that it is always a discourse for the other: "For it is a universal habit for the inquirers to aim not at the object itself but at the contradictor; and even when one inquires by himself he advances until he is no longer able to contradict himself" (Aristotle *De Caelo* 294 b). See P. Aubenque (above n. 19), p. 114.

(The Muses . . . whom in Pieria did Mnemosyne [i.e., Memory] . . . bear in union with the Father, son of Kronos, to be forgetfulness of evils and rest from cares.)

The juxtaposition of Μνημοσύνη and λησμοσύνη at the beginning of these lines is conscious and purposeful.[36] The song of the Muses conjures up the past, the present, and the future (*Th.* 38). It is therefore memory, but at the same time this memory diverts the mind and causes forgetfulness of the self, for it is "a forgetting of ills and rest from sorrows . . ." (*Th.* 55). The song of memory is also a song of forgetfulness in the same way that the straight *logos* is devious and that no mark distinguishes true from false discourse. The *logos*, the strange entity that at once evokes and makes present what is not there, what is not itself, encompasses evidently the polarity Memory and Forgetfulness as well.[37] The song of memory is also a song of forgetfulness in the deep sense, that of life and death, that memory and forgetfulness acquire in Greek mystical and religious thought.[38]

Now we can add a new polarity, Memory : Forgetfulness, to the set of other polarities comprehending the *logos*:

Truth	: Falsehood
Straightness	: Crookedness
Steadfastness	: Erring
Memory	: Forgetfulness

The left column—truth, straightness, steadfastness and memory—represents the qualities of a *logos* or song conforming to Hesiod's desire. The correspondence between the true and the straight has already been shown. We should now demonstrate the connection between truth (straightness-steadfastness) and memory. In *Theogony* 233 ff., Nereus, the good old man of the sea, is praised for his virtues:

---

[36] West calls this juxtaposition "a conscious paradox."

[37] A different but parallel explanation is proposed by J. P. Vernant, *Mythe et Pensée chez les Grecs* (Paris, 1965), p. 59, who states that the forgetfulness of present sorrows is brought forth by the recalling of the past. Analogously, Detienne, pp. 9-27.

[38] Cf. Vernant, p. 60 ff.

Νηρέα δ'ἀψευδέα καὶ ἀληθέα γείνατο Πόντος
πρεσβύτατον παίδων· αὐτὰρ καλέουσι γέροντα
οὕνεκα νημερτής τε καὶ ἤπιος, οὐδὲ θεμίστων
λήθεται, ἀλλὰ δίκαια καὶ ἤπια δήνεα οἶδεν.

(And Pontos begat as the eldest of his children Nereus, the man without lies and truthful. Men call him the Old Man for he is infallible and kind, and he does not forget the judgments; he knows just and kind thoughts.)

Nereus' truthfulness (ἀληθέα) is connected, among other things, with the fact that "he does not forget the ordinances or the judgments" (οὐδὲ θεμίστων λήθεται).[39] West (p. 233), while calling attention to line 235, develops the argument that Nereus' ἀληθέα is contrasted with the Λήθη (Forgetfulness) of line 227. The text mentions—among many other evils—Λήθη as a child of Eris (Discord). Here are some lines of that gruesome catalogue (*Th.* 226 ff.):

αὐτὰρ Ἔρις στυγερὴ τέκε μὲν Πόνον ἀλγινόεντα
Λήθην τε Λιμόν τε καὶ Ἄλγεα δακρυόεντα
Ὑσμίνας τε Μάχας τε Φόνους τ' Ἀνδροκτασίας τε
Νείκεά τε Ψεύδεά τε Λόγους τ' Ἀμφιλλογίας τε
Δυσνομίην τ' Ἄτην τε, συνήθεας ἀλλήλῃσιν
Ὅρκον θ', ...

Forgetfulness is therefore in the unpleasant company of hardships and labors of all kinds, such as Fight and Struggle, and also of such intellectual calamities as Falsehood, Discourses (Λόγους), and Disputes. Here, therefore, forgetfulness and falsehood are connected by belonging to the same family and, accordingly, they are posited against Nereus' truthfulness and lack of λήθη (233 ff.). Concerning the etymological play a-ληθ-, West (p. 233) writes: "'Αληθής, -εια are often thought of in this etymological way, and so associated with remembering, cf. *Il.* 23.351 and many later

---

[39] We should not press this point too much, for *forgetfulness* of crooked, unjust decisions (*Erga* 264) would rank forgetfulness with truth and straightness. But like Nereus, Zeus is characterized by lack of λήθη in *Erga* 268-269:

καί νυ τάδ', αἴ κ' ἐθέλῃ ἐπιδέρκεται, οὐδέ ἑ λήθει
οἵην δὴ καὶ τήνδε δίκην πόλις ἐντὸς ἐέργει.

Here λανθάνω has the normal active meaning of "escape notice."

examples collected by E. Heitsch, *Hermes* 1962, pp. 26-30."[40] The juxtaposition of ἀψευδέα and ἀληθέα in line 233 might even support the idea of a conscious etymological play; in this way ἀληθέα— taken as a negative term, ἀ-ληθέα—and ἀψευδέα would constitute an elegant symmetry.[41]

Nereus' truthfulness is defined by his lack of forgetfulness or neglect (235). The praise of Nereus' truthfulness follows upon a catalogue of the evil children of Eris in which forgetfulness and falsehood are connected. From this evidence, we can extrapolate a set of correspondences as follows:

Truth	: Memory	= Falsehood : Forgetfulness
(Alethea)	(Mnemosyne)	(Pseudea) : (Lethe)

This set of correpondences confirms our set of polarities. Truth and memory are in the column opposed to falsehood and forget-fulness.[42]

---

[40] An important paper by M. Detienne on the relationship between Ἀλήθεια and Λήθη appeared in *REG* 73 (1960), 27 ff. See also *Les maîtres*, pp. 9-27, 105 ff. Krischer (above, n. 9), connects ἀληθής of *Th.* 233 with λήθη of 227, pp. 161-174, and in particular p. 165, n. 1.

We should make it clear that today the accepted etymology of ἀλήθεια mainly derives from the active meaning of λανθάνω "to pass unnoticed, unperceived," though the connection of ἀλήθεια with λήθη, λανθάνομαι "forgetfulness, to forget" is supported by scholars (see Luther, *Archiv*, pp. 35 f.) and in fact it is empha-sized by the Greek texts since *Il.* 23. 361. Luther (p. 36) reconciles both etymo-logical connections.

On the matter of being true as "being uncovering" see M. Heidegger, *Being and Time* (New York, 1962), pp. 262 ff.

[41] The Greek taste for the alliteration of negative words is well known. In Hesiod see *Th.* 277, 489, 797, 944.

P. Friedlander, *Plato* 1. 2d ed. (Berlin, 1954), p. 235, denies that the Greeks felt in living language the etymological origin of ἀλήθεια. Detienne (*REG*, p. 33) states that the relationship between the two religious representations πεδίον Λήθης and πεδίον Ἀληθείας "nous réstitue un plan de la conscience où l'a-privatif avait sa pleine valeur, et c'est le plan mythique." H. D. Rankin in *Glotta* (1963), 51 ff., infers from Plato's usage of the same two expressions an awareness of the negative force of ἀλήθεια. Luther (*Archiv*, p. 33) convincingly argues from *Od.* 13. 254 f. that the living language felt the negative formation of ἀλήθεια.

[42] One should become aware that the polarity, memory forgetfulness, also implies the polarity, self other. The memory of the Muses—the song of the other—effaces the self. This is true in a double sense: the poet forgetful of himself is simply repeating the song the Muses taught him, and his listeners

At this point we should realize how the Muses' ability to cause forgetfulness (even only forgetfulness of evils, λησμοσύνη κακῶν *Th.* 55) narrows their claim to truthful utterance (*Th.* 28). For the Muses' *logos* effaces (see ἐπιλήθεται *Th.* 102) the truth of the mind, of the self and turns the mind towards the truth about past heroes and blessed gods. This *logos* numbs the sense and the perception of what is there present in the mind and creates an artificially induced serenity. Thus the truthful *logos* of the Muses is also a discourse *effacing* some truth, the truth of the self and of the present. Moreover forgetfulness stands in the column containing falsehood and crookedness. By now no one should be surprised at this, for the lack of demarcation in the polarity, Memory : Forgetfulness, simply repeats the lack of real (i.e., within the text) demarcation between the terms of the other polarities, straight : crooked, and truth : falsehood. The paradox of the Muses as daughters of Memory and causes of forgetfulness corresponds to the paradox of the Muses uttering false discourse identical to a truthful one, or to the paradox of a straight *logos* that persuades by deviousness. In these cases the paradox results from the same basic contradiction; the distinction is made and the polarity is shaped and maintained in defiance of the text, which first, declares the impossibility of distinguishing a false *logos* from a true one, second, does not consistently support a neat separation between straightness and crookedness, and, finally, plays consciously on the coincidence of memory and forgetfulness. This perplexing situation is too consistently structured to result from chance; it must depend on a coherent principle. As we have already suggested, the polarities are in some way the result of Hesiod's writing. The poet's desire for a word that is firm, stable, straight, truthful, corresponds to his desire to interpret and speak for justice and Zeus, to become the voice repeating their voices. In the wake of this desire a clear distinction is made: *logos* is viewed as truthful and false, straight and crooked. Yet beneath these clear distinctions (and often beyond Hesiod's consciousness) intrudes the real nature of lan-

---

forget themselves. But as the Muses constitute the hypostatization of Hesiod's self, the polarity is turned into a self that aims at possessing the others and making them forgetful of themselves.

guage: a vicarious entity, hinting at what it means rather than telling it, and becoming meaning by a deviating movement. This movement effaces over and over the polarities continually shaped and maintained by the impulse of Hesiod's desire.

The Logos as a Remedy

The truthful, straight, remembering *logos* of the Muses produces a healthy effect on the anguished soul by softening the truth (γλυκερὴ ... αὐδή *Th.* 97, μαλακοῖσι ... ἐπέεσσιν), by deflecting the mind, and by inspiring forgetfulness. The paradox is particularly marked and, as we have seen, obeys a rigorous necessity. Let us comment on the paradoxical quality of this *logos*. Already in Homer clear evidence posits the poetic *logos* as a source of pleasure; in the *Odyssey* the poet goes so far as to say that this pleasure (τέρπειν) does not necessarily stem from the gratifying narration of glorious deeds, but it comes rather from the song of the poet, wherever it might wander, even to the sad and inglorious returns of the heroes (νόστοι *Od.* 1. 346 ff.). These ideas expressed by Telemachos receive the necessary stress from their context, for Penelope had asked Phemios to sing what is pleasing to men (ἄλλα βροτῶν θελκτήρια *viz.* ἔργ' ανδρῶν τε θεῶν τε 1. 337f.) and to avoid sad and inglorious matters (340 f.). Yet only Hesiod's text provides all the stages of a complete argument on this pleasurable effect of the poetic *logos*. If we start from the discourse of the Muses, which looks like truth but is in reality difference, we begin to understand the rigor of Hesiod's thought. As a false imitation of reality, as honey which runs from the mouth of the poet, this discourse is difference and deferment, a supplementary structure added to reality, which replaces and displaces just as it evokes reality. By this process, evidently, the discourse allays sorrows and introduces forgetfulness into the minds of men. The *logos* of the poet begins to sing the glorious deeds of past men and the blessed gods in Olympus (*Th.* 100-101):

κλεῖα προτέρων ἀνθρώπων
... μάκαράς τε θεούς

as befits the theme and also the epic subject of the *Theogony*. The

glorious deeds of heroes[43] and gods are the pleasant themes
Penelope would like to hear instead of the *nostoi*, and also Achilles'
subject, when he sings in Book 9 of the *Iliad* (189):

τῇ ὅ γε θυμὸν ἔτερπεν, ἄεισε δ᾽ ἄρα κλέα ἀνδρῶν.[44]

As the poet sings these themes, evidently true since they are
inspired by the Muses, what is present to men absents itself, what
is deep inside men is distracted and turned away. It is not perhaps
a matter of sheer chance—even so, chance becomes somehow
meaningful—that the Muses teach the poet to sing of the past and
of the future (not of the present):

... ἵνα κλείοιμι τά τ᾽ ἐσσόμενα πρό τ᾽ ἐόντα   [*Th.* 32].

but the Muses themselves sing past, present, and future:

εἴρουσαι τά τ᾽ ἐόντα τά τ᾽ ἐσσόμενα πρό τ᾽ ἐόντα   [*Th.* 38].

The two forms might well be equivalent, as West maintains in his
commentary, but one should notice the different emphasis produced by variation of the formula. Thus, by inspiring forgetfulness
of the present and of the self, the Muses deny just what they claim
to teach, *aletheia*. Hesiod is not aware of the oblivious, negative,
absenting side of his restoring *logos*, but seems to emphasize the
divine attribute of song and its glorious theme. He is convinced
that he is singing the truthful song of the Muses, and because of
this the poet does not notice the movement of difference and
paradox that ensues. By the same token, he hints that a serenity of
mind will be fully restored. For the Muses are described as ἀκηδέα
θυμὸν ἐχούσαις (61) with a non-Homeric formula that also designates
in the *Erga* the heroes in the blessed islands and the happy people
of the golden race (170 and 112). By removing the anguish from
νεοκηδέι θυμῷ, the song of the Muses restores the full serenity which
belongs to the gods and which belonged to men before their
parting with the gods. As befits a song coming from the gods, it

---

[43] The πρότεροι ἄνθρωποι are the heroes; see *Erga* 158-160, *Il.* 5. 637.
[44] See also *Od.* 8. 73:

μοῦσ᾽ ἄρ᾽ ἀοιδὸν ἀνῆκεν ἀειδέμεναι κλέα ἀνδρῶν οἴμης.

produces divine effects, it annuls the difference in every sense of this word, even the discrepancy between men and gods.

The oblivious, devious and absenting side of his *logos* escapes the poet, but without this facet of his text there would be no restoration of serenity. Our analysis has shown that, connected with this absenting of the present and of the self and with the forgetfulness of *lethe*, are violence and death. For the sweetness and the gentleness of Nereus and of the poet inspired by the Muses are attributes of the true, reminding *logos*. The *logos* of *lethe* is a son of Eris and therefore a brother of Hunger and Anguish, Struggle, Battle, Murder, Homicide, and Quarrels, Lie, and Dispute (*Th.* 226 ff.). Truly Hesiod's poetic *logos* as such implies violence. First of all, it suggests the rejection of the old Homeric poetry (if the usual interpretation is correct), or, in any case, the poetry of others, which is scorned as imitation of truth and difference from truth and condemned by a gesture of bitter refusal. For the Muses are not sweet at all when they insult the shepherds and call them obtuse and vulgar (*Th.* 26). The Muses' bold, violent gesture of rejecting all earlier poetry constitutes their first teaching to their pupil Hesiod. Second, this *logos* inspires forgetfulness, the absenting of the present and the self. This effect might be viewed in connection with the murderous relatives of *logos* (*Th.* 226 ff.) and might therefore prompt the suggestion that it reveals the fear and the presence of death. Consequently, the *logos* of the Muses takes its form in the wake of death as a deferment of death.

The pleasant, idyllic effects of the *logos* are brilliantly celebrated by the poet, whereas the side effects are simply mentioned in the same passage or recorded in other contexts and are almost hidden. But the structure of the negative effects counterbalances perfectly that of the pleasant ones; this precise balance shows the pertinence of our reconstruction. Indeed, this reconstruction shows the coherence and inner logic of the text. For ultimately the text in these hesitations and tensions, in this strategy we have illustrated, reveals the great force of the desire for godlike serenity combined with the desecrating movement of difference. And thus the metaphysical desire for a divine *logos* takes shape also as the *logos* presents itself, as a son of Eris.

Nemean 7 and the Theme of Vicissitude in Pindar

G. M. KIRKWOOD

Most readers find themselves troubled by the inescapable presence of the poet in *Nemean 7*. Pindar's presence in his poems does not usually trouble us. When at the end of *Olympian 1* he links himself with the victor, and in *O. 6* indicates that he has by his poem shown himself to be free of the rustic boorishness of the "Boeotian pig" (90),[1] we accept in these as in many similar passages the poet and his art as legitimate parts of the encomiastic whole. The presence of the artist in his poem is part of the χάρις of the celebration of victory. But in *N. 7* there is a note of urgent self-justification that deeply affects and modifies the encomiastic tone and raises questions of relevance and poetic unity.

Answers to some of the most interesting and perplexing of these questions can be made more adequately if we use in our interpretation a very important yet often neglected aspect of Pindar's comprehension of myth and human experience: his brooding consciousness of fluctuation or vicissitude in human fortunes. This aspect of the Pindaric outlook has been observed by a number of critics, but it has not been used much for the understanding of his poetry in general and has been applied very little in the exegesis of *N. 7*.[2] Enough points of doubt are left unsolved by this approach

---

[1] References to the *Epinicians* are to the Snell-Maehler Teubner text, *Pindari Carmina I* (Leipzig, 1971). For the fragments the corresponding text, Snell's third Teubner edition (Leipzig, 1964), is used. Both are hereafter cited as Snell. Translations are my own.

[2] John H. Finley, Jr., *Pindar and Aeschylus* (Cambridge, Mass., 1955), makes "Vicissitude" one of four principal "themes" of Pindar's odes, and on pp. 59-77 discusses six odes (not including *N. 7*) as exemplifying this theme. C. M. Bowra, *Pindar* (Oxford, 1964), makes a number of good observations; see especially

to discourage any broad "smile of triumph,"[3] but the general meaning of the poem, the relevance of its main parts, and the interpretation of some of its most problematical passages are substantially illuminated by its application.

The poet invokes Eileithyia, goddess of birth (1-6), and moves on to praise of the victor, Sogenes, and Aegina, his home (7-10); then comes the theme that deeds well done call for songs of praise (11-16). Transition to the myth is made by way of a difficult passage, beginning with the statement that *sophoi* foresee a wind that will come in two days and are not ruined by profit. After the aphorism that rich and poor alike must die, the passage continues with the statement that Homer's account of Odysseus exaggerates his worth by its charming untruths, and that most men are easily misled; otherwise Odysseus's reputation would not have been so high, and Ajax would not have taken his own life. From Ajax Pindar moves to Neoptolemus, and an explanation that his death at Delphi was a fulfillment of destiny. There is much emphasis on the honored place that he has at Delphi, as θεμισκόπος ἡροΐαις πόμπαις (46-47). This, the main mythic section, brings us to a point about half way through the poem and into Triad 3. The myth ends with praise of the Aeacids, and then, by way of another puzzling transition and maxim, gets back to the present occasion, turning to Thearion, the victor's father, and to asseverations of Pindar's friendship with him.

Triad 4 continues the personal theme, at a higher emotional pitch. Pindar exclaims that "an Achaean man from beyond the Ionian sea" (64-65) will not blame him; that is, no man from the district of Epirus, where the descendants of Neoptolemus rule, will blame Pindar; he does not at this point say what they might blame him for. Pindar is, he goes on to tell us, their *proxenos*. Then, beginning with the assertion that he has said nothing amiss, Pindar

---

pp. 250-252. Ernst Tugendhat, "Zum Rechtfertigungsproblem in Pindars 7. Nemeischen Gedicht," *Hermes* 88 (1960), 385-409, discusses the matter of vicissitude in *N.* 7 especially on pp. 406-409. Hermann Fränkel, "Man's 'Ephemeros' Nature According to Pindar and Others," *TAPA* 77 (1946), 131-145, makes important general observations on the topic.

[3] B. L. Gildersleeve, *AJP* 31 (1910), 126: "Commentator after commentator has retired baffled; baffled even when they have worn a smile of triumph."

proceeds to an elaborate metaphor drawn from the games and to the declaration that if he has raised his voice too high, he is ready to "set down" a favor for the victor.[4]

Triad 4 ends, and 5 begins, with a brief passage in praise of Zeus, the god of the Nemean games, and his son Aeacus, and Aeacus's brother Heracles, who, it appears, had shrines neighboring on Thearion's house. This personal note, with a return to the victor, is followed by four lines in which Pindar speaks defensively about his poetic treatment of Neoptolemus. With this troubled and abrupt passage the poem ends.

In its general proportions and subject matter the poem is not unusual. There is praise of the victor and his family, a prominent place for the poet and his art, and a passage of myth. All this is customary; if the attention given to the poet himself, in Triad 4, is more than usually extensive, such a disproportion is itself readily paralleled; the epinician form has no set proportions. Where the poem departs from the Pindaric norm, and in the opinion of many critics from any acceptable norm of poetry, is in the intensity of Pindar's insertion of himself in the poem and the domination of the poem by a self-justifying emphasis on his treatment of Neoptolemus.

In comment on the poet's exclamation, at the very and of the poem (102-104), "Never shall my heart declare that I have abused Neoptolemus with inflexible words," one editor was moved to declare that Pindar was afflicted with "a returning attack of egoism."[5] If this comment is justified, the implications are disastrous for the poem; a passage that is to be explained solely as a manifestation of the poet's egoism is very bad encomiastic poetry indeed.

Farnell, the editor in question, may simply be wrong in his judgment; that is a question which will arise later in this study. But Farnell is not without company in his view, and not without substantial grounds for believing that the passage is to be inter-

[4] My interpretation assumes the punctuation of lines 75-76 in Snell and in the text of C. M. Bowra, *Pindari Carmina cum fragmentis* (Oxford, 2d ed. 1947), and A. Turyn, *Pindari carmina cum fragmentis* (Oxford, 2d ed. 1952). A different punctuation would make line 75 mean, "If I have raised my voice too high in praise of the victor."

[5] L. R. Farnell, *The Works of Pindar* (London, 1930), I, 209.

preted as an intrusion by the poet and his emotions. The scholiasts tell us that not only this passage but other aspects of the treatment of Neoptolemus in *N.* 7 were conditioned by Pindar's desire to defend himself and to justify his references to Neoptolemus in *Paean* 6. The Aeginetans had, according to the scholia, taken strong exception to the lines in that poem (to which we shall return) in which the death of Neoptolemus at Delphi is described.

But why would Pindar devote part of an epinician ode to a defense of himself? What is its relevance? Are we to think that Pindar's interpretations of myth are so shifting and ephemeral that he denigrates Neoptolemus in one poem in order to glorify Apollo, and then praises him when next he has occasion to write for an Aeginetan patron? If this is so, why is Pindar so passionately defensive, in *N.* 7, about his treatment of Neoptolemus? Gilbert Norwood would have it that "Pindar for his own utterly irrelevant purpose foists the original 'hero' Neoptolemus upon poor Sogenes and his ode, proceeding to explain away the offensive paean by a cool insistence that he has not said what he had said therein."[6] Norwood's misrepresentation of the spirit of *N.* 7 at once demolishes the force of his assertion. There is nothing like a "cool insistence" here; that is what there ought to be, for Norwood's view to be right. On the contrary there is a deeply troubled and personally involved defense of Pindar's attitude toward Neoptolemus.

Several recent critics have asserted[7] that the scholiast who made the connection between *N.* 7 and *Paean* 6 and explained lines 102-104 thereby was only making a literary-critical inference.

---

[6] Gilbert Norwood, *Pindar* (Berkeley, 1945), p. 84.

[7] See E. L. Bundy, "Studia Pindarica I," *University of California Publications in Classical Philology* (Berkeley, 1962) pp. 4, 29, and Erich Thummer, *Pindar: Die Isthmische Gedichte, I* (Heidelberg, 1968), 94-98. Thummer does not discuss the scholia but agrees with Bundy in regarding the references to Neoptolemus and to Pindar's attitude toward this hero as pertaining only to *N.* 7. He refers to the comparison of the two treatments of Neoptolemus as "interesting but not important" for the interpretation of *N.* 7 (p. 96). Since my purpose is to show that the principle of vicissitude is crucial to the interpretation of both poems, I regard the comparison as important, even if one declines to accept the ancient account of their historical connection. Neither Bundy nor Thummer, I think, adequately explains the urgent tone of certain passages of *N.* 7.

Aware of this other poem in which Pindar mentions Neoptolemus,[8] the ancient critic assumed, it is argued, that the apparent strangeness of expression in some passages of $N.$ 7 reflects the poet's desire to insist that the unflattering references to Neoptolemus in *Paean* 6 were not an attack on him. The critic would presumably have been led to his interpretation not only by the emotional tone and apparent personal nature of the passages themselves but also by the strikingly different presentation of Neoptolemus in the two poems.

It does not matter to the argument of this essay whether the scholiast's reference to *Paean* 6 is a literary-critical inference or conveys a literary-historical tradition. Nevertheless, it seems worthwhile to register a protest against too easy a general dismissal of what the scholia say; the Pindaric scholia are too important to be slighted.

In the first place, we all accept some information conveyed by the Pindaric scholia which cannot be explained as inference; the scholia are our principal source for the dating of a number of poems. Since nobody has ever suggested that the dates given by the scholia are confections of the scholiasts and since some of these dates can in fact be confirmed by external evidence,[9] it is clear that the Pindaric scholia draw on historical information not always available to us. And we should of course expect so, since we know that many of these notes go back to conscientious and able critics.[10]

In the second place, lines 102-104 of $N.$ 7 need explication. To say, as E. L. Bundy says, that "the authors of the scholia had only the odes to aid them," and to dismiss the information as "one guess reported by the scholia," is to shrug off a legitimate question of scholarship much too lightly; and to characterize the reference here to Neoptolemus as merely an assertion that the poet "has

[8] Neoptolemus is mentioned by Pindar only in these two poems and in $N.$ 4, where he is merely listed in an enumeration of the places of power of various Aeacids. All the other Aeacids, Peleus, Achilles, Telamon, and Ajax, as well as Aeacus himself, are mentioned far more often.

[9] For example, the dates of $O.$ 12 and $O.$ 13 given by the scholia are confirmed by other sources. For references see Camille Gaspar, *Essai de Chronologie Pindarique* (Brussels, 1900), pp. 123, 142.

[10] Aristarchus and Didymus are repeatedly cited as authorities. Jean Irigoin gives a brief description of the traditions of the scholia in *Histoire du Texte de Pindare* (Paris, 1952), pp. 102-105.

done justice to this hero and to the other laudandi of the ode"[11]
is unconvincing. It strains credence to maintain that the words
οὐκ ... ἀτρόποισι Νεοπτολέμου ἐλκύσαι ἔπεσι are a way of
saying "I have praised Neoptolemus well," and the one parallel
passage adduced by Bundy, *O.* 2. 95-100, is itself far too unclear
to clarify the interpretation of *N.* 7. 102-104.[12]

Admittedly, many interpretations offered in Pindaric scholia
are transparent inferences, and some of them are extremely bad.
But the form of the scholium, not only its quality, is likely to betray
this fact. When, for example, a scholiast asserts, at line 82 of *N.* 3,
that the words κραγέται δὲ κολοιοὶ ταπεινὰ νέμονται refer specifically to Bacchylides, the suggestion is intrinsically bad. The
passage, clearly a metaphor of excellence contrasted with inferiority, needs no external explanation, and the scholiast's introduction
of Bacchylides is a lame copy of the tradition concerning the
difficult passage, *O.* 2. 87, in which "a pair of chattering crows"
are often taken to represent Bacchylides and Simonides. In the
N. 3 passage, not only is the intrinsic inferiority of the interpretation clear, but the introductory word of the note, δοκεῖ,
indicates that the critic is speculating, not reporting a historical
tradition. Similarly, a scholium to the first line of *N.* 7, on the
invocation of Eileithyia, suggests special circumstances in the
occasion of the ode which account for the invocation of the
goddess of birth in an ode for athletic victory. Again, no such
accounting is needed; as we shall see later, features and emphases
of the poem make the invocation of Eileithyia especially appropriate, but the simple fact of the invocation is not surprising.
Eileithyia is a kind of Moira, a dispenser of fate; as such she is

[11] Bundy (above, n. 7), pp. 4, 9, 29.

[12] *O.* 2. 95-100 is a difficult passage, and Bundy's interpretation, in which
the μάργοι are excessive eulogizers, rather than those resentful of another's praise,
is dubious. If, as he maintains, κόρος means excessive praise, it is hard to make
sense out of οὐ δίκᾳ συναντόμενος, line 96, or of θέλων, line 97. Bundy's objection
to connecting κόρος with envy is ill-founded, since κόρος conveys the notion of
satiety and ill-will at *P.* 8. 32 and *N.* 10. 19. Cf. R. W. B. Burton, *Pindar's
Pythian Odes* (Oxford, 1962), p. 107.

W. J. Slater, *Classical Quarterly* 63 (1969), 91-94, arrives at much the same
meaning as Bundy for 102-104, but only by dint of implausible straining of the
of the sense of the words.

appropriate to the context of success through natural endowment. The form of the scholium reveals clearly that it presents a literary-critical inference, not a piece of historical information:

Some say that Thearion was a priest of Eileithyia, but there is no evidence for this. Others, that there was a neighboring shrine of Eileithyia; this is not recorded either. Others say that it is because Pindar always praises those good by nature, rather than by training, and Eileithyia endowed Sogenes with athletic skill from his very birth; other gods give blessings to those who are already growing, but Eileithyia at the very outset. But to this it can be said: Why then does he adduce Eileithyia particularly in the case of Sogenes, and not for others distinguished for natural endowment? Aristodemus, the pupil of Aristarchus, says it better thus (βέλτιον οὕτω φησί): Sogenes was born when Thearion was already advanced in age and had prayed to the goddess; the birth of the child is a sort of favor of Eileithyia.

To say that Aristodemus "says it better," and to follow this with a piece of information containing a most improbable intimacy of detail, especially the matter of Thearion's prayer, is to imply that the writer is recording speculative suggestions, not historical traditions.[13]

The references to the tradition of Aeginetan resentment of *Paean* 6 are not couched in such ambiguous terms, and Aristarchus is given as the authority for it.[14] Aristarchus need not be right, but to dismiss his notes as mere guesses is unwarranted.

It cannot be proven that the tradition of Aeginetan resentment

[13] For a valuable and entertaining analysis of scholiastic speculations, see Hermann Fränkel, "Schrullen in den Scholien zu Pindars Nemeen 7 und Olympien 3," *Hermes* 89 (1961), 385-397.

[14] Bundy (p. 4) quotes only the scholium to line 102. But the relevant information is given also in a note to line 48, where it is ascribed to Aristarchus. The fullest reference, but without ascription to Aristarchus, is in a scholium to line 64; in this note there is some speculative interpretation about other matters but no indication that the tradition of Aeginetan resentment of *Paean* 6 is speculative. David C. Young, "Pindar *Nemean* 7: Some Preliminary Remarks (vv. 1-20)," *TAPA* 101 (1970), 633-643, expresses reservations about the ascription of the tradition to Aristarchus, on the grounds that "there are considerable difficulties in ascribing the scholiasts' explanations to their proper author" (n. 2). The discussion by S. L. Radt, *Pindars zweiter und sechster Paian* (Amsterdam, 1958), p. 85, n. 4, to which Young refers for confirmation of his doubts, argues for ascription of this information to Aristarchus.

is historically valid. In any case, the fervor with which Pindar in *N.* 7 defends his presentation of Neoptolemus and the strikingly different ways in which Neoptolemus appears in *Paean* 6 and *N.* 7 are necessary and important considerations for the understanding of *N.* 7 It can be shown, I think, that these are in fact crucial considerations and that they are, moreover, manifestations of the concept of the mutability of fortune.

The suggestion that Pindar was conscious of the mutability of human fortunes presents nothing new. No concept is more prevalent in the archaic Greek outlook, and there is no more famous example of the outlook than the closing lines of *Pythian* 8.[15] It is probably not an exaggeration to say that this outlook is one of two main elements of Pindar's understanding of human fortunes, of what accounts for a man's success or failure. The second element is his conviction that superior natural endowment is necessary for success. Both these tenets are characteristic of archaic Greece, but they are, partially at least, in conflict, and their joint presence in Pindar's view of life creates a tension and balance in which each outlook conditions the other. In this as in many respects the central mythological symbol of the Pindaric epinician is Heracles,[16] whose career is one of toil but whose divinity also is part of the heroic essence; Heracles always performs κατὰ δαίμονα, as in *O.* 9. 27-35. But the emphasis on hereditary endowment tends to predominate in the impression created by Pindar's poetry. This is perhaps inevitable in poetry that concerns itself with successful achievement, but if we over-emphasize this aspect and do not perceive the recurrent patterns of vicissitude, we are likely to obscure some of the most moving and profound themes and passages in the odes. Along with the aristocratic insistence that—in victor as in poet—only he who performs φυᾷ, by the power of his inborn ἀρετά (*O.* 2. 86, σοφὸς ὁ πολλὰ εἰδὼς φυᾷ;[17] *O.* 9. 100, τὸ δὲ φυᾷ

[15] The passage is the starting point of Fränkel's article, "Man's 'Ephemeros' Nature" (above, n. 2).

[16] Cf. *N.* 1. 33-34: ἐγὼ δ' Ἡρακλέος ἀντέχομαι προφρόνως/ἐν κορυφαῖς ἀρετᾶν μεγάλαις.

[17] For discussion of the apparently traditional admiration of the man who "knows many things," and of the criticism of that tradition by Archilochus, Heraclitus, and others, see Michael C. Stokes, *One and Many in Presocratic Philosophy* (Cambridge, Mass., 1971), pp. 88-89 and n. 11.

κράτιστον ἅπαν), can achieve greatness, there is also present, in the Pindaric view, a recognition that all human beings are ἐπάμεροι (*P.* 8. 95) and burdened with more woes than blessings (*P.* 3.81-82). Pindar is not only the heir of the traditional epic, chivalric confidence in the excellence and success of the ἀγαθός; he has also the Archilochian perception (Fr. 67a), οἷος ῥυσμὸς ἀνθρώπους ἔχει.

The Pindaric perception of the mutability of fortune is far more developed and articulated than this archaic outlook of Archilochus. Along with the Pindaric concept goes a complex understanding of myth that belies the somewhat simplified interpretation that we may think we are seeing, if we consider only the Pindaric presentation of deity.

To say, as is often said, that Pindar habitually avoids speaking of evils in his treatment of myth is a half truth. His refusal, in *O.* 1, to accept the divine cannibalism of the usual story of Tantalus and Pelops is familiar. In the many references to the career of Heracles throughout the odes there is hardly a word about Hera's persecution of the hero, though this detail of the legend is recurrent and as old as the *Iliad* (19. 95-133). In the one poem where the birth of Heracles and the strangling of the snakes that attacked him in his cradle are the main features of the myth (*N.* 1) the fact that Hera sent the snakes (37-40) is mentioned, but the emphasis is on the prowess of the infant Heracles. The poet is frank in ascribing heated emotions to the goddess, but he does not, here or anywhere, suggest the abiding and vindictive hatred usually ascribed to her in connection with this incident. In *O.* 9 there is a puzzling passage about the encounter of Heracles with Poseidon, Apollo, and Hades; it is not clear whether Pindar is expressing disbelief in this story (or group of stories); if he is not, it is clear that Heracles can oppose deity only because he acts κατὰ δαίμονα (28), and the passage therefore cannot be taken as questioning divinity's inviolability in relation to man.

Pindar avoids incidents of myth that attribute to the gods discreditable actions or motives. Thus far the belief that the poet avoids evil in myth is true; but it is by no means true that he declines to attribute evil, much less misfortune and disaster, to the human persons of myth.

Two families of mythology seem, along with Heracles, to have a specially strong and personal significance for Pindar: one is the Theban family, from Cadmus to the grandsons of Oedipus; the other is the Aeginetan group, Aeacus and his descendants. Both attachments are understandable; Theban stories are home territory, while Aegina and its heroes represent, in Pindar's view, a particularly powerful and touching example of the aristocratic tradition of moral and physical ἀρετά. Pindar wrote far more epinicians for Aeginetans than for victors of any other state, and an air of intimacy and affection prevails in the Aeginetan odes. The closing lines of one of these, *P.* 8, contain a roster of Aeginetan heroes of mythology whose names seem to symbolize the ultimate in human excellence.

In the mythology of Thebes the presence of sorrows can hardly be ignored. In *O.* 2, Pindar lists a series of Theban stories of disaster: Semele died "at the roaring of the thunderbolt" (25-26), Laius's "fateful son" (38) met and killed his father, and Oedipus's "Erinyes killed with mutual slaughter his warrior offspring" (41-42). But Pindar emphasizes the alternating moments of success: Semele "lives in Olympian realms" (25); Ino, whose troubles are only implied, has life immortal with Nereus's daughters; and Polyneices' son Thersander achieves power and honor. Moreover, in this poem Pindar makes the explicit point that the bright succeeds the dark and vanquishes it (23): "Sorrow yields, heavy though it is, before a good that is stronger than it." Pindar by no means denies the existence of the dark themes in these stories, but sees Theban myth as a woven pattern of dark and bright strands.[18]

The mythology of Aegina is not without its areas of darkness.[19]

[18] My metaphor is not meant to imply that Pindar's image for vicissitude is always or mainly lightness/darkness. In *O.* 2 Theban vicissitude is prominently expressed as the reversals of some kind of encounter (lines 20-24, 37, 43). But brightness is so typical and recurrent a Pindaric image for success that it seems appropriate to use this image as shorthand for the whole range of metaphors used to express this theme.

[19] In the following discussion of vicissitude I have not distinguished systematically between the darkness of misdeeds and that of misfortune. For the pattern under discussion I do not believe that the distinction is significant, but of course I do not mean to imply that Pindar saw no difference.

There is, of course, Neoptolemus's slaughter of Priam. There is
also Ajax's madness and suicide, but Pindar's attitude to this
disaster is so sympathetic and justificatory (in *N*. 8 as well as *N*. 7)
that it can hardly be called an acceptance of evil in the Aeacid
family. The only evil that Pindar sees here is in Odysseus. But
there is, also, the less familiar incident of the murder of Phocus by
his brothers Peleus and Telamon, one of the least attractive
moments of Aeacid history. In *N*. 5 Pindar is particularly concerned with Peleus in exile and hence finds occasion to refer to the
cause of exile, the murder. He accepts it, with a shudder, and
passes rapidly on to the better, with a *praeteritio* that stresses the
horror more than it hides the fact (14-18):

> Shame forbids me to mention a strong deed
> > That was not undertaken with justice,
> How they left the glorious island, and some divinity drove
> Those men of valor from Oenone.
> I shall stop; not every truth
> Is the better for showing its face unflinching;
> And silence is often the wisest thought for a man.

That silence becomes misdeeds is the corollary of the more
common Pindaric statement that silence cheats great deeds of the
glory they deserve. Both expressions are devices of stress, not of
concealment. Had Pindar wanted to conceal here he would have
omitted the incident, or at least avoided the moral judgment that
his horrified reference to the deed emphasizes. Pindar ensures that
his audience will recall the murder quite specifically by mentioning
the name of Phocus, just two verses before the passage quoted.

   Aeginetan tradition has, then, its sorrows and darkness, but here
too Pindar spends most of his time on its chapters of glory: on
Aeacus, who was χειρὶ καὶ βουλαῖς ἄριστος (*N*. 8. 8); on the
incorruptibility of Peleus despite the proffered charms of Acastus's
wife (*N*. 5); on Telamon as the helper of Heracles at Troy (*N*. 4);
on the might of Ajax (*Isthmian* 6) and the brilliance of Achilles
(*I*. 8).

   Thus in Aeginetan myth as in Theban myth, Pindar recognizes
the dark areas and emphasizes the bright. Moreover, he often

represents dark and bright as an alternating pattern: the murder of Phocus is followed by the moral excellence of Peleus in exile, just as in the pattern of *O.* 2 each Theban sorrow or failure is followed by joy or success. Brightness follows darkness and makes amends for it. The amends do not always come to the same person as the sorrow; Oedipus and his sons are mentioned only for the disasters that befell them, but these are balanced and amended by the success of Thersander.[20]

The same pattern is evident in other Pindaric myths. *O.* 7, the mythic history of Rhodes, has a series of three incidents in which some error or sorrow is followed by success: Tlepolemus killed Licymnius in a rage, but the exile to which he was thereby forced brought him glory and success in Rhodes; the sons of Helius erred in their sacrifice to Athena and Zeus, but then were favored by Zeus and endowed by Athena with extraordinary skill; Helius missed the division of provinces among the gods, and thereby later got Rhodes. *P.* 11 stresses an inglorious chapter of myth, Clytemnestra's murder of Agamemnon, but then, though only marginally and largely implicitly, brings in the moral integrity of Orestes. In *O.* 13, with a *praeteritio* like that of *N.* 5, Pindar alludes briefly but intensely to the unhappy ending of Bellerophon's story, and at once adds an application of the usual principle of bright following dark that on this occasion borders on the comic. Pegasus fared better, for (92), "The primal mangers of Zeus on Olympus received him."[21]

Pindar accepts the presence of evil in myths, but this does not deny that he often chooses a version or alters a detail to enable him to glide lightly over possible sorrows and flaws. In *N.* 10, in place of the usual story of the rape of the daughters of Leucippus, the trouble of the Dioscuri with Idas and Lynceus is rather vaguely ascribed to "some anger about cattle" (60); in *O.* 1 the version of

[20] The strong sense of "solidarity of the family" which prevailed in Greece in Pindar's time makes the compensation by the success of a later generation the more acceptable, the more truly compensating, than it would be in some societies. Cf. E. R. Dodds, *The Greeks and the Irrational* (Berkeley, 1951), pp. 33-34.

[21] In *I.* 7 Pindar refers again to this incident and this time speaks explicitly of Bellerophon's reprehensible effort to reach heaven, lines 44-47.

the chariot race between Pelops and Oenomaus omits all suggestions of treachery, and even of Myrsilus, who is in other versions
the faithless charioteer of Oenomaus. In these odes of victory it is
natural for Pindar to choose what is bright and good to symbolize
the success attained. That he nevertheless so often modifies this
choice by a recognition of sorrow, failure, and wrong, and presents
myth as an alternating pattern is the more remarkable and
characteristic. His treatment of myth is sometimes not far in spirit
from the refrain written by his great contemporary, in the parodos
of *Agamemnon*: αἴλινον, αἴλινον εἰπέ, τὸ δ' εὖ νικάτω.

The transience of prosperity and the unpredictability and
inevitability of fate are commonplaces in the literature of the
archaic age. What is not commonplace but is in close accord with
the alternating pattern in the presentation of myth is the idea of a
fluctuation, more or less by generations, between success and
failure, or between glory and obscurity. Pindar's most precise and
impressive statement of this generalization is in *N*. 11 (39-43):

> Neither in constant series do the dark fields give crops,
> Nor is it willed that trees in every annual cycle
> Give equal wealth of fragrant blossoms;
> Instead, they alternate. And a like fate
> Guides the mortal race.

In *N*. 6, speaking of a boy victor whose success follows in his
grandfather's footsteps, Pindar expresses the same idea with the
same metaphor (8-11):

> Now Alcimidas gives visible evidence of his inborn nature,
> In the manner of crop-bearing lands, which in alternation
> Now give forth from their plains abundant living for men,
> And now by pausing gather strength.

And in *I*. 3/4, a family that has lost grievously in war has its
fortunes restored by an athletic victory (34-37):

> The cruel snowfall in one day of war deprived
> This blessed hearth of four men.
> But now again after the darkness of winter's months
> It is as if the flowering earth bloomed with red roses
> By the will of the gods.

This concept of the fluctuation of fortune, both in myth and in contemporary reality, holds deep meaning for the poet. At times, clearly, even natural endowment, φυά, is in eclipse.[22] In contemporary life as in myth, one man's sorrow or failure is not necessarily balanced by a following success of that man. As in the case of Oedipus of Thebes in *O. 2*, a man in his career may be a dark moment in the fortunes of his family.

A number of passages revealing Pindar's observation of the principle of vicissitude have been quoted. Substantial elements in the matter and structure of several poems are based on this same perception. In *O. 2* the alternation of disaster and triumph in the myth-history of Thebes is followed by eschatological vision of life after death in which the basic pattern is a succession of lives spent alternately ἐν τᾷδε Διὸς ἀρχᾷ (58) and κατὰ γᾶς until the souls have lived in complete justice ἐστρὶς ἑκατέρωθι (68-69) and win their way to the "tower of Cronus" and a life of bliss (70-77). This is not the place to discuss the many specific uncertainties of this remarkable passage;[23] its continuation of the pattern of alternation is clear.[24]

P. 8 is perhaps even more designed to the pattern of alternation. The ode, the latest datable poem of Pindar (446), is in honor of a wrestler. Its principal myth is the story of the Epigoni, who

[22] Tugendhat (above, n. 2), p. 407, n. 2, observes that Pindar's use of φυά in this sense of endowment is limited to the dative case, and suggests that for Pindar the word indicates not so much specific talent as inherited bent. Cf. Young (above, n. 15), p. 638, n. 24. The observation is interesting, but the distinction is sometimes slight if it exists at all; e.g. *P. 8*. 44-45.

[23] Some of the principal discussions of it are: Farnell (above, n. 5) 2. 16-21; Erich Thummer, *Die Religiosität Pindars* (Innsbruck, 1957), pp. 121-130; Erwin Rohde, *Psyche* (1925 ed. of the English translation), pp. 414-419 and 442, n. 35; Leonard Woodbury, "Equinox at Acragas," *TAPA* 97 (1966), 597-616; Kurt von Fritz, "Ἐστρὶς ἑκατέρωθι in Pindar's Second Olympian and Pythagoras' Theory of Metempsychosis," *Phronesis* 2 (1957), 85-89.

[24] Norwood (above, n. 6), who has good comments on the pattern, pp. 133-134, makes the symbol of the poem the wheel, representing the κύκλος γενέσεως which the eschatology of the poem describes, and arising from the similarity of the initial *theta* of Theron's name to a four-spoked wheel. The specific symbol is dubious; the passages quoted in support, lines 21-22, 23-24, 35-37, can as well or better be explained as metaphors of a wrestling match or similar struggle (cf. 19-20), but the pattern of the poem can certainly be comprehended in these terms.

triumphantly reverse the ill-fated attack of the Seven against
Thebes, a reversal that has in its success failure too. Pindar
emphasizes success and failure in the person of Adrastus, leader of
both attacks. Amphiaraus prophesies of him (48-50),

> He who was felled by disaster before
> Is now sustained in report
> Of happier omen

but (51-52)

> Will suffer reversal
> Closer to home,

because his son, alone of the attackers, will die. Yet, the prophecy
continues, Adrastus will, τύχą θεῶν, bring his army home to Argos
(otherwise) unscathed (53-55). The myth is followed by reflections
on the vicissitudes of human fortune couched in metaphorical
terms that suggest the action of wrestling (76-77),

$$δαίμων δὲ παρίσκει$$
$$ἄλλοτ' ἄλλον ὕπερθε βάλλων, ἄλλον δ' ὑπὸ χειρῶν.^{25}$$

Then, most unusually, Pindar mentions specifically—though
briefly—the victor's wrestling contests, with emphasis as much on
the sorrow and shame of the defeated opponents (83-87) as on the
joy of victory (88-92). This rather subdued tribute is followed by a
generalization—again couched in metaphors of reversal and
suggestive of the alternating throws or falls of wrestling—on the
transience of human joy (92-93):

$$ἐν δ' ὀλίγῳ βροτῶν$$
$$τὸ τερπνὸν αὔξεται. οὕτω δὲ καὶ πίτνει χαμαί,$$
$$ἀποτρόπῳ γνώμą σεσεισμένον.$$

The celebrated conclusion of the poem, with its statement of the
insubstantiality of man, continues the pattern. It is not just a
melancholy assessment of man's worth; human frailty is transformed by divine favor and, though man is σκιᾶς ὄναρ (95), he

---

[25] Cf. Burton (above, n. 12), p. 187. Gildersleeve, *Pindar: The Olympian and
Pythian Odes* (New York, 1885), in his note *ad loc.* thinks of balls thrown up
and caught; but ὑπὸ χειρῶν does not suggest this metaphor.

can become radiant with a λαμπρὸν φέγγος (97). The poem ends with a list of the great Aeginetan and Aeacid heroes of myth, a final assertion of man's potential for excellence.

In this poem of vicissitude and a melancholy that is only alleviated, not subdued, by the hope of accomplishment through human excellence supported by divine favor, it is significant that the Pindaric belief in the importance of inherited greatness is conspicuous too. Amphiaraus prophesies the destined success of the Epigoni in these words (44-45):

φυᾷ τὸ γενναῖον ἐπιπρέπει
ἐκ πατέρων παισὶ λῆμα.

The two observations are by no means mutually exclusive in a Pindaric presentation of human success; they are, rather, two inevitable circumstances of it.

In *O.* 12, the goddess *Τύχα* is invoked. The short poem is for Ergoteles of Himera, an exile from Crete, and its theme is the unforeseeable nature of human events: had not Ergoteles been uprooted by *stasis* from his native Cnossus, he might never have achieved the glory of Olympic victory. The emphasis on the ups and downs of human life suggests the motion of a ship, an appropriate image for the fortunes of a man whose fate has taken him from island to distant island.[26] The poem, narrow though it is in scope, exemplifies especially clearly one aspect of Pindar's perception of mutability. The figure of *Τύχα* here and the concept of τύχα (the concept is far more common in Pindar than its personification as a divinity, found only here in the *Epinicians*) do not have the suggestion of capricious or incomprehensible chance that is usual in later writers. Pindar uses the word most commonly in such phrases as τύχᾳ θεῶν (*P.* 8. 53), τύχᾳ δαίμονος (*O.* 8. 67), σὺν τύχᾳ πότμου (*P.* 2. 56), which suggest divine dispensation: οἱ θεοὶ τεύχουσιν.[27] What comes by τύχα is unforeseeable and mysterious, but it is managed by divine will, not by random chance. As in other Pindaric expressions of mutability, there is in

[26] Gildersleeve (p. 225): "The poem rocks like a ship." Cf. Norwood, pp. 105-106.
[27] Cf. Fr. 141, θεὸς ὁ πάντα τεύχων βροτοῖς / καὶ χάριν ἀοιδᾷ φυτεύει.

this poem of Τύχα a strong underlying sense of divine control and stability.

O. 7, with its triple shadow of failure or error preceding success, and its shifting breezes at the conclusion, has, in spite of the opulence and glory of its beginning, this feeling for vicissitude. In *P*. 1 (50-54), Hieron is likened to Philoctetes, the crippled hero who is nevertheless the sacker of Troy (55): ἀσθενεῖ μὲν χρωτὶ βαίνων, ἀλλὰ μοιρίδιον ἦν. Once again the shadow of suffering is lifted by divine favor. In *N*. 5 the story of Peleus moves from the dark chapter of the murder of Phocus to the moral rectitude of Peleus's rejection of the unchaste Hippolyta and the splendor of his marriage with Thetis. Even in *O*. 1, where the emphasis is on the success of Pelops over Oenomaus, with the loving aid of Poseidon, there is also the failure and punishment of Pelops's father Tantalus and the initial rejection of Pelops, sent back from immortality to the ταχύποτμον . . . ἀνέρων ἔθνος (*O*. 1. 66).

Turning back now to *Paean* 6 and, in more detail, to *N*. 7, I shall undertake to show that comprehension of the poetic structure and meaning are deeply dependent on recognition of this pattern of fluctuation. But an important qualification should be added to what has been said. Again and again the progression of the pattern is from darkness to light, from failure to success, from the σκιᾶς ὄναρ to the λαμπρὸν φέγγος. This direction is of course appropriate in encomiastic poetry in praise of the victory of excellence. But the victor's progress from toil and difficulty to success, and the mythical hero's glorification after adversity are not automatic. These successes need strenuous effort as well as inherited excellence and divine favor. The victor must invest δαπάνα and πόνος (*I*. 6. 10-11; cf. *O*. 5. 15), and the success of the hero requires the braving of danger. The Argonauts, in *P*. 4, are ready (186-187),

> Even at the price of death
> To find with their fellows
> The fairest essence of their own valor.

Moreover, it is the part of a wise man to accept the vicissitudes of human life and concentrate on the good, and Pindar makes a principle of this (*P*. 3. 81-83):

> The immortals distribute to men two sorrows
> For every blessing. Foolish men cannot
> Bear this with dignity
> But good men can, turning the beautiful outward.

The human response is therefore no more a matter of haphazard chance than is the τύχα θεῶν.

The picture of Aeginetan myth in *Paean* 6 has the same balance and alternation of dark and bright, ill fortune and good, that has been illustrated as a basic and typical part of the Pindaric reading of myth and comprehension of the human lot. The evidence for the pattern is complicated both by the fact that the myth presumably concerned primarily Apollo, not the Aeginetan heroes, and that large parts of the poem are lost. Of the three triads, the second is best preserved, with its antistrophe and epode essentially intact. They tell how Apollo brought death to Achilles and Neoptolemus. Triad 3, fragmentary after the first seventeen verses, was apparently devoted mainly to the birth of Aeacus and his career as a celebrated man of justice. The closing lines of the poem are extant, and in them a tribute to the excellence of the Aeacids is linked with an address to Apollo by his title of *Paian*. It may be that Triad 1 (of which thirty-one lines are missing) contained other aspects of Apollo's decisive role in the story of Troy. The relevance of the story of Aeacus, in Triad 3, cannot be determined from what is left. There may have been some mention of the role of Aeacus as the partner of Apollo and Poseidon in the building of the wall of Troy; the same connection, accompanied by the linking of the Aeacids with the beginning and the end of Troy, is made in *O. 8*. However this may be, the order in which Pindar treats the Aeginetan heroes in *Paean* 6 is significant: Aeacus, who is here the chapter of brightness and success, follows in the poem, though of course not chronologically, Achilles and Neoptolemus, who were Apollo's victims. The poet, led by his Apolline theme to portray a dark chapter of Aeginetan mythology, balances it with a contrasting story of Aeginetan success and excellence. The darkest moment of all, the description of how Apollo killed Neoptolemus while he "quarreled with attendants concerning customary (or

"destined") honors"[28] is followed immediately by a warm tribute
to Aegina (124-125):

ὀνομακλύτα γ᾽ ἔνεσσι Δωριεῖ
μεδέοισα πόντῳ
νᾶσος, ὦ Διὸς Ἑλ-
λανίου φαεννὸν ἄστρον.

Island of illustrious name,
Mistress of the Dorian sea,
Bright star of Zeus of the Hellenes.

Neoptolemus's death is a parallel to that of Achilles, narrated
before it; and while it is more darkly told, with emphasis on
Neoptolemus's killing of Priam, it must be taken in its context, in
the pattern of the poem, which narrates failures and glories of
both the Aeacids and Apollo. For even Apollo must accept defeat,
in the capture of Troy. While Neoptolemus's death is presented as
a punishment for his slaughter of Priam (113-116), it also has its
part in the design of the poem.[29] The complete design cannot be
determined in the fragments that remain, but the pattern of
alternating fortunes is clear. Moreover, Pindar's treatment of
Neoptolemus here is not a unique instance of telling only the worst
part of a hero's story. He does the same with Oedipus in *O. 2* and
with Bellerophon in *I. 7*; and clearly Pindar had no general view
of Bellerophon as an example of human failure and immorality,
since in *O. 13* a full account of that hero's successful exploits is
given.

It is time now to go back to *N. 7*. Above, I quoted Norwood's
assertion that the myth of Neoptolemus is irrelevant to the victory
of Sogenes. Other critics have expressed themselves almost as

[28] The scholium to *N. 7* quoting this passage has μυριᾶν. The papyrus of
Paean 6 has only the letters YP, with the P uncertain. Snell accepts Boeckh's
conjecture μοιριᾶν, as does Radt (above, n. 14), whose discussion of the whole
passage (pp. 163-170) is valuable. With the Y of the scholium confirmed by
the papyrus, I prefer Housman's κυριᾶν.

[29] Tugendhat (above, n. 2) comments that "In Pindars Paian wurde dieser
Tod des N. als Strafe Apollons für die Zerstörung von Ilion und insbesondere
für die Ermorderung des Priams gedeutet" (p. 385). This is true, but it leaves
out an essential point: a basic element in the description of Neoptolemus's
death is its contribution to the design of the poem.

decidedly. Two aspects of Pindar's use of myth are pertinent to the
general relevance of the particular myth of *N*. 7. First, Pindar's
practice in the choice of myths is extremely varied. The myth
may give a prototype for the victor, as Perseus is in *P*. 10, and
Antilochus in *P*. 6 (more exactly, in this case, for the victor's son).
Or it may be one of several kinds of origin story: of the family, in
O. 6, with the story of Iamos; of the state, in *O*. 7, with the myth-
history of Rhodes; of the sanctuary of Olympia itself, as in *O*. 1
with the story of Pelops; or of the Olympic Games, in *O*. 10, with
Heracles' establishment of the first contest. It may take the form
of a more purely symbolic celebration of the spirit or the excellence
of the victor's state or family, as in *O*. 13, with its story of
Bellerophon for a Corinthian victor, and *O*. 14, with its celebration
of the Graces for a victor from Orchomenus, the city of the Graces.

The second point about Pindaric myth is this: in the numerous
odes for Aeginetans the poet virtually always uses Aeacus and his
heroic descendants as his myth material (the one exception is *P*. 8).
He usually mentions several of the Aeacids and then gives special
attention to one; thus, in *I*. 6, for example, a general section is
followed by praise of Achilles. But sometimes there is only a
panorama or parade of Aeacids (*N*. 3, *N*. 4); and sometimes only
a small space is devoted to the general group, while the story of
one or two of the heroes is given in some detail: thus *O*. 8 concen-
trates on the Aeacids at Troy, *N*. 8 on Ajax.

To assert that the material of the myth of *N*. 7—the story of
Neoptolemus, preceded by some account of Ajax—is irrelevant
would be to deny the relevance of Pindar's customary use of myth.
What Norwood and the others who find this myth irrelevant mean
to suggest, I think, is that the tone of it, with its stress on Pindar's
self-justification, is unsuitable for encomium. This criticism too is
largely unjustified. If we listen properly to the poem, we find that
nearly everything falls into a place relevant to the whole. We shall
not necessarily find that the poem is a successful artistic unit, but
nothing in it cannot be understood in the usual terms of Pindar's
encomiastic style.

If what has been said above about the pattern of mythology in
Paean 6 is correct, Pindar might well have regarded it as of the

utmost importance to enlarge on his interpretation of the career
of Neoptolemus, assuming that the story of Aeginetan anger is
true. It was not simply a matter of losing friends and epinician
contracts; the treatment of Neoptolemus in *Paean* 6 exemplifies
one vital aspect of the poet's comprehension of myth and of human
fortunes. To justify *Paean* 6 meant not merely defending a poem;
it meant justifying something broadly important to Pindar's art,
to his conception of human fortunes in myth and in contemporary
life, and hence to the tribute he is paying in *N.* 7 to Sogenes of
Aegina.[30]

Pindar could have said with fairness that he was no more
attacking Neoptolemus here than Oedipus in *O.* 2; the violence
and perhaps impiety of Neoptolemus's attack on Priam at the
altar represented indeed a dark moment in the mythology of
Aegina and were so used in *Paean* 6, balanced by the immediately
following story of Aeacus; moreover, there was no implication
that this is all that could be said about Neoptolemus, any more
than the incident of Bellerophon's impious attempt to rise to
heaven is all that could be said about Bellerophon. Rather, it is
all that Pindar needed for a particular pattern of myth in a
particular poem. We ought not to accuse Pindar of being a facile
sycophant when in *N.* 7 (75-76) he says, "It is not hard for me to
set down a favor for the victor if I was carried away and shouted
too high." If, that is, Pindar in praising Apollo did Neoptolemus
less than justice, the story of Neoptolemus affords material with
which his greatness can be recorded, material that constitutes an
appropriate χάρις for an Aeginetan victor.

Lines 102-104 do not indicate a contradiction between the two
poems. As Tugendhat has observed,[31] the adjective ἀτρόποισι

---

[30] Those who resist the evidence of *N.* 7. 102-104 and of the scholia might
argue that *Paean* 6 is no more relevant to *N.* 7 than *I.* 7 to the other poem
dealing, in very different terms, with the story of Bellerophon, *O.* 13. There is,
however, a conspicuous difference between the two pairs; there is no suggestion
in *O.* 13 that the poet is concerned about the acceptability of his attitude to
the hero, whereas in *N.* 7 there is clearly such a concern, whatever its cause
is judged to be.

[31] See p. 404.

means "inflexible," "unchangeable." Pindar is not ready to retract what he has said about Neoptolemus; but Neoptolemus's career can be interpreted with an entirely different emphasis when the context makes it fitting; and this is the case in *N.* 7. Analogously, in lines 20-30, Pindar broods resentfully over the underestimation of Ajax and the undue prestige of Odysseus, given by Homer and by common repute. But in *I.* 3/4 Pindar balances Ajax's unhappy fate with Homer's poetic recompense (53-57).

The treatment of Neoptolemus in *Paean* 6 was in keeping with a fundamental Pindaric outlook, and it was therefore a matter of vital importance to Pindar to correct the impression that he was attacking Neoptolemus. *N.* 7 honors Sogenes by its implicit comparison of the honor that he brings to Aegina by his victory in the pentathlon with the honor that Neoptolemus brought to the Aeacids and to Aegina by his heroic place at Delphi. The poet is concerned to show that the story of Neoptolemus can be used to illustrate the same viewpoint, the same alternation of darkness and brightness, and the same emphasis on ultimate brightness as the myth of *Paean* 6 does. There is no irrelevance and no dishonor; Sogenes is given the treasured depths of Pindar's comprehension of myth and of life.

Tugendhat's study suggests that in fact Pindar viewed the story of Neoptolemus as a difficult and delicate subject for encomiastic treatment,[32] and that the poem is a *tour de force* of the encomiastic art. Clearly Tugendhat is right in stressing the dominant place of Pindar's art, but it is more likely that the choice of myth rests with other considerations, which are in this instance beyond the horizon of our perceptions. In some poems we know the external circumstances that caused Pindar to choose a particular myth or impart a particular emphasis. Quite clearly in *P.* 3 the emphasis on healing arises from Hieron's sickness, as in *P.* 1 the lame Philoctetes symbolizes the physically impaired Hieron; some of the emphasis of *P.* 4 arises from the special purpose of the ode in connection with the restoration of Damophilos to Cyrene. More often, we cannot know the situation, as in *O.* 2 and *N.* 7, but it is reasonable

---

[32] "In dieser heiklen Sache," p. 399.

to believe that something in the circumstances of the victor or the
occasion influences Pindar's choice of style and material.

Enough has been said about the general form and style of the
ode. A number of the principal difficulties of detail are eased when
the poem is read with this basic pattern in mind, and, conversely,
several passages confirm the pattern.

The invocation of Eileithyia, goddess of birth, need not occasion
any difficulty of interpretation. The general relevance of Eileithyia
in an epinician is made clear by the context; and an ancient
scholiast comments sensibly that Eileithyia is addressed as a kind
of Moira, or dispenser of fate. The sense of lines 2-6 is: "Without
you we cannot live and attain to your sister goddess, fair-limbed
Hebe. We do not all breathe the breath of life on equal terms (or
"for equal ends"). Varying fortunes, yoked to *potmos*, hem each of
us in." The emphasis on Eileithyia as the goddess who makes it
possible for us to reach Hebe, youthful maturity, is especially
appropriate in a poem for a youth who is presumably just arriving
at that age. Next comes the declaration (to which the introduction
has been building) that the victor has achieved glory σὺν τίν,
"with your aid." Farnell[33] speaks of the broad powers that are
elsewhere ascribed to Eileithyia, and of her connection elsewhere
with *potmos* or *moira*. An emphasis on the role of those deities that
dispense our portions is suitable to a poem which stresses the
concept of τὸ μόρσιμον. In the presentation of the checkered
career of Neoptolemus with its ultimate glory at Delphi, this concept is the leading theme, as indeed it is likely to be in poetry of
vicissitude and as it is in *Paean* 6 (93): μόρσιμ᾽ ἀναλύεν Ζεὺς ὁ
θεῶν σκόπος οὐ τόλμα.

This is all clear and simple, and the dubious guidance of
Aristodemus's inference about the late birth of Sogenes to the aged
Thearion can be dismissed as a fiction useless for the understanding
of the proemium and mischievous for the understanding of the
poem as a whole.

One of the crucial passages of the poem begins with the epode
of Triad 1:

---

[33] See above, n. 5, II, 203.

> Wise men know of a wind to come
> On the third day; they are not brought to harm by the persuasion
>   of profit.
> Rich and poor alike come
> To death's boundary marker. I believe that
> The report about Odysseus is greater than his experience was,
> Through the art of sweet-tongued Homer.
> For upon his lies, by his soaring craftsmanship[34]
> A dignity is cast; and poetic skill
> Deceives and seduces with its tales. Most men
> Are blind at heart.

Otherwise, the poet goes on, Ajax would not have been deprived of the armor of Achilles and taken his own life.

Since antiquity, the first part of this passage has often been taken to mean that men of judgment will not hesitate to spend money commissioning epinician odes, realizing that their riches will not otherwise avail against mortality. In itself this is an acceptable Pindaric outlook, and it follows naturally enough from the preceding thought, that only poetry brings virtue its proper glory. But what follows would be grotesquely inappropriate; we have to believe that Pindar first advises spending money for poetry that glorifies, and then immediately follows this with a strong warning about the deceptiveness of Homer's poetry glorifying Ajax.

The entire passage can best be interpreted as a rather involved but quite intelligible transition to the story of Neoptolemus.[35] The poet is aware that he is broaching a delicate topic, on which he must set the record straight, and he begins with a maxim, as he does in other similar contexts: *O.* 1. 28-35, for example, in introducing his correction of the story of Tantalus and Pelops, and *N.* 5. 17-18, in alluding to the murder of Phocus. Here the maxim

---

[34] I follow Erasmus Schmid (1616), supplying γε rather than Hermann's τε.

[35] Adolf Köhnken, *Die Funktion des Mythos bei Pindar* (Berlin, 1971), pp. 42-60, maintains that there are two myths, the first being what I regard as transitional, the second being, of course, the story of Neoptolemus. In Köhnken's rather elaborate analysis of the first, "Odysseus-Ajax" myth, Odysseus turns out to be the σοφός of line 17, because he takes care of his fame after death. I find Köhnken's analysis and interpretation generally overelaborate, strained, and unpersuasive.

alludes to some sea tradition about the prediction of winds.[36]
Skillful mariners will not suffer harm by sailing at the wrong time,
because they have foresight and are prudent enough not to let
desire for profit mislead them; human prosperity is anyway
transient; just so, men of discriminating mind will refrain from
hasty judgments; in their assessment of character or the stories of
mythology, they will not judge by only a part of the story, and
will not be misled, even by the seductive charm of Homer, to
overvalue Odysseus or undervalue Ajax; but because men as a
rule judge superficially and blindly, Ajax was undervalued by his
fellows and took his life, though he was the greatest of the
Achaeans at Troy after Achilles. There is also the suggestion that

[36] Traditions of the sea have an affinity for threes. There is the third wave
and the drowning man who goes down three times; veterans of sailing speak
of a "three-day blow." Boeckh, *Pindari Carmina quae supersunt* 3. 420, gives
references to two traditions that bear so substantial a resemblance to our
passage as to indicate fairly clearly that it reflects a sailing tradition. Strabo
(6. 2. 10) reports that differences in volcanic activity on the island of Ther-
messa, one of the Lipari group, enabled men to predict a sailing wind two days
hence (προσημαίνεσθαι καὶ τὸν εἰς ἡμέραν τρίτην πάλιν μέλλοντα ἄνεμον πνεῖν . . . γενομένης
ἀπλοίας προειπεῖν . . . τὸν ἐσόμενον καὶ μὴ διαψεύσασθαι). Pliny (3. 9. 94) speaks of a
volcano on Stromboli, "cuius fumo quinam flaturi sint venti in triduum
praedicare incolae traduntur."
    In the first instance, then, the *sophoi* of line 17 are sailors, and to recognize
this and the fact the whole sentence of lines 17-20 is a maxim in praise of
prudent sailors is crucial to the right approach to this passage. Efforts to find
in the maxim a specific reference to poets or their patrons have clouded understanding. Gian Franco Gianotti has even argued in "La Nemea Settima,"
RFIC 94 (1966), 385-406, that Pindar is rejecting the wisdom of the *sophoi* of
lines 17-20, "Saggi di una falsa *sophia* che perdono lo splendore del κέρδος
ὕψιστον" (p. 403) in contrast with what follows, ἐγὼ δέ . . . (line 20). There is no
basis in Pindar's words for any such contrast. Gianotti's argument carries to
an extreme the misleading notion that the maxim directly concerns *sophoi* other
than sailors. These *sophoi* are prudent *sailors*; wider application comes by
analogy and implication.
    Who, then, are the implied *sophoi*? *Sophoi* in Pindar are those of judgment
and discrimination, including but not restricted to those who possess poetic
judgment. Cf. Burton (above, n. 12), pp. 45, 72, 100, 120, on Pindar's use of
sophos. Poets are not excluded from the implications of this passage: the true
poet sees the whole story. Homer's report of Odysseus is ψεύδη, Pindar's of
Neoptolemus is a true report, a λόγος which brings τιμά after death. But the
main emphasis of the passage is on the prudence of all men of discriminating
judgment, who are implicitly likened to the prudent, weather-wise sailors of
the maxim.

wise men will accept, as the victor does, the need for μόχθοι, keeping in mind the ἄποινα of victory. A further implication, in this poem of which neither Odysseus nor Ajax but Neoptolemus is the principal figure, is present: one must not judge Neoptolemus blindly, by only a part of his story. There is perhaps also the hint that one must not judge poetry by seizing on one point, such as the death of Neoptolemus in *Paean* 6; there was more to *Paean* 6, and there is more to the story of Neoptolemus. The whole passage is based on the idea of the fluctuation of fortune and the lessons to be drawn therefrom. Haste is destructive, blind, and unproductive; it fails to recognize that mutability which is the common lot of man. The mention of the winds[37] and the mariners and the maxim about death are an introduction to the concept of prudent judgment; the implications of prudence extend from the sailors of the maxim to the poet and his audience and all men of good judgment. The mention of Homer and Odysseus emphasizes the picture of the underestimated Ajax, which in turn leads to the mention of Neoptolemus.

Transition from one Aeacid to another is common in the *Nemeans*, but here the link is especially close, through the unhappy deaths of the two men. The analogy of their fates accounts for the introduction of Ajax. With a further maxim, that the wave of Hades comes alike to him who expects it and to him who does not[38]

---

[37] For a good presentation of the Pindaric use of the winds as an image for the fluctuations of fortune, see Gilbert Lawall, "The Cup, the Rose, and the Winds in Pindar's Seventh Olympian," *RFIC* 39 (1961), 33-47, especially 44-45. See also Gianotti (above, n. 36), p. 391.

[38] Πέσε δ' ἀδόκητον ἐν καὶ δοκέοντα (31). The conjecture δοκέοντι is wrong; cf. Douglas Gerber, *AJP* 74 (1963), 182-188. To have the first of two words dependent on a preposition precede that preposition is a common Pindaric idiom; cf. Gildersleeve (above, n. 26), p. 394, for references to examples. Support for the interpretation "on the obscure and the famous alike," espoused most recently by David C. Young, "A Note on Pindar Nemean 7. 30 f.," *California Studies in Classical Antiquity* 4 (1971), 249-253, is thought by some to be found in *Trag. Adesp. Frag.* 482, Nauck, 2d ed. Pointing out that it is difficult to take the word δοκέοντ' in that fragment to mean "him who expects," with no indication of what he is to expect, Young disregards the equal difficulty of taking the single word to mean "the esteemed." Δοκέοντα is "him who expects" or "him who seems"; in either case something has to be supplied, and ἀδόκητον everywhere else is concerned with "expectation," though apart from these two

and that honor accrues to those of the dead whose *logos* deity
causes to flourish, Pindar brings us to Neoptolemus, who is, of
course, the one on whom the wave of Hades comes unexpected.
For indeed, Pindar continues, Neoptolemus came to Delphi "as a
helper," βοαθῶν.[39]

The story of Neoptolemus, briefly told, follows next. It mentions
the sack of Troy in words that do not state but do not conceal the
fact that Neoptolemus killed Priam (Πριάμου πόλιν). There is
stress on Neoptolemus's death at Delphi as a fulfillment of his
πότμος: τὸ μόρσιμον ἀπέδωκεν. Then follows an emphatic statement, again put in terms of what was inevitable (ἐχρῆν), of the
honored position that Neoptolemus holds at Delphi. As presented
in this poem, the story of Neoptolemus is a classic example of
Pindar's concept of the fluctuation of fortune. The emphasis on
fate in the proemium and the structure and imagery in the
transitional passage about Odysseus and Ajax introduce and
emphasize this same pattern.

The myth is now completed, and another transitional passage,
difficult to interpret in detail, follows. It begins with the statement
(line 48) that "three words will suffice for justice of fair name."
Critics ancient and modern have undertaken to specify what the
three words can be. Aristarchus suggests that they are the three
points about Neoptolemus's fate emphasized by Pindar: that his
death was μόρσιμον, that it was destined for an Aeacid to be

---

passages the sense is always passive. The choral tag that comes at the end of
five plays of Euripides with a phrase similar to this one in Pindar has to do
with expectation; thus the evidence of usage is overwhelmingly in favor of
"on him who expects and him who does not." The metaphor echoes that of
the maxim that rich and poor die alike (19-20); the ring-like echo marks the
close of the story of Ajax, and by linking him with Neoptolemus makes the
transition to the following passage on Neoptolemus. Also, with the subsequent
clause on the achievement of τιμά, this maxim again emphasizes the idea of
fluctuation and the need for judging a man by the true and entire λόγος about
him.

[39] Farnell's minute change from the MSS βοαθόων and his consequent repunc-
tuation of the sentence are convincing. For a different view of this passage,
see Charles Segal, *TAPA* 98 (1967), 445-450, who keeps βοαθόων and reads
μόλον, and Thummer (above, n. 7), who reads βοαθόων with μόλον or μόλε
(imperative). Snell now has βοαθῶν and μόλον, which was an ancient variant.
I consider that both MSS evidence and sense favor μόλεν.

buried in the shrine at Delphi, and that Neoptolemus was to receive heroic honors there. Another ancient critic links the three words with the triadic structure of the poem. It seems more reasonable to suppose that the reference to three words here is a form of the usual Pindaric theme of *kairos* or *metron*: there is no need, Pindar is saying, for great length in telling of great deeds; a brief record ("three words") is enough when a great poet is the witness.[40] And there may well be a hint here of the contrast between the epic lies of Homer and the succinct truth of Pindar.

A sentence in general praise of Aegina and its heroes follows, and then the poet continues (52-58):

> But respite is sweet in all things,
> Even honey, even Aphrodite's flowers bring surfeit.
> Each of us differs by nature in the life he attains.
> Men and their lots are various; no one man can hit upon
> And win complete good fortune. There is no man
> Whom I know, to whom Moira has given this outcome
> Unchanging. But, O Thearion . . .

and Pindar then goes on to praise Thearion, the victor's father, and to declare his own friendship for him.

From antiquity there has been a wayward but persistent effort to find personal references in this passage: that Thearion was unsuccessful, his life an ἀνάπαυσις, a respite from glory, that he was in disrepute;[41] even that Thearion, or young Sogenes, was over-amorous, a suggestion induced by the mention of the surfeit of Aphrodite's flowers. No such imaginative sallies are needed or acceptable, and the chief support adduced for some of them in the ancient notes is Aristodemus's bright suggestion about the invocation, that Sogenes came as a consolation to his aging father.

It is far more germane to the movement of the poem as a whole to see the beginning of this passage as referring still to the Aeacids. The train of thought in this part (48-53) is then as follows: the

---

[40] Cf. *P.* 9. 78-79: ὁ δὲ καιρὸς ὁμοίως / παντὸς ἔχει κορυφάν. *P.* 4. 247-248 uses a different metaphor to express the same formula.

[41] The notion of Thearion's disrepute is induced also by the mention, in line 61, of the poet's protecting him from blame. But this is, of course, a recurrent Pindaric convention of praise; cf. *O.* 8. 55, *P.* 1. 85, *N.* 1. 24.

truth is quickly told, and I have told it; I tell no lies about the
Aeacids—they need no Homeric lies, such is their native glory;
moderation is good, even when material for praise is abundant,
just as moderation is good even in the joys of life. Then, in words
that clearly recall the opening strophe of the poem (lines 54-55
echo strikingly the thought of lines 5-6) and that reintroduce the
theme of fluctuation, Pindar makes transition to the victor's
circumstances and addresses the victor's father, Thearion. In view
of the emphasis on vicissitude in the following lines, it is inevitable
that lines 52-54 suggest, in addition to the theme of moderation
in praise, the concept of fluctuating fortune, which then continues
in lines 55-58. The passage as a whole can be paraphrased thus:
in every series of events there must be some respite, some recess
from glory, as with the manner of Neoptolemus's sack of Troy and
his death; this too was *morsimon*, and no man's life, and no family's
history, can be all success and brightness; such pauses are the
common lot; I know no man to whom Moira has granted all. The
train of thought is strikingly close to that of the invocation, with
Moira here resembling in her powers Eileithyia of the invocation
and recalling as well the mention of the Moirai in line 1; it is close
also to the spirit of the myth. The idea that the victor's family too
has experienced the same kind of fluctuation is no more than an
assumption.[42]

The rest of Triad 3 (lines 58-63) praises Thearion in a manner
familiar from other odes: Moira has granted Thearion a due
measure of success and "courage for the accomplishment of good
things" ($\tau \acute{o} \lambda \mu \alpha \nu \ldots \kappa \alpha \lambda \hat{\omega} \nu$), along with wisdom; Pindar wards off
"the darkness of blame" (the blame that springs from the envy
that is an inevitable concomitant of achievement); the poet's
praise is likened to streams of water, as in line 12, and as it is to a
$\kappa \hat{\upsilon} \mu \alpha$ at *O*. 10. 10, and to $\ddot{\upsilon} \delta \omega \rho$ at *N*. 1. 24.

Up to this point in the poem no reference has been made to the
picture of Neoptolemus in *Paean* 6. The insistent justification of

---

[42] A very probable assumption, in my opinion, since we know that Pindar
elsewhere adapts his myths to particular circumstances: Philoctetes in *P*. 1,
Jason and the theme of restoration in *P*. 4.

Neoptolemus and the emphasis on fluctuation make us conscious
that another, less favorable report could be made of Neoptolemus,
and if we have read *Paean* 6, we shall be especially aware of this
other picture, which *N.* 7 incorporates and transcends. In the final
two triads several passages, in addition to the apparent overt
reference in lines 102-104, seem, *prima facie*, to refer to another
picture of Neoptolemus and have usually been so interpreted. It is
possible, I suppose, to interpret all of them, except 102-104,
without external reference, but it seems to me both artificial and
unnecessary to do so. These triads are dominated by references to
Pindar's art in relationship to Sogenes and his family; they are
intense, emotional, and highly personal. To reject the story about
the Aeginetans and *Paean* 6 does not alter this aspect of the poem;
acceptance of the story helps us to understand it, and to a very
considerable extent it fits in with the domination of the poem by
the theme of the fluctuation of fortune, especially in the interpretation of the principal remaining passage that raises severe
difficulties of interpretation, lines 70-76. A consideration of these
lines will bring us close to the end of our examination of this
Pindaric theme in *N.* 7.

Triad 4 begins with a reintroduction of Neoptolemus, in a
reference to Pindar's relationship to the people of the traditional
kingdom of Neoptolemus's descendants (64-69):

> If an Achaean man is near, who
> Lives beyond the Ionian sea, he will not censure me.
> I trust in my proxeny; among my demesmen too I look with clear
>   gaze,
> Without excess and keeping all violence from before my feet. May
>   time to come
> Be kindly. He who understands will say
> Whether I come speaking discord and words that go astray.

As the ancient scholia observe, the "Achaean man" whose
presence at the victory celebration is (perhaps improbably) supposed is presumably an Epirote, since Epirus was reached
by sailing north on the Ionian Sea. In Molossia of Epirus
Neoptolemus ruled briefly, and there his descendants ruled, as we

have been told in lines 38-40.[43] Whether Pindar was in fact *proxenos* for the Molossians or uses the word only figuratively to suggest his good will need not concern us. The passage as a whole proclaims Pindar's confidence in the harmony of his relationship with the people of Neoptolemus as with his fellow Thebans. The emphatic assertion that he will not be censured by countrymen of Neoptolemus and that his words are not discordant suggests that Pindar is concerned to defend his presentation of Neoptolemus. The topic is continued in the next lines (70-74):

> ἀπομνύω
> μὴ τέρμα προβαὶς ἄκονθ' χαλκοπάραον ὄρσαι
> θοὰν γλῶσσαν, ὃς ἐξέπεμψεν παλαισμάτων
> αὐχένα καὶ σθένος ἀδίαν-
>   τον, αἴθωνι πρὶν ἁλίῳ γυῖον ἐμπεσεῖν.
> εἰ πόνος ἦν, τὸ τερπνὸν πλέον πεδέρχεται.

> I swear
> That I have not overstepped the barrier and hurled
> My swift voice like that bronze-cheeked javelin
> That sends a man's neck and strength
> Unsweated from the wrestling, before his limbs fall below the sun's blaze.
> If there was toil, the pleasure that follows is greater.

A reasonable explanation of these lines is as follows: I have not said anything to disqualify me from praise of Neoptolemus or Aegina, as a man is disqualified from completing the pentathlon by participating in the wrestling if he oversteps the limit in throwing the javelin; like you, Sogenes, who competed in all the events of the pentathlon and followed this *ponos* with the greater pleasure of victory, so I follow the *ponos* of being misunderstood by the pleasure of praising Neoptolemus, Aegina, and Sogenes. Once again the theme of fluctuation takes a prominent place, and here, as usual, the brightness that follows is greater than the darkness that precedes: the poet's joy is greater than his former distress, and Sogenes' joy is greater than his toil in the pentathlon, just as

---

[43] Cf. also 98-101. There is a very brief allusion also in *Paean* 6. 109-110. The greater emphasis on this heritage in *N.* 7 is in line with the theme of vicissitude that marks the story of Neoptolemus in this poem.

Neoptolemus's glory at Delphi is greater than the dark moment of his death.[44]

There is no explicit reference to *Paean* 6. But, clearly, Pindar is being vehemently defensive about his poetry, and, in view of the preceding lines and the theme of the poem as a whole, we can hardly avoid thinking specifically of his presentation of Neoptolemus. Nothing in *N.* 7 calls for vehement defense; the picture of Neoptolemus in *Paean* 6 might well occasion the need for defense. We are told on as good ancient authority, Aristarchus's, as we could hope for, that it did. It is not contrary to Pindar's style to introduce personal themes, and in this case the personal theme has a profound relevance to the myth and the thought of *N.* 7. It is therefore appropriate to make the connection between this passage and *Paean* 6.

The triad continues (75-77):

> Give way to me, for I am ready to set down a favor
> For the victor, if carried away I raised my voice too high.
> To weave garlands is a light task; strike up a prelude.

Then follows mention of constructing a crown of gold, ivory, and coral. Both figures refer, of course, to aspects of poetry. The first part of the passage means, if our line of interpretation is right,

---

[44] My interpretation of 70-73 is almost entirely in accord with that of Charles Segal, "Two Agonistic Problems in Pindar," *GRBS* 9 (1968), 31-45. But I do not agree with his and Edwin D. Floyd's ("Pindar's Oath to Sogenes," *TAPA* 96 [1965]) rejection of the meaning "overstepping the barrier" for τέρμα προβαίς. Τέρμα is used elsewhere by Pindar for the turning post of a chariot race (*O.* 3. 33); therefore it need not mean limit in the sense of goal, and can mean a barrier not to be crossed. Προβαίνειν as "overstep" is strange, but since Hesychius states that it can have the meaning ὑπερβαίνειν, there is some justification for so interpreting here.

For line 74, Segal, *TAPA* 98 (1967), 436-440, proposes the meaning "if there was toil, it (the toil) seeks after joy the more." The meaning is not basically changed, but the proposal strikes me as resorting to a rather strained understanding of the Greek to avoid an imaginary problem. The problem, according to Segal, is that πεδέρχεται ought to be transitive, but if τὸ τερπνόν is subject, it is here intransitive. But I take it that there is an understood direct object, "it," referring to πόνος. The word order decidedly favors τὸ τερπνόν as subject. The verb when transitive need not imply "seek out" or "pursue"; it means "come to" at *Odyssey* 16. 314 and Euripides *Electra* 56.

that if in praising Apollo in *Paean* 6 I did less than justice to
Neoptolemus, I am ready to make amends now. There is nothing
dishonorable or inconsistent here; the poet declares himself
entitled to stress different aspects of a myth in different contexts.
But what of the statement that "to weave garlands is a light task"?
Usually Pindar takes a much more esoteric attitude toward the
art of poetry: it is a task only for those who by natural talent can
"plough the field of the Graces." But Pindar here means not poetic
composition but the ease with which suitable material can be
found for the praise of Sogenes. A victory always provides suitable
material for a poet's art and to say so is a convention of Pindaric
encomium; *I*. 1. 45-46 provides a close analogy: κούφα δόσις
ἀνδρὶ σοφῷ / ἀντὶ μόχθων ... ἔπος. When Pindar turns, as he does
at once in *N*. 7, to a more specific reference to composition,
esoteric skill is implicitly suggested in the imagery of the triple
diadem, imagery which, as John Finley says, shows the poet's
awareness that "his poetry is elaborate and difficult."[45]

The rest of Triad 4 and most of the final triad need not detain
us. Only the closing reference to Neoptolemus, in lines 102-104, is
integral to the problems raised in this essay. A few words in
enlargement of what was said earlier are necessary. Interpretation
of this passage has traditionally been guided—misguided in fact—
by a scholiast's suggestion. In this final declaration about his
treatment of the myth of Neoptolemus, the poet exclaims,
"My heart will never declare that I have dragged (ἑλκύσαι)
Neoptolemus ἀτρόποισι ... ἔπεσι." 'Ατρόποισι has traditionally
been taken to mean "unseemly," "offensive," or the like, following
the ancient gloss ἀπεοικότως. Tugendhat properly argues that
ἀτρόποισι can be taken in the much more normal meaning of
"inflexible," not in the sense of "irrevocable," as Bury has it, but
of "unchangeable". A different context can call for a changed
description of Neoptolemus, not because Pindar retracts what he
has said elsewhere but because different aspects and emphases of
Neoptolemus's career elicit changing descriptions.[46] Again the

[45] *HSCP* 60 (1951), 78.

[46] Tugendhat (above, n. 2), p. 404; J. B. Bury, *The Nemean Odes of Pindar*
(London, 1890), p. 144.

concept of mutability lies at the heart of the poet's language and treatment of the myth.

I conclude with a brief recapitulation of my argument. The theme of fortune's alternations is pervasive and important in Pindar's outlook, and in some instances dominates the poetic structure. I have argued for the presence of this theme in *Paean* 6 and *N.* 7, and have undertaken to exploit the theme in the interpretation of *N.* 7 as a whole and of a number of its notorious problems. There is room for much difference in the understanding of this poem, but I hope to have established one crucial point, that the theme of vicissitude explains and justifies the strange and troubled tone of the poem. Pindar is not merely defending a single poem (though the argument of this paper supports the traditional belief that he alludes, in fact, to *Paean* 6), he is explaining a vital aspect of his encomiastic art. Since in Pindar's view the poet's art is an essential reward for the victor's excellence, there can be no irrelevance in its prominence. The story of Neoptolemus's fluctuating fortunes, ending in ultimate glory, stands as a type of Aeacid and Aeginetan ἀρετή, fit reward for the πόνος of Sogenes. But the reward can only be achieved by the πόνος and the ἀρετή of the poet, and by his wisdom in interpreting the meaning of the vicissitudes of mythological tradition and contemporary experience.[47]

[47] Is there any evidence for the date of *Paean* 6 and *N.* 7 from Pindar's emphasis on the theme of fluctuation? Wilamowitz, in "Pindars siebentes nemeisches Gedicht," *Pindaros und Bakchylides* (Wege der Forschung 134 [Darmstadt, 1970]), pp. 127-158 (originally published in the *Sitzungsberichte der Preussischen Akademie der Wissenschaften*, 1908, 328-353), took them to be early, dating *N.* 7 at 485. Snell and Turyn accept this dating. But the argument for it is extremely weak, consisting only of the dubious assumption that words in the proemium of *P.* 6 (the date of which is 490), ἑλικώπιδος Ἀφροδίτας ἄρουραν ἢ Χαρίτων ἀναπολίζειν, resemble the proemium of *Paean* 6, with its reference to Aphrodite and the Graces. But ἀναπολίζειν need not mean to "plough again," but simply to plough, and both the Graces and Aphrodite are referred to so frequently by Pindar that the combined reference (which is Hesiodic) is not remarkable.

John Finley (above, n. 45) has urged the acceptance of a date between 476 and 460, on the grounds that the general outlook of these poems resembles the reflective and complex thought of the mature Pindar rather than the tranquility and self-confidence of early poems. Bowra (above, n. 2), pp. 410-411, is influenced by this argument in suggesting 467 as a tentative date for *N.* 7.

I confess total uncertainty. Some of the most striking presentations of the fluctuation of fortune come in poems of Pindar's maturity: *P.* 8, in 446, is the most conspicuous of all, and *N.* 11 is probably late also. But *O.* 2, with its highlights and shadows of Theban myth was written in 476. Moreover, the earnestness with which Pindar in *N.* 7 undertakes to clarify the meaning of his mythological interpretation shows perhaps the naïveté of youth.

A Lucretian Paragraph : III. 1-30

MICHAEL C. STOKES

In offering this essay to James Hutton I recall with special gratitude the kindness with which he has welcomed an Englishman to Cornell, and I hope that, being himself *utriusque linguae doctissimus*, he will welcome no less kindly this excursion by a Hellenist into the field of Latin poetry. Lucretius, as the most extensive source for our knowledge of Epicureanism, has attracted many Hellenists; for them the philosophy, not the poetry, has been the honey on the cup. But the more one studies Lucretius the more futile it seems to consider either his poetry or his philosophy separately. Any separation of the two in this paper will be for reasons only of convenience and not of conviction.

Cicero's famous agreement with his brother, that Lucretius displays high craftsmanship as well as many highlights of genius,[1] has inspired surprisingly few studies of Lucretius' art. "On the poetical techniques of Lucretius," E. J. Kenney has recently said, "existing commentaries leave much to be desired."[2] Scholars in

The following works are referred to throughout by editor's name only: T. Lucreti Cari, *De rerum natura*, Latin and German by H. Diels (Berlin, 1923-1924); Lucrèce, *De rerum natura: Commentaire*, by A. Ernout and L. Robin (Paris, 2d ed. 1962); T. Lucreti Cari, *De rerum natura, libri sex*, by C. Giussani (Torino, 1896-1898); T. Lucretius Carus, *De rerum natura, Buch III*, ed. R. Heinze (Leipzig, 1897); Lucreti, *De rerum natura, libri sex*, ed. W. A. Merrill (New York, 1907); T. Lucretius Carus, *De rerum natura, libri sex*, ed. H. A. J. Munro (London, 4th ed. 1886).

[1] Ad Q. Fratr. ii. 9, 3: *Lucreti poemata, ut scribis, ita sunt multis luminibus ingeni, multae tamen artis.* The temptation to insert a negative in the sentence (so still G. Jachmann in *Athenaeum* N.S. 45 [1967], 89-118) should be resisted.

[2] Lucretius, *De Rerum Natura*, Book III (Cambridge, 1971), p. vii; see Kenney's analyses at pp. 26-28. I have drawn on his notes from time to time in this essay and agree with more than seemed relevant in my context. See

this century have devoted more time to the order than to the manner of Lucretius' composition. But Kenney's own edition of Book III represents a long step forward, and he has finely illustrated his positive remarks with two analyses of widely differing parts of the Book. The present essay concerns itself with the analysis of the first preface to Book III and its connection with the following paragraph. Deeply indebted to previous scholarship, it may nevertheless serve to illustrate one kind of thing remaining to be done, or at least needing to be collected into continuous studies of continuous passages.

Here then is the text of Book III, lines 1-40:

O tenebris tantis tam clarum extollere lumen
qui primus potuisti inlustrans commoda vitae,
te sequor, o Graiae gentis decus, inque tuis nunc
ficta pedum pono pressis vestigia signis,
non ita certandi cupidus quam propter amorem   5
quod te imitari aveo; quid enim contendat hirundo
cycnis, aut quidnam tremulis facere artubus haedi
consimile in cursu possint et fortis equi vis?
tu, pater, es rerum inventor, tu patria nobis
suppeditas praecepta, tuisque ex, inclute, chartis,   10
floriferis ut apes in saltibus omnia libant,
omnia nos itidem depascimur aurea dicta,
aurea, perpetua semper dignissima vita.
nam simul ac ratio tua coepit vociferari
naturam rerum, divina mente coorta,   15
diffugiunt animi terrores, moenia mundi
discedunt, totum video per inane geri res.
apparet divum numen sedesque quietae
quas neque concutiunt venti nec nubila nimbis
aspergunt neque nix acri concreta pruina   20

also Anne Amory, "*Obscura de re lucida carmina*; Science and Poetry in *De Rerum Natura*," in *Yale Classical Studies* 21 (1966), 145-168. On repetitions see Wayne B. Ingalls, "Repetitions in Lucretius," in *Phoenix* 25 (1971), 227-236, and M. F. Smith in *Hermathena* No. 102 (1966), 77-82, both dealing with repetitions from one passage to another, and, for repetitions of neighboring words, R. Deutsch, *The Pattern of Sound in Lucretius* (Bryn Mawr, 1939), and C. Bailey, *Lucretius* (Oxford, 1967), I, 155-158.

cana cadens violat semper⟨que⟩ innubilus aether
integit, et large diffuso lumine ridet.
omnia suppeditat porro natura neque ulla
res animi pacem delibat tempore in ullo.
at contra nusquam apparent Acherusia templa   25
nec tellus obstat quin omnia dispiciantur,
sub pedibus quaecumque infra per inane geruntur.
his ibi me rebus quaedam divina voluptas
percipit atque horror, quod sic natura tua vi
tam manifesta patens ex omni parte retecta est.   30
    Et quoniam docui, cunctarum exordia rerum
qualia sint et quam variis distantia formis
sponte sua volitent aeterno percita motu
quove modo possint res ex his quaeque creari,
hasce secundum res animi natura videtur   35
atque animae claranda meis iam versibus esse
et metus ille foras praeceps Acheruntis agendus,
funditus humanam qui vitam turbat ab imo
omnia suffundens mortis nigrore neque ullam
esse voluptatem liquidam puramque relinquit.   40

A prominent feature of this passage, and one with which we shall be much occupied, is the poet's repetition of words, sounds, and ideas. This strikes us right at the start not only with the alliteration of the first line,[3] but with the repetition of the sonorous *O* from the beginning of the first line to line 3.[4] This anaphora, with the accompanying postponement of the vocative after the initial *O*, helps first to create and then to resolve suspense. The whole address, as in that to Venus at the opening of the poem, is underscored by anaphora. There follows *te sequor . . . inque tuis nunc . . . quod te imitari aveo*, and the renewed repetition, again with the aid of the possessive adjective, *tu, pater, es rerum inventor, tu patria nobis . . . tuisque ex, inclyte, chartis*. The symmetry of the two sets of

[3] See Ernout-Robin *ad loc.* Ernout seems somewhat hostile in his comments generally on the whole passage; for example, on line 4 he says "L'expression est embarrassée." Heinze was more just: "man sieht, wie die Metapher *sequor* sich zum Bilde ausgestaltet hat." And Kenney's analysis of the placing of swallow, swan, goat, and horse is more helpful than Ernout's curt denigration of the "clumsy" periphrasis *facere consimile in cursu* at lines 7-8.

[4] See Timpanaro and West cited by Kenney *ad loc.*

repetitions goes further than this; the form of the possessive is the same, *tuis*, in lines 3 and 10, and in each case the form is governed by a preposition and the resulting phrase is linked by *que* to what precedes. Each in addition contains, if line 9 is rightly punctuated, a parenthetic vocative.[5] Each of these anaphoric addresses is followed by a comparison with the animal world, the first by the images of swallow and swan, goat and horse, and the second by the bees. Within the second is another repetition, as *pater* is picked up by the derivative *patria*. The bees just mentioned bring Lucretius' reader back by way of the repeated *omnia* of lines 11 and 12 to the writings of Epicurus.

Anaphora, though not confined to hymns, is a common feature of them:[6] and this is a fact which gains in significance when we examine the epithet "golden" applied by the poet to Epicurus' writings. The double repetition *omnia . . . omnia* and *aurea . . . aurea* is very unusual and therefore prominent. The repetitions, despite their resemblance in metrical placing, are of two very different kinds, distinguished most obviously by the fact that the second *aurea* occupies the same syntactical position as the first, whereas *omnia* is repeated in different clauses. The repetition of *omnia* is

[5] Some editors, notably Bailey and Kenney, punctuate *tu pater es, rerum inventor*, following Giussani's slightly eccentric *tu, pater es, rerum inventor*, and his argument that only with *pater* as predicate is the parallel with *tu patria* brought out. This seems, like most of the arguments brought to bear on this passage, subjective: Munro felt no difficulty with *pater* as an address, commenting "9 *patria* is said with reference to *pater*: thou, o father, like a father"; Ernout labelled the passage "anaphoric" while putting commas round *pater* in the Budé text. Heinze went perhaps too far in saying "*pater* nur als Anrede, nicht als Prädikat denkbar." Merrill's suggestion that Giussani's punctuation was "inconsistent with L.'s plainness" ignores the question whether Lucretius is being plain here. Heinze was surely right in noting the interlacing at 4 as characteristic of the high style. But, allowing for excesses, editors have not convinced me that it is necessary to saddle Lucretius with what seems to me the awkwardness of *rerum inventor* either as an address or in apposition to *pater*. However, if *rerum inventor* is an address, then not only is it too parallel to *Graiae gentis decus*, as a parenthetic vocative, but also it is a vocative of the same general structure, a noun with dependent genitive.

[6] See especially Kenney *ad loc.* and Karl Büchner, *Lukrez und Vorklassik*, Studien zur römischen Literatur I (Wiesbaden, 1964), p. 69, "Lukrez ihn wie einen Gott in Hymnenstil Vater nennt und von seinen göttlichen Funden spricht."

purely for emphasis, to bring out forcibly a point in which the
simile is specially appropriate in a way that might otherwise
escape the reader's attention.[7] The repetition of *aurea* is perhaps
also partly emphatic. But this kind of repetition may have the
function of attaching an explanation more clearly to the word it
explains,[8] and in this case may also be due to the dual function of
the epithet "golden." The felicity of *aurea* as a transitional expression from Lucretius' relation with Epicurus to the effects of
Epicurus' philosophy, lies in these points: that honey, the food of
the bees, is golden in color, and the poet is feeding like the bees
(the metaphor is carried on with *depascimur*); and that what is
golden was characteristic in ancient poetry, from Homer on, of the
divine ambience, which leads naturally into the next point
Lucretius wishes to make.[9] Lucretius broaches the question deli-
cately. He follows up the hint of the epithet "golden" with the
statement that Epicurus' sayings are "*forever* worthy of *perpetual*
life" (my emphasis). With this emphatic, partly redundant statement we may be sure Lucretius intended two effects on his
reader.[10] The language is reminiscent of the motif, recurrent in
ancient literature, of the *monumentum aere perennius* raised by the
poet or historian to himself or others. But if we ask the pertinent
question who or what has eternal life, the answer is obviously "the
gods." The poet is leading up to the ascription of divinity to the
mind of his philosophic mentor; one step on the way is to portray
the philosopher's sayings as worthy of eternal life. In the next two
lines the divinity of Epicurus' mind becomes explicit; his philosophy no sooner began to speak than the terrors of the mind were
dispersed—and that philosophy arose from a divine mind. The
reader has been subtly prepared for this assertion, which makes a

---

[7] See Heinze *ad loc.*

[8] Consult Merrill's examples.

[9] See J. Duchemin, in *REG* 65 (1952), 52-58 (I owe this reference to G. M.
Kirkwood). Duchemin refers to H. L. Lorimer in *Greek Poetry and Life*: *Essays
presented to Gilbert Murray* (Oxford, 1936), pp. 14-33, on compounds of χρυσο-
in Greek lyric. See for golden chariots Page, *Sappho and Alcaeus* (Oxford, 1955),
p. 7, on Sappho 1. 8.

[10] W. S. Maguinness discusses this type of redundancy in *Lucretius*, ed.
D. R. Dudley (London, 1965), pp. 76 f.

climax. Such preparation of the reader's mind is no unusual occurrence in Lucretius' poetry.[11]

Lucretius thus leaves no stone unturned to beguile his reader into accepting the divinity of Epicurus' mind, and this alone, even without the asseveration in the proem to Book V, *deus ille fuit, deus . . .* , shows Lucretius to have been at least more than half serious in suggesting it, "in the metaphorical sense of Hellenistic theology."[12] But Lucretius' sentence is not yet complete, and the rest of it is constructed with equal care. As Epicurus speaks, the terrors of the mind flee, the walls of the world part, and Lucretius himself sees things moving on through the void. The cluster of repetitions and symmetries exhibited here deserves analysis. The chiasmus *diffugiunt . . . terrores, moenia . . . discedunt* is superbly pointed by the assonance in the first words of each line, di*ffugi*unt . . . di*sced*unt, thrown into sharper relief by the fact that *diffugiunt* is not the most obvious compound to use of "terrors." The assonance here is matched by the rhyming terminations, at caesura and line end, of *animi* and *mundi*. More potent still is the alliteration of *moenia mundi*, with the repetition of *m* and *n*, found already (in reverse order) in *animi*. The *un* of *mundi* repeats sounds from the endings of *diffugiunt* and *discedunt*, and like them is followed by a dental. The effect is characteristic of archaic Roman poetry, but it is especially typical of Lucretius.

What Lucretius says he sees is (to cite Bailey's translation) "things moving on through all the void." The word "all" here is vital to the structure of the subsequent lines and cannot be obscured in translation or paraphrase without obfuscating that

---

[11] One may compare the way in which *validis* agreeing with *ventis* at 509 is prepared for by *validis* at 494 in a simile, thus helping to give it its full force at 509.

Büchner, *Lukrez und Vorklassik*, pp. 97-101, is unconvincing in placing the proem to Book III later than that of V. Particularly unconvincing is the argument that III. 15 is more deeply understood when the result of the proem to V is "vorausgesetzt." The delicacy of Lucretius' approach in III would then be wasted, and Lucretius was not so incompetent a poet as to compel his readers to read him backwards in order to understand him deeply.

[12] "Im metaphorischen Sinn der hellenistischen Theologie," H. Diller in *SIFC* 25 (1951), 11.

structure.[13] The succeeding section of the preface falls into two unequal parts from 18 to 24 and 25 to 27. The division between the two is marked by yet another repetition of words, *apparet* in line 18 and *nusquam apparent* in line 25.[14] The first part describes the vision of the gods' abode, usually placed above the earth and implicitly placed there by Lucretius in this passage, where (doubtless as a concession to popular superstition) the cloudless *aether* shines on them. The poet knew his readers would be thinking of the part of the universe above the level of the earth's surface. The second part of this section refers to the spaces below the earth, where the dead were supposed to go. The spaces above and below the earth exhaust the universe, and this is the point of *totum* in line 17.[15] The sub-paragraph so constructed is rounded off neatly by the echo of line 17 *per inane geri res* in the words of line 27 *per inane geruntur*.[16]

Less verbally obvious, but none the less significant, is the repetition of ideas from the first line of the divine abode's description to the last. What Lucretius emphasizes in this description is the peace and quiet of the divine existence. He starts with *quietae* at the end of 18 and rounds off with *animi pacem* at line 24. The Epicurean gods reflect the Epicurean ideal of tranquillity. The need in his philosophic context for this emphasis goes far to explain some features of the way in which Lucretius in this sub-section adapts the Homeric description of the gods' dwelling-place. Homer wrote as follows:

ἡ μὲν ἄρ' ὣς εἰποῦσ' ἀπέβη γλαυκῶπις Ἀθήνη
Οὔλυμπόνδ', ὅθι φασὶ θεῶν ἕδος ἀσφαλὲς αἰεὶ
ἔμμεναι · οὔτ' ἀνέμοισι τινάσσεται οὔτε ποτ' ὄμβρῳ
δεύεται οὔτε χιὼν ἐπιπίλναται ἀλλὰ μάλ' αἴθρη
πέπταται ἀνέφελος, λευκὴ δ' ἐπιδέδρομεν αἴγλη.

[13] In his paraphrase Bailey unfortunately replaced it by "vast," which is not the point here, though a genuinely Lucretian sentiment.

[14] Noted, e.g., by Robin (Ernout-Robin *ad loc.*), and G. Müller, "Die Problematik des Lukreztextes seit Lachmann," *Philologus* 103 (1959), 75, n. 2.

[15] See again Heinze *ad loc.*

[16] Giussani's judgment (*ad loc.*) that 26-27 include "una certa ingrata repetizione di 17" shows only how distant some modern attitudes to repetition are from the ancients.

(She then, grey-eyed Athena, with these words departed for
Olympus, where, they say, is the seat of the gods, a safe seat
forever: it is neither shaken by winds nor ever drenched with
rain, nor does snow draw near, but indeed a cloudless sky is spread
there, and a brilliant light runs over it.)

Homer's conventional reference to the seat of the gods as safe
forever is replaced in Lucretius by the description of a peaceful
seat: tranquillity, not security, is fundamental to the Epicurean
gods.[17] Objection is sometime taken to Lucretius' substitution of
metaphor for the moving directness of Homer's statements, but
this seems to miss the point.[18] Lucretius is elaborating the Homeric
ἀσφαλές, in keeping with the Epicurean association of pleasure
and tranquillity. The violence of the verb *concutiunt*, the sharpness
explicit in *acri* and audible in the alliteration *concreta . . . cana
cadens* which repeats sounds from *concutiunt*, and the renewed
violence of *violat* are all means of expressing the negation of that
tranquillity.[19] The implications of *violat* are easily seen on comparing (with Merrill) IV.134 *mundi speciem violare serenam*. As
Heinze well said, "Die Schnee . . . fällt nicht nur, sondern *cana
cadens violat*: so wird das Unerfreuliche seinen Wirkung ausge-
malt."

Lucretius' further metaphor, the "smile" of the aether on the
gods' abode, replaces a different one in Homer. Both poets could
rely on their readers' minds being stocked with anthropomorphic
gods. But Lucretius here makes use of this fact. The reader's
sensibility transfers the smile from the aether to the gods, and the
smile is in itself a mark of gentle tranquillity. Homer's metaphor

[17] F. Giancotti, *Il Preludio di Lucrezio* (Messina and Florence, 1959), p. 88,
seems confused about this in suggesting that "nell'una e nell'altra (sc. in the
Homeric and Lucretian passages) attributi della sede degli dei sono la quiete
imperturbata." I am not sure whether Kenney means what I have said when
he remarks of *quietae* that it is "more pointed than Homer's ἀσφαλές"; to me
it seems that the points made by the two poets are different, though made with
equal sharpness.
[18] See David A. West, *Imagery and Poetry of Lucretius* (Edinburgh, 1969),
pp. 31-33.
[19] Giancotti (p. 88) notices the alliteration at least from *nix* to *violat*.

of running no doubt struck Lucretius as less well adapted to Epicurean purposes.[20]

The description is built out of a negative and a positive statement. The harassments that the gods are spared are balanced by the enjoyments they have. It is characteristic of Lucretius, and certainly no accident or technical flaw, that the antithesis between negative and positive is sharpened by another verbal repetition. The *aether* of line 21 is cloudless, *innubilus*, in direct opposition to the *nubila* of line 19 which scatter—or rather do not scatter—showers. The effect is doubly reinforced; the sounds of the first *nubil-* are impressed on ear and eye by the alliterative *nimbis* which follows it; and the two occurrences of *nubil-* are placed in precisely the same position in the hexameter, despite the sense being otherwise differently divided in the two lines concerned. Ancient readers perhaps objected less to casual repetition than most modern readers of English, but were certainly sufficiently sensitive to allow this kind of effect.[21]

It is important in this context to realize the extent to which the poet relies on verbal repetitions for his effects, since there are others in the present passage which have passed, so far as I know, unnoticed, and which are crucial to the understanding of it. In that stirring first line we find ourselves at once in the contrast between light and darkness, a contrast which for all its frequency

[20] The comparison of Lucretius with Homer has been weighed down with value judgments. One of the more interesting is D. E. W. Wormell's in *Lucretius* (ed. D. R. Dudley), p. 45: "a borrowing from Homer, but with enhanced dignity (the majestic peace of the setting is but the outward manifestation of the majesty and peace of its inhabitants.)" With much of this I agree, but I am at a loss to see how the majesty of Lucretius' gods or their dignity is greater than that of Homer's gods, unless it be because of what Giancotti has called Lucretius' "maestà di ritmo" (p. 89). Further, it is not fair to compare the weight of the spondees in Lucretius' version with the tripping dactyls of Homer without mentioning the generally higher proportion of spondees in Latin than in Greek hexameter poetry; Lucretius' spondees here would not stand out as heavy in his context any more than the Greek dactyls would seem specially light in Homer's.

[21] West (p. 31) finds here a technical flaw. But if this repetition of sound and stem is a flaw, what shall we think of the poet who so frequently points his argument with this kind of device?

loses here none of its poetic power.[22] The light of Epicurean philosophy, illuminating the advantages of life, opposes the darkness of
superstition. We learn as we read on to appreciate the divinity of
Epicurus' mind. We are then offered a picture of the place where
a truly divine mind would belong, the place where the divine
powers (*divum numen* with a surely intentional vagueness) actually
dwell. It is natural, but none the less effective, that it is light,
generously spread, with which that dwelling smiles. The reader's
ear, already attuned to echoes, catches the echo in *diffuso lumine* of
the *lumen* in line 1. How consciously he does so, or is meant to do
so, are of course difficult questions to answer, but the repetition is
there, and interpretation must take account of it. As the light of
philosophy was contrasted in line 1 with the darkness of ignorance,
so now the gods' dwelling-place is contrasted with the darkness of
the underworld. The divine philosopher enjoys the light, a light
closely analogous to the light which shines on the gods. The ideal
human life, the *commoda vitae* of line 2, is the closest possible
approach to the generous illumination (*large diffuso lumine*) of the
divine existence. To some degree heaven, like hell, is on earth.[23]
True, the underworld is contrasted with heaven only to be denied.
Nowhere do they appear, the temples of Acheron. But that,
evidently, is because the light of true philosophy has banished
them. In such great darkness Epicurus has raised so bright a light.
The idea is beautiful, and exquisitely pointed; it is a pity that
translators sometimes deface it by using different words to render
lumen in line 1 and *lumine* in line 22.[24]

Translators tend also to obscure the further repetitions which
in their subordinate place assist the fundamental one of the idea

---

[22] Ernout (Ernout-Robin on III. 2) finds the image "banal," but G. Müller
more justly writes "Dieser sachlich so entscheidenden und dichterische so
wirkungsvollen Gegensatz" (*Darstellung der Kinetik bei Lukrez* [Berlin, 1959],
p. 10).

[23] Two Italian scholars have seen this point, without, however, bringing out
the evidence from the text which establishes it. Giussani wrote that the divine
life "è anche un ideale della vita del sapiente," and Giancotti (p. 89) says
"La pace degli dei si configura quindi come l'ipotiposi della pace interiore che
l'uomo può conquistare rispondendo al messaggio di Epicuro."

[24] So (to name only a few of the most illustrious) Munro, Diels, and Bailey.

of light. Where Lucretius has *suppeditas* at line 10 and *suppeditat* at line 23, Bailey, for instance, has first "dost thou vouchsafe" and in the second place "nature supplies."[25] Lucretius intends here to throw into yet sharper relief the parallel between the light of philosophy and the light of the gods' dwelling. As Epicurus' thought "supplies" the precepts which cause the terrors of the mind (animi *terrores* 16) to disperse, so the gods are "supplied" by nature with all they need for peace of mind (animi *pacem* 24). Perhaps this last is accidental; perhaps certain words were running not unnaturally in Lucretius' mind as he composed. But at least we should be clear that, as J. D. Denniston once wrote in a somewhat similar context, "such accidents do not befall inferior writers."[26]

Lucretius, however, is not finished with the image of light and dark. As he began the proem with the vision of a *clear* light raised in the darkness, so he begins the transition to the book proper, after summarizing progress so far, by pointing out that the next thing for him to do is, in accordance with the atomic theory of the first two books, to *clarify* the nature of the soul. The verbal parallel should be observed between *clarum extollere lumen* and *claranda*.[27] The use of *clarare* is not frequent, and this fact might, under certain conditions, bring the link between the proem and the transition more forcibly to the reader's attention.[28] This link is followed up

[25] Bailey is again accompanied by Diels and Munro.

[26] *Greek Prose Style* (Oxford, 1952), p. 41.

[27] Kenney notices the repetition of the idea of illumination, but not the verbal point, of a kind frequent in Lucretius, nor the linking function of such repetitions.

[28] Ernout (Ernout-Robin *ad loc.*) does not fail to point out the rarity of *clarare*. If this part of the Book was written in the order we possess, the word's rarity is an argument in favor of the supposition that Lucretius not only intended this repetition of stem and sound but wanted to draw the reader's attention to it as sharply as possible. But I refrain from pressing the point further, first because one should avoid chronological assumptions however reasonable, and second because the fact that the word is used by Cicero as well as in one other passage by Lucretius (see Ernout-Robin) would render the argument, however plausible, inconclusive.

For the connection of *clar-* with light, compare the balance between *clarius audi . . . obscura* (I. 921-922) and *obscura de re tam lucida pango carmina* at I. 933-934, on which see Müller, *Kinetik*, p. 13. It is worth noting, while we are

in the transition by a reference to the fear of Acheron that must be driven out. This refers back, as has long been recognized, to the *Acherusia templa* of the proem which are nowhere to be found.[29] The superb image that follows has been well analysed by West, following Heinze. The darkness of death, traditionally associated with the underworld, becomes at line 39 the *mortis nigror* which is stirred up from the bottom of the river or the pool of life, leaving none of its waters pure. It is not for nothing that we have this switch from light and dark *simpliciter* to the darkness of stirred up mud immediately after a mention of one of the *rivers* of the underworld. Acheron is frequent as a metonym for Hades, but its use here none the less serves as a good starting point for the image.

At the end of the transition from proem to Book, we find at lines 87-90 the famous simile, repeated elsewhere, of the children afraid of the dark. The vanity of adult fears is compared to the vanity of children's in the dark. This terror of the mind and darkness, Lucretius says, must be dispersed by the *naturae species ratioque*, the "outer view and inner law of nature" as Bailey translates. Here the darkness is still that of superstition, and it has become mere childishness. At the same time the *Acherusia templa* of line 86 are obviously the things feared by adults in line 88, and they too are presumably dark. In this are several features that recall the opening of the Book: the juxtaposition of the *Acherusia templa* and the darkness of the superstitious mind (compare lines 25 and 37-39), the phrase *terrorem animi* (compare *animi terrores* at line 16), and the association of *ratio* with *natura* at line 93 (*naturae ratio*) with lines 14-15 *ratio tua coepit vociferari naturam rerum*. The extent to which the whole, proem and transition, form a unity, has not always been recognized. Unfortunately the effect is weakened, to my taste, by the occurrence of the same image of light and dark in a different kind of context in the middle of the transition at

---

connecting a proem with the following paragraph, that *tenebras* at II. 54 picks up *tenebras* at II. 15 (see Büchner, *Lukrez und Vorklassik*, p. 67).

[29] Giussani thought the connection weak. Editors have long neglected the connections between Lucretian paragraphs; I cannot find one (for example) who notices the reference back (by way of contrast) with *victus* at I. 103 to *victor* at 75 and *victoria* at 79.

lines 75-76. But the link between proem and transition remains
and is further strengthened by the application of the epithet
liquida at line 40 to pleasure. It is fitting that pleasure should be
metaphorically clear or bright after divinity has been associated
with light at lines 18-22, and pleasure with divinity at line 28.

Line 28 and the two following lines constitute indeed a poetic
summing up of the proem. The work of Epicurus' divine mind is
such as to produce a divine pleasure, presumably a calm akin to
that of the gods' dwelling. The mind which discovered the truth
about the gods and the mind which receives the message are alike
divine. Pleasure is accompanied by *horror*, another master stroke
of the poet. For generations men had shuddered at the darkness of
Acheron and the dread abode of death. Lucretius shudders also,
but with a pleasurable excitement at no longer having to fear the
after life. This shudder is different; perhaps the poet meant us to
read *divina* with *horror* as well as *voluptas*. So far Lucretius has
summed up his words from line 18 to line 27. The words *ex omni
parte* at line 30 call back to mind the emphasis on the "whole"
void at 17. The idea of revelation implicit in the rest of line 30,
tam manifesta patens . . . retecta est, as Kenney well remarks, "returns
the reader to the point of departure in 1." The nature of things
which Epicurus cries aloud at line 15 is brought back by *natura* at
29. Finally the phrase *tua vi* at the end of line 29, recalling the
person of Epicurus to the reader's attention, reminds us of two
earlier points in the proem. First, the earlier use of the possessive
tuus, and especially its occurrence at line 3 in the same conspicuous
position as in 29, namely just before the line ends with a monosyl-
lable (compare *inque tuis nunc* with *tua vi*). Second, the comparison
of the trembling goat Lucretius with the mighty strength of the
horse at 8, the resemblance again being shown up by the placing
of *vis* in line 8 and *vi* in line 29, both as final monosyllables.

Such, in outline, is the verbal structure of one Lucretian paragraph, and of its juncture with the next. Not, perhaps, a wholly
typical paragraph, for the Prefaces have long been seen to be
especially fine-wrought work. But it is less untypical than might
be supposed. There is a great deal of the same kind of analysis
waiting to be done or to be collected. To hark back once more to

the famous sentence of Cicero to which allusion was made at the
outset, we shall not understand the genius of Lucretius until we
take the pains to study his craftsmanship. Not that such categories
are adequate in the face of a craftsman of genius.

[30] I am grateful to my colleagues Gordon M. Kirkwood and Frederick M.
Ahl for reading and helpfully criticizing an earlier draft of this paper. They
are not responsible for errors of commission or omission.

Pound's Propertius :
The Homage and the Damage

GORDON M. MESSING

The study of ancient authors, whatever scoffers may say, is not a form of ancestor worship; a concern with the past can no longer exclude the present. Since at least the turn of the present century a classical scholar has had to acknowledge, however gloomily, that he inhabits the contemporary world. Like his colleagues in other humanistic studies, he bears within himself the uneasy self-consciousness proper to modern man, and thus it is with a modern awareness that he must now confront his ancient texts. They have not changed greatly, but he has changed. For their interpretation, he cannot simply rely upon tradition as in days gone by. There are new oracles to be consulted. Inevitably, some of these new Pythias and Sibyls have been engendered by the social sciences, currently enjoying an enormous intellectual prestige as the most reliable guides to human behavior: anthropology, psychology, demography, sociology (in Browning's words, "Greek endings, each the little passing bell/That signifies a faith's about to die"). Other serviceable hints have come from the professors of modern literatures, whose techniques of close reading are seen to be equally applicable to the ancients.

But, fortunately or unfortunately, a classicist wishing to heed the stern injunction to "make it new" finds at least one promising avenue of research blocked off: we do not know enough about the public life, let alone the private life, of ancient authors. Even if the ancients were not averse to literary gossip,[1] they were far from

---

[1] And they were not, as Moses Hadas has gracefully demonstrated in his *Ancilla to Classical Reading* (New York: Columbia University Press, 1954).

sharing our own insatiable curiosity for the minutiae of existence. Sheer ignorance prevents us from writing a life of Sophocles or Catullus[2] comparable in their detail to, let us say, Leon Edel's voluminous assessment of Henry James or Sartre's mammoth analysis of Flaubert, still incomplete, but dwelling at inordinate length upon the elusive psychological factors of his hero's childhood. It is inconceivable that we will ever stumble upon any list of the customers who bought produce from Euripides' mother or the school exercises that Horace wrote out for Orbilius, not to mention that private journal of Caesar's, which Thornton Wilder so cunningly reconstituted in *The Ides of March*.

In default of all such multifarious biographical data from our own age of copious newsprint and ubiquitous photography, those who would update the classics have had to concentrate not on the authors but on their writings. Following an unstated hypothesis, unknown to the ancients but certainly no less legitimate for that reason, that every real work of art is infinitely complex, the new scholarship has been at pains to search for undetected subtleties in the works of antiquity. The diligent expositors of Joyce, Yeats, and Proust have of course been carefully observed and lovingly imitated; ancient authors too can be interrogated and made to yield up their folklore motifs, their borrowings and echoings of predecessors, their meaningful imagery and pervasive symbols. Nor is there any closed season for hunting down the favorite big game of so many critics, irony and ambiguity. Above all, a modern psychological analysis of an ancient composition will reveal the personality of the author, because we surely can claim that human beings have always responded more or less constantly to the same stimuli.

---

[2] Even if biography is defined in less demanding terms, Wilamowitz remarks that Cicero is the first ancient whose life is well enough known to permit a biography; in ancient times, thanks to the still extant correspondence, such a biography of Aristotle or Epicurus could have been possible. However, "eine wirkliche Biographie wie Justis Winckelmann, können wir von keinem Hellenen schreiben, weil dazu das Material für uns fehlt," (U. von Wilamowitz-Moellendorff, *Euripides Herakles* I [Darmstadt: Wissenschaftliche Buchgesellschaft, 1969; 1st ed. 1895], p. 1).

As a result of these new techniques and our own altered emphasis, we have witnessed a striking reappraisal of many classical reputations and a heightened interest in some writers, perhaps neglected in the past, who seem despite their remoteness from us in time to be peculiarly our contemporaries. Propertius certainly belongs in this happy band: "There is something in the Umbrian poet that appeals to the modern mind," as Georg Luck has rightly observed, "whether it is the rich texture of his imagery or rather the desire to avoid the banal and conventional at all costs."[3] Not that the revaluation of Propertius had no harbingers: almost a century ago J. P. Postgate in the introduction to his school edition called attention to the poet's modern spirit ("in his employment of sentiment Propertius is modern and even romantic") and, more surprisingly, to "a vein of humour which we should not have expected."[4]

In the present essay, dedicated to my distinguished colleague James Hutton, who is at home in so many literatures, I shall dwell only incidentally upon the much vaunted modernity of Propertius. Instead, at the risk of entering an arena still strewn with the prostrate forms of earlier combatants, I shall address myself to the lifelike and ultramodern hero of Ezra Pound's *Homage to Sextus Propertius*, who bears so astonishing a resemblance to Pound himself.

The passage of years has only slightly muffled the harsh cries of both Pound's detractors and admirers, those who reject his rendering as a travesty of Propertius and those who extol it as "creative translation," and a model to inspire future translators. No mediator could hope to arbitrate such conflicting claims. My modest hope is to redefine the issues and restate a few obvious truths that may have been drowned out by all the shouting. Propertius says, "in magnis et voluisse sat est" (2. 10. 6), which, suitably ex-Pounded, is: "In things of similar magnitude the mere will to act is sufficient."

---

[3] *The Latin Love Elegy* (London: Methuen, 2d ed. 1969), p. 121.
[4] *Select Elegies of Propertius* (London: Macmillan, 1881); modern spirit, pp. lxxv–lxxvii; humor, pp. lxxxvi–lxxxvii.

I

Judged purely as a poem within the Pound canon, *Homage to Sextus Propertius* (hereafter, *Homage*) is indeed an adjunct to the Muses' diadem. Splendid passages like Section III ("Midnight, and a letter comes to me from our mistress") or IX. 2 ("Persephone and Dis, Dis have mercy upon her")[5] show Pound at his almost unrivaled best. There are many characteristic touches, mordant phrases, dazzling flashes of wit and pathos. A close relationship obviously exists between *Homage* (1917) and *Hugh Selwyn Mauberley* (1920); in both a sensitive poet is with some irony portrayed in disgruntled retreat from a strident and vulgar society, a theme long congenial to Pound ("Lovers of beauty starved, thwarted with systems").[6] J. P. Sullivan sees the more complex *Mauberley* as in essence a popularization of *Homage*,[7] and Pound himself made an identical assertion to his young friend Michael Reck.[8] Both are "works of self-justification, concerned with the fate of the artist in an age unsympathetic to his art."[9]

A problem of a very different order arises when we consider *Homage* as a translation from Propertius in its own right. T. S. Eliot in his well known introduction to Pound's *Selected Poems* touched gingerly upon his reason for excluding *Homage*: "I felt that the poem . . . would give difficulty to many readers because it is not enough a 'translation' and because it is, on the other hand, too much a 'translation' to be intelligible to any but the accomplished student of Pound's poetry."[10] Although in his postscript for a reissue of *Selected Poems* (1948) Eliot indicated that he "should

[5] References here and throughout are to the critical text prepared by J. P. Sullivan and included, together with the Latin text of L. Mueller utilized by Pound, in Sullivan's *Ezra Pound and Sextus Propertius* (Austin: University of Texas Press, 1964 hereafter *EPSP*), pp. 107-171. I call attention to two misprints in the Latin text, *tropae* for *tropaea*, p. 120, line 8, and *Titans* for *Titanas*, p. 134, line 19.

[6] "The Rest" in *Lustra*.

[7] *EPSP*, p. 27.

[8] Michael Reck, *Ezra Pound: A Close-Up* (New York: McGraw-Hill, 1967), p. 160.

[9] John J. Espey, *Ezra Pound's Mauberley: A Study in Composition* (London: Faber and Faber, 1955), p. 102.

[10] London: Faber and Faber, 1928, 2d ed. 1948.

now write with less cautious admiration" of *Homage*, yet in an essay on Pound, written in 1946 and revalidated in a postscript of 1950, he went a step further: "I am aware of the censure of those who have treated it as a translation; and if it is treated as a translation, they are of course right."[11]

But if *Homage* is not a translation, what is it? When Pound in an early poem complained that his sleep was troubled by "the thought of what America would be like if the Classics had a wide circulation,"[12] he was undoubtedly assigning himself the arduous mission of putting the classics back into circulation. That he later felt himself frustrated in this task can be assumed from the meaningful wording of Mauberley's resigned deference to his philistine public: "better mendacities / Than the classics in paraphrase."[13]

Pound originally called *Homage* a translation; he did not persist, however, and in fact renounced the term under fire as early as 1920,[14] after classical scholars, starting with William Gardner Hale, began to challenge his qualifications as a translator. Understandably, *Homage* is not included in Pound's collected translations. But "paraphrase" will not do either, for *Homage* is not simply a loose rewording of Propertius. Again it was Eliot, in the same preface to *Selected Poems*, who came up with the *mot juste*: "It is not a translation, it is a paraphrase, or still more truly (for the instructed) a *persona*."[15] Alas, *persona* nowadays is a word to make one wince; it has passed through the pens of too many criticasters and come out sadly faded. All the same, *persona* it must be, and then Pound's strategy becomes clearer. While *Homage* is in part a translation, often close, occasionally even too close to the Latin, Pound, by screening out some lines, focussing on others, and above all by emphasizing certain attitudes or if need be even incorporating them into his version, has created a Propertius of his own

---

[11] Included in the volume, *Ezra Pound*, ed. Peter Russell (London and New York: Peter Neville, 1950), p. 33.

[12] "Cantico del Sole," *Instigations* (1920).

[13] It is doubly significant that this line occurs in the first section of the poem entitled "E. P. Ode pour l'Election de son Sépulcre."

[14] Details in *EPSP*, pp. 4-12.

[15] See above, n. 10.

and made the Roman elegiac poet into a convenient spokesman for himself. As Elio Pasoli remarks, Pound surmised that Propertius had something to say to the man of today, and in *Homage* "rivelò quanto affini al suo proprio talento poetico fossero alcuni aspetti della poesia properziana, con cui il Pound volle in certo senso rivaleggiare."[16] More realistically, G. S. Fraser notes that *Homage* "will send you . . . to Propertius, looking for a wry humour, which is perhaps only Pound's, or which anyway no one would have seen in Propertius until Pound had read it into him."[17] Whether Pound's Propertius is identical with Propertius' Propertius or only with Pound's Pound is a troubled question which I shall put off for the moment.

Translation, paraphrase, *persona*, or a combination of these, *Homage* glaringly displayed one further feature which from the outset startled and dismayed many readers with classical tastes. I refer of course to certain weird mistranslations, whether deliberate or accidental, which bear Pound's special hallmark. A good example is Propertius 3. 1. 15-18:

> multi, Roma, tuas laudes annalibus addent,
> qui finem imperii Bactra futura canent.
> sed, quod pace legas, opus hoc de monte sororum
> detulit intacta pagina nostra via.

This comes out disconcertingly as:

> Annalists will continue to record Roman reputations,
> Celebrities from the Trans-Caucasus will belaud Roman celebrities
> And expound the distentions of Empire,
> But for something to read in normal circumstances?
> For a few pages brought down from the forked hill unsullied?

Robert Graves, who has always been contemptuous of Pound, wrote a stinging skit to demonstrate with the help of these lines

---

[16] *Sesto Properzio: Il Libro Quarto delle Elegie* (Bologna: Riccardo Pàtron, 2d ed. 1967), p. 3.

[17] From an essay, "Pound: Masks, Myth, Man" (1950), included in the book cited above, n. 11.

that Pound was a pretentious ignoramus.[18] It should surprise no one that A. Alvarez triumphantly seized upon this identical passage as a welcome indication that *Homage* "is also an ironic survey of Pound's own time and place" in which "the Roman becomes curiously modern."[19] Another Pound fancier, Lawrence Richardson, was thrilled to discover that the second line of the English is a pure invention inspired by the words *Roma, laudes,* and *Bactra*; he warmly approved Pound's occasional readiness to replace normal translation by "the garbled collage of sense possible if one takes only a few words and fits them on to what has gone before."[20]

This is another topic to which I shall later revert, for here I think Pound's idolaters have done him almost as great a disservice as his fiercest calumniators. Unfriendly critics quite naturally see these wilder flights into the blue as spectacular misinterpretations, differing only in degree of conspicuousness from the multitude of Pound's other ineptitudes. Friendly critics justify some or all of the extraordinary deviations; but if they are wise, they will freely admit that Pound's rendition swarms with what they will usually qualify as unimportant slips. Some of these minor slips, I believe, may turn out to be of some importance in gauging Pound's competence and his understanding.

To J. P. Sullivan, whose *Ezra Pound and Sextus Propertius* is the only full-length treatment of the entire problem, all scholars must be doubly indebted, whether or not they agree with his arguments: first, because he has printed a *texte jumelé*, a reliable *Homage* plus its resected and sutured Latin original, something which facilitates a minute comparison of the two; second, because he has boldly presented almost, but not quite, the most outrageous claim yet advanced in defence of *Homage* as a true translation and a valid criticism of Propertius.

---

[18] "Dr. Syntax and Mr. Pound" in *The Crowning Privilege* (London, 1955). This satiric sketch was inspired by an anonymous article praising Pound's translations in *The Times Literary Supplement* (18 Sept. 1953), p. 596; G. S. Fraser later revealed himself to be its author.

[19] *Stewards of Excellence* (New York: Scribners, 1958), p. 54.

[20] "Ezra Pound's Homage to Propertius," *Yale Poetry Review*, No. 6 (1947), p. 23.

II

Propertius is not the only author to be translated by Pound, who was a polyglot constantly quoting, translating, and paraphrasing. It is legitimate to enquire, as a guide to his competence in Latin, with what skill he has accomplished his translations from other languages. The answers are divergent. It is fair to say that the same old criticisms have always been leveled at him: he frequently does not seem to be in complete control of the language of his original.[21] Those languages which he studied in the usual academic way, French, Italian, and Provençal, come out the best, but even in the Romance sector his scholarship has been impugned. *The Spirit of Romance* (1910), his first prose volume, was "faulted for blunders in translation and inaccuracy in quoting from, or using in English phrases from, foreign languages."[22] Pound's Greek, one strongly suspects, was never up to his Latin—he himself once commented facetiously (Canto 105) "I shall have to learn a little greek to keep up with this / but so will you, drratt you"—but even Hugh Kenner gently points out some flaws in a version of Sappho[23] and objects to the swapping of colloquial styles in *The Women of Trachis* (1956).[24] Michael Reck confesses that Pound's "Greek was not large; it was mainly read with the help of the Loeb Classical Library translations."[25]

German is clearly one of Pound's weaker languages. Jeannette Lander, a German speaker, fastened with some asperity upon an elementary mistake in grammar (Canto 51, "zwischen *die* Völkern") and a misquoted and misapplied German saying (*ABC of Reading*,[26] "wie in den Schnabel gewachsen").[27] At Saint

[21] G. S. Fraser in *Ezra Pound* (Edinburgh and London: Oliver and Boyd, 1960) says: "The case of the scholars against Pound as a translator is that he perpetually shows signs of not knowing properly the language he is translating from" (p. 64).

[22] Fraser, p. 11.

[23] *The Pound Era* (Berkeley and Los Angeles: University of California Press, 1971), pp. 55-56.

[24] Kenner, p. 526.

[25] Reck (see above, n. 8), p. 118.

[26] Reprint, London: Faber and Faber, 1951, p. 36.

[27] Jeannette Lander, *Ezra Pound* (New York: Frederick Ungar, 1971), pp. 78-79.

Elizabeth's, Pound told Michael Reck that he had read little
German since translating Heine around 1910.[28] In one of those
translations he confused *Leid* and *Lied* and "would not have been
interested," according to Kenner, "had he read correctly."[29] In
ABC of Reading (p. 36) Pound claimed, and his admirers have often
repeated, that "the German verb corresponding to the noun
Dichtung meaning poetry" was fittingly rendered by the Italian
verb *condensare*, since "poetry is the most concentrated form of
verbal expression." Whatever the rhetorical truth of this bold
statement, it is sheer etymological nonsense.[30]

The critics have predictably wavered in their verdict on Pound's
translation of *The Seafarer*, which swarms with inaccuracies, both
errors of interpretation and omissions (probably deliberate) of
Christian references in the Old English original.[31] Nonetheless,
many, myself included, have admired its somber account of lonely
wandering and exile; Michael Alexander dedicated his own
volume of translations from Old English to Pound and called the
latter's *Seafarer* "miraculous, however many howlers be proved
against it."[32] Howlers there are, for example, the notorious
"Waneth the watch, but the world holdeth" where the text means
"the weaker sort live on and control the world." Such mistakes are
ascribable to Pound's tenuous grip on Old English and his reluc-
tance to verify the accuracy of his translations.[33]

Finally, there are the wonderful Chinese translations in *Cathay*
(1915) which led T. S. Eliot to call Pound "the inventor of Chinese

[28] Reck, (see above, n. 8), p. 118.

[29] Kenner, (above, 23), pp. 142-143.

[30] There are of course two word families at issue, one cognate with Eng.
tight (*dicht, dichten, Dichtung*), the other with Eng. *indite* (*dichten, Dichter, Dichtung*), and never the twain shall meet.

[31] Donald Davie, *Ezra Pound: Poet as Sculptor* (New York: Oxford University
Press, 1964), pp. 25-26. Christine Brooke-Rose finds "a great deal of Pound's
version ridiculous" but chiefly faults his attempts to duplicate Anglo-Saxon
scansion; see *A ZBC of Ezra Pound* (Berkeley and Los Angeles: University of
California Press, 1971), pp. 86-89.

[32] *The Earliest English Poems* (Penguin Books, 1966), p. 159.

[33] It was the ninth-century sounds which intrigued him, according to Hugh
Kenner; see the essay, "Blood for the Ghosts," in Eva Hesse, ed., *New Ap-
proaches to Ezra Pound* (Berkeley and Los Angeles: University of California
Press, 1969), pp. 332-334.

poetry for our time."[34] These include without any doubt some of Pound's most highly praised compositions, yet many Sinologists have been unhappy with them judged simply as renderings of the Chinese original. Unlike the other translations, however, these drew upon a detailed and annotated version in English; when Pound came into possession of the manuscripts of Ernest Fenellosa, he was completely ignorant of Chinese (and of Japanese, in which a phonetic transcription of the Chinese characters had been provided).[35] In later years, Pound did acquire a certain amount of Chinese, but his versions of the Confucian prose classics and the classical anthology of Chinese poetry are less relevant to my purpose. Fenellosa had formulated, and Pound eagerly endorsed, a theory of translation arising out of analysis of the Chinese originals and published by the latter under the title, *The Chinese Written Character as a Medium for Poetry*, in *Instigations* (1920). Sinologists dismiss the theory in the main as arrant nonsense, however stimulating to Pound's own poetical practice, for it contains, *inter alia*, the following two pseudo-linguistic principles: first, that the characters themselves, over and above their phonetic values, have an additional poetic meaning as pictograms;[36] second, that the structural organization of Chinese in itself has some sort of aesthetic value which can and should be duplicated by an English translator, for example, word order and use of transitive verbs.

Although Hugh Kenner ironically offers a "canonical list" of *Cathay's* "derelictions" plus a plausible explanation of how and where they occurred,[37] doubts arise, like those inspired by *Homage*, as to the success of *Cathay* in recapturing the tone of the original. I have fortunately been permitted to read an unpublished essay by

[34] Preface to *Selected Poems* (see above, n. 10), p. 14.

[35] Kenner is especially informative on the contents of Fenellosa's papers; see his chapter, "The Invention of China," in *The Pound Era*, pp. 192-222.

[36] I do not find it pertinent to assert, as does Brooke-Rose, in defence of this claim, that "many of us are aware of the original meanings of, say, *Psychosomatic* or *hydro-electric*, or that *silly* once meant 'blessed'." We need none of this information when we read a connected text, and in any case a more valid comparison might concern the constituent letters forming these words as well as their etymology. See *A ZBC of Ezra Pound*, pp. 101-103.

[37] Cf. above, n. 35.

Wu Hsin-min (hereafter, Wu),[38] a Chinese reader of Pound who is thoroughly familiar with the Chinese poems. She gives *Cathay* very high marks for general effectiveness. Nonetheless she finds, comparing each poem with a literal version of her own, that there are a great many inaccuracies, only a few of which figure on Kenner's list. Here are two almost at random. In "The River Merchant's Wife: A Letter," which Wu considers a brilliant rendering, when "The monkeys make sorrowful noise overhead," the noise is not audible over the young wife's head, as Pound imagines. She is imagining the gibbons chattering over her husband's head by the gorges of western China. Again, in "Exile's Letter," the line "And then I was sent off to South Wei, smothered in laurel groves" is a reversal of the sense ("I went to the south of Huai River to search for cassia boughs"), for while cassia boughs signify passing the imperial examination (as laurel groves signify obtaining literary fame), Pound suggests his writer succeeded and in fact he did not.

Sometimes, more importantly, Pound has not duplicated the original mood. The very first poem of *Cathay*, "Song of the Bowmen of Shu," is composed in his wonted conversational style whereas the original is highly formalized. It consists, Wu says, of six stanzas, each with eight lines, and each line with four characters; there is rhyme, and each line has three definite stresses. "Though on a small scale, it beats out its rhythm like a funeral march, and this Pound misses." (She notes elsewhere that most classical Chinese poetry is too stylized to lend itself to a more unbuttoned rendering.) Wu makes another useful comment apropos of "Poem by the Bridge at Ten-Shin" (a lesser achievement, since many of the allusions have been muffed): Li-po wrote, "If at the height of success (one) does not retire, / From ancient times much disaster has been bred." This bit of moralizing is vital, since the Chinese poet goes on to cite three famous *exempla* of persons who either followed or disregarded it. Pound simply cut the line out, perhaps because of a distaste for this and similar moral apothegms.

[38] I am grateful to my colleague Harold Shadick, Emeritus Professor of Chinese, for showing me this paper, dated 1951, from his former student Wu-Hsin-min (Mrs. John Brohm).

III

The evidence collected in the preceding section on the accuracy of Pound's translations from languages other than Latin shows that he has been repeatedly and successfully challenged for philological inadequacy. In dozens of renderings, he has either mistaken the meaning or deliberately altered it for reasons of his own; this inveterate *traduttore* has been proved to some degree a *traditore*.

Returning now to the original point of departure, I should like to examine much more closely Pound's credentials as a Latinist. In doing so, I have no intention of playing either of the little games habitual to critics of *Homage*. Unlike the adulators, I shall not automatically credit Pound with extraordinary subtlety and wit every time he deviates from the Latin; on the other hand, I shall not follow Robert Graves or the other scoffers when they detect schoolboy errors in what is clearly whimsy or persiflage. I wish merely to observe some of Pound's slips when he is functioning as a conventional translator, when we can exclude any sly winks or high jinx. According to Lawrence Richardson, clearly a fervid admirer, "Pound's knowledge of Latin is considerable though it is untidy . . . he has disrespect for the finesse of scholarship."[39] Still, how considerable is considerable, and how untidy is untidy?

In the essay, "A Retrospect,"[40] Pound advised a prospective poet to "fill his mind with the finest cadences he can discover, preferably in a foreign language, so that the meaning of the words may be less likely to divert his attention from the movement." In at least one passage of Section XII, however, Pound himself has tripped up from failing to pay attention to the fine cadence of the hexameter; "utque decem possint corrumpere māla puellas" (2. 34. 69) becomes "and how ten sins can corrupt young maidens."

Tense distinctions offer another easy criterion and are not always, *pace* Sullivan, "non-functional."[41] In Section III a past

[39] *Yale Poetry Review* (see above, n. 20), p. 21.
[40] *Literary Essays of Ezra Pound*, ed. T. S. Eliot (Norfolk, Conn.: New Directions, 1954), p. 4.
[41] *EPSP*, p. 97.

event, "peccaram semel, et totum sum postus[42] in annum"
(3. 16. 9), has unaccountably been shifted into the future: "*And
I shall be in the wrong, and it will last a twelve month.*" A
fundamental distortion occurs in Section V where again an action
in the past, "bella canam, quando scripta puella meast" (2. 10. 8),
is projected into the future: "*and I will also sing war when this
matter of a girl is exhausted.*" Propertius makes no such stipula-
tion; he will sing of wars (and proceeds to do so) *since* he has
finished writing about Cynthia (and has perhaps parted from
her).[43] Whether conscious or not, this change of tense crucially
alters the meaning and artfully pushes Pound's Propertius in a
particular direction.

A subjunctive has been mishandled in Section V. 2. The lines
"quod mihi si tantum, Maecenas, fata dedissent / ut possem heroas
ducere in arma manus" (2. 1. 17-18) are rendered by "Thus much
the fates have allotted me, and if, Maecenas, / I were able to lead
heroes into armour," with the result that "thus much" is wrongly
made to look backward instead of forward.

Apropos of tenses, "Amities," IV, in *Selected Poems*, an amusing
fling in homemade Latin, is famous for the form *gaudero*, evidently
intended to be a future to *gaudeo*. Like the Ovidian epigraph in
Mauberley, "vacuos exercet aera morsus" (which cannot be translated unless one inserts a missing *in* before *aera*),[44] or the spelling
Polydmantus for *Polydamas* in *Homage*,[45] these were errors which no
amount of persuasion could ever induce Pound to renounce. In
this as in some far less trivial matters, he reminds one of Sergius in

---

[42] So *EPSP*. But in fact L. Mueller in his Teubner edition of 1892, like
E. A. Barber in the latest Oxford Classical Text (2d ed. 1960), and indeed like
most editors, read *pulsus* with the manuscripts FLP against *portus*, the reading
of manuscript N. Barber in his *apparatus* attributes the emendation *postus* to
J. S. Phillimore, whose first edition was not published until 1901 (2d ed. 1907).
H. E. Butler and E. A. Barber, *The Elegies of Propertius* (Oxford: Clarendon
Press, 1933) indicate in their preface (p. lxxxi) that "we have also followed *y*
[i.e. FLP] at III. xvi. 9, though with grave misgivings."

[43] See W. A. Camps *ad loc.* in his *Propertius: Elegies II* (Cambridge: University Press, 1967), pp. 108-109.

[44] Espey, (above, n. 9), p. 22.

[45] *EPSP*, p. 97.

Shaw's *Arms and the Man,* who habitually folded his arms like an automaton and announced haughtily, "I never apologize."

Mistaken identification of case forms is rare in *Homage,* only because such examples invariably include more basic misinterpretations of meaning. I find one in the notorious *facetiae* about "Welsh mines" (to which I shall return); "et benefacta Mari" (2. 1. 24) is translated sportively in Section V. 2, as "and the profit Marus had out of them." The joke does not extend to "Marus." In Section VI Pound correctly inserted "Marius" into his poem twice, working in each case from an unambiguous "consule cum Mario"; "Marus," extracted from *Mari,* is surely the slip of someone not at his ease in Latin accidence. (As a parallel example, one of the pieces in *Polite Essays*[46] flaunts a title clearly designed to be a sarcastic sally: "Prefatio [*sic*] aut Cimicium Tumulus." But *cimex* is not an *i*-stem, as Pound could easily have verified.)

Let me turn now to erroneous collocations of words. To begin at the very beginning, there is "Coan ghosts of Philetas" for "Coi sacra Philetae" (3. 1. 1). Sullivan is convinced that "the line succeeds rhythmically and the meaning is not changed,"[47] but he is noticeably uneasy about Richardson's flashier defense of it. The latter argues that retention of the Latin word order is itself a desideratum,[48] surely a claim without any foundation, even if Pound himself believed it. In an inflected language like Latin a freer word order is permitted than in an analytic language like English. The illusory goal of copying a Latinate word order in English can appeal only to pseudo-linguists, like the Fenellosa theories about copying Chinese structure in English. "Coan ghosts of Philetas" is a long way removed from "the rites of Philetas of Cos."

In Section I we read "For Orpheus . . . held up the Threician river" where Propertius wrote "et concita dicunt / flumina Threicia sustinuisse lyra" (3. 2. 2-3). The adjective *Threicia* should go with *lyra* (left untranslated), and this is not without importance,

---

[46] Norfolk, Conn.: New Directions, 1940.
[47] *EPSP,* p. 98.
[48] Richardson, (above, n. 20), p. 22.

for Orpheus' blocking of rivers need not have occurred in Thrace. One suspects, incidentally, that the Latin spelling of "Threician" was retained because Pound did not know it was the same as Thracian and naturally did not waste time looking it up. (It would be petty to insist that Propertius spoke of rivers in the plural; in another such interchange of number, Pound himself defended "Oetean gods" for the singular, "Oetaei dei," as improving the verse rhythm.)[49]

Further on in the same section, to render "quin etiam, Polypheme, fera Galatea sub Aetna / ad tua rorantes carmina flexit equos" (3. 2. 5-6), the English runs "And you, O Polyphemus? Did harsh Galatea almost / Turn to your dripping horses, because of a tune, under Aetna?" Needless to say, it was Aetna which was *fera*, not Galatea. She was the opposite of harsh if she, as Propertius describes, turned *her* horses in response to *his* melodies (*tua* is also transposed). Meaning has been seriously impaired, and one wonders whether to attribute this to carelessness, to ignorance, or to Latin word order prevailing over scansion and sense. The extra "almost" with which Pound thought to hedge his bets is also intriguing.

Another transferred epithet may be found at the beginning of Section II, where Pound wrote "I had been seen in the shade, recumbent on cushioned Helicon" to translate "Visus eram molli recubans Heliconis in umbra" (3. 3. 1). It may be, as Thomas Drew-Bear maintains,[50] that *molli*, which properly goes with *umbra*, has been deliberately and dexterously switched in the translation—"cushioned Helicon"—to stigmatize conventional poetic aspirations. One wonders, though, how an effect so shrewd can occur in conjunction with the elementary blunder of rendering *visus eram* by "I had been seen." (Another passage of Section X confirms that Pound had difficulties with this simple idiom. In the line, "talis visa mihi somno dimissa recenti" (2. 29. 29), his only recourse was to take *visa* as a noun: "such aspect was presented to

---

[49] *EPSP*, p. 97.
[50] "Ezra Pound's 'Homage to Sextus Propertius'," *American Literature* 37 (1965), p. 206.

me, me recently emerged from my visions."[51] By compounding of error, this has wandered very far from the literal meaning, "so she appeared to me as she awoke from recent sleep.")

I come now to various acts of mayhem committed against the Latin original where again I shall eschew both trifling mistakes and intentional jocularity. First, some *faux amis*. *Miror* has twice been confused with its Romance offspring (especially, Span. *mirar*, It. *mirare*); in Section I *miremur* does not mean "we must look into the matter" nor in Section V. 2, does *miramur* mean "we look at the process." *Rigare* of course means "to wet." Pound has confused it with the family of *rigeo*, *rigidus* in Section II, where "ora Philetaea nostra rigavit aqua" (3. 3. 52) is converted into "Stiffened our face with the backwash of Philetas the Coan." For Sullivan, to be sure, no mistake is involved: "Pound relies here on the connotation of 'rigid' in English and intensifies the simple meaning of the Latin to give the line an overtone of the stiffening of a poetic resolve. There is in fact no need to postulate a theory for these changes or bad philology."[52] Unfortunately for this confident assertion, Pound fell into the same trap twice. When "non operosa rigat Marcius antra liquor" (3. 2. 14) becomes in Section I "Nor are my caverns stuffed stiff with a Marcian vintage," it is hard to invoke any brilliant poetic overtone to justify so palpable a slip; bad philology is obvious in any case since *Marcius liquor*, far from being a vintage, is water from the aqueduct of Marcius, which Propertius himself elsewhere (3. 22. 24) praises as "aeternum Marcius umor opus."

In Section II Pound speaks of "lares fleeing the 'Roman seat' " and has manifestly confused *fugantes* with *fugientes* in his original: "Hannibalemque Lares Romana sede fugantes" (3. 3. 11). Thomas Drew-Bear, inexcusably to my mind, protests that Pound is merely "careless of the literal meaning of the Latin, since for the average American reader the image of the Lares frightening

---

[51] Pound may have been deceived here by assuming that Propertius was still under the spell of the scene described earlier in the poem according to Mueller's text. Today, editors prefer to divide the poem in two since the contents are virtually irreconcilable.

[52] *EPSP*, p. 100.

someone carries with it no automatic associations different from
the image of the Lares fleeing . . . Pound felt free to ignore the
details."[53] There is less strain on our credulity if we assume that
Pound nodded, both in this transparent example, and in turning
"nervis hiscere posse meis" (3. 3. 4) into "shall be yawned out on
my lyre." The apologists are ecstatic about this (admittedly most
amusing) line. Sullivan remarks that "*hiscere* ('tell of', for only
chasms 'yawn' with this word in Latin) suffers a sea-change to
express Pound's distaste for epic Roman subjects."[54] Drew-Bear
characterizes *yawn* as "a neat device for retaining both the literal
sense of Propertius' verb and a pointed satire on the fashionable
hacks."[55] May I suggest, much more prosaically, that Pound knew
hiscere only in the sense "to yawn" and as usual did not look it up;
he needed a transitive verb and saved the situation by converting
"yawn" into "yawn out."

Certainly, no witticism is intended in the solemn peroration of
Section IX. 3, yet a curious error occurs there which I think can
easily be accounted for. Propertius tells his mistress

> munera Dianae debita redde choros
> redde etiam excubias divae nunc, ante iuvencae. [2. 28. 60-61]

This becomes in *Homage*

> Go back to great Dian's dances bearing suitable gifts,
> Pay up your vow of night watches to Dian goddess of virgins.

Concerning the "suitable gifts" I cannot refrain from pointing out
that the woman has made a vow to participate in the *chori* and
that this in itself is her gift to the goddess. In the next line, the
night watches are naturally not payable to Diana but to Isis as
identified with Io "who is goddess now, but formerly a heifer,"
and is unforgettably if inaccurately described in Section VIII
("Io mooed the first years with averted head"). I have a strong
suspicion that in Pound's mind *iuvenca* and *iuvenis* were blurred,
and I can present one small piece of confirmatory evidence in the

---

[53] Drew-Bear, p. 209.
[54] *EPSP*, p. 104.
[55] Drew-Bear, p. 209.

essay cited above.[56] There Pound wished to deprecate those who considered him an obstreperous youth. Characteristically, he thought it amusing to replace the English phrase by an impromptu Latin equivalent, and just as characteristically, he came up, not with *strenuus iuvenis* but *strenuus iuventus*. If he was able to confuse these two, my guess is that he took *iuvenca* to mean "young girl" and construed "divae . . . ante iuvencae" as "goddess who stands in front of a maiden."

Another example is even more revealing of Pound's slipshod treatment of the Latin. Propertius wrote:

> tristis erat domus, et tristes sua pensa ministrae
> carpebant, medio nebat et ipsa loco. [3. 6. 15-16]

In return, Pound offers in Section IV:

> Sadness hung over the house, and the desolated female attendants
> were desolated because she had told them her dreams.
> She was veiled in the midst of that place.

While the phrase about the "desolated female attendants" is mock-heroic, there is no reason to suspect any deliberate infidelity. Perhaps by mentally equating *pensa* to French *pensées* and stretching that to include reverie, Pound arrived at "dreams" and then, logically enough, took *sua pensa carpebant* to be "they gathered her dreams," a periphrasis for "she had told them her dreams." *Sua*, which should have been a barrier, did not deter him in his headlong rush to portray the wrong scene. Had he paused, he might have found the true scene more picturesque: the desolated female attendants, drawing off their stints of wool from the distaff; their mistress, in true Roman matronly fashion, spinning (*nebat*) in their midst. ("She was veiled," I take it, was sheer guesswork on Pound's part.)

When *Lustra* first appeared, Pound supplied on the title page a definition of *lustrum*[57] taken from Lewis' elementary Latin dictionary, "offering for the sins of the whole people, made by the

---

[56] Pound, *Polite Essays* (above, n. 46).

[57] London: Elkin Mathews, 1916. It is omitted in the American edition (New York: Alfred Knopf, 1917), but reappears in *Selected Poems*.

censors at the expiration of their five years of office." Thinking still perhaps of that definition, and without this time consulting Lewis, Pound in Section V translated "sed tempus lustrare . . . Helicona" (2. 10. 1) as "Now if ever it is time to cleanse Helicon."

Flagrant mistakes of this kind—and the number could without effort be greatly increased—make one less inclined to give Pound the benefit of the doubt in more ambiguous contexts. In Section XII, for example, Pound, in his rage at British imperialism, made Virgil the innocent target for numerous envenomed darts. At one point Propertius refers gracefully to the *Eclogues*:

> felix intactum Corydon qui temptat Alexin
> agricolae domini carpere delicias!
> quamvis ille sua lassus requiescat avena. [2. 34. 73-75]

Pound begins harmlessly enough, "Corydon tempts Alexis," and then, incredibly, he writes: "Head farmers do likewise, and lying weary amid their oats." Is he being funny? It certainly looks as if he has read *agricolae domini* as "farmers who are masters," hence "head farmers," and has construed *carpere delicias* as "gather delights" and therefore, with a sidelong glance at what has gone before, "do likewise." Those for whom Pound can do no wrong are free to exonerate him and declare he is surely spoofing his readers; I am not so certain. Carelessness and haste can be invoked as readily as playfulness and bravado. And is "lying weary amid their oats" another private joke? After reading *Homage* against the Latin line by line, I would not put my hand in the fire to warrant that Pound really did know that *avena* meant "reed pipe." Two lines further there pops up a famous Poundian witticism, suitably earmarked as such: "Go on, to Ascraeus' prescription, the ancient, respected, Wordsworthian," a light-hearted updating of "tu canis Ascraei veteris praecepta poetae" (2. 34. 77). But "Ascraeus" inevitably reminds one of "Marus," that other unhappy phantom. It is crystal-clear that Pound understood the Latin to mean "the precepts of the old poet, Ascraeus," rather than "the poet of Ascra." Great sport, I admit, to twit Wordsworth for sometimes sounding like a sort of farmer's almanac; but at the time Pound certainly had no inkling of "Ascraeus" ' real identity.

My last example stands on a razor's edge between mistaken translation and deliberate mistranslation, but the two realms are not hermetically sealed off from each other. In several passages, notably but not exclusively in Sections V and XII, there is a mere pastiche of Propertius, a phrase here, a phrase there, selected haphazardly from the Latin and handled impressionistically. Pound was bored or thought his readers would be, and he flipped over the pages rapidly. In other passages it amused him to play word-games rather than to translate, and so he perpetrated the famous "howlers." If only because a detailed comparison of *Homage* with the Latin reveals so many great and small uncertainties in Pound's comprehension of the niceties of grammar, syntax, and sense—I have necessarily offered only a sampling—I suspect that at least some of these started in a faulty initial interpretation. An embryonic example might be "unde pater sitiens Ennius ante bibit" (3. 3. 6) and "father Ennius, sitting before I came" in Section II. A translator who is capable of confusing *rigare* and *rigere* might equally well have wavered just for an instant between *sitiens* and *sedens*, given the added temptation of the English "sit." I am inclined to believe that Pound caught the slip and then retained it because it tickled his sense of humor. To judge more elaborate constructions, we must advance in a progression. First are the outright gaffes ("she had told them her dreams"). Then comes a border zone where we must pick our way with caution: is "head farmers" for *agricolae domini* a blunder? Or again, how about another line which has caused many brows to wrinkle: "nocturnaeque canes ebria signa fugae" (3. 3. 48)? In Section II this emerges as "Night dogs, the marks of a drunken scurry." Sullivan after tentatively dismissing a theory of intersecting homophones that might have intrigued Pound (*canes* as noun and verb), claims rather defiantly that the imagery is more vivid in the English version, but admits it might be just a simple mistake.[58] (If the latter is true, it is of course not just a *culpa* but a *felix culpa!*)

Finally, all the way over the edge, may be found the truly bizarre mistranslations, which must be intentional even though

[58] *EPSP*, pp. 99-100.

they are clinically related, so to speak, to the errors I have hitherto been discussing. Here belong such an outré rendering as that mentioned above: "Annalists will continue to record Roman reputations . . ." or the following three all-too-famous passages:

> carminis interea nostri redeamus in orbem,
> gaudeat in solito tacta puella sono. [3. 2. 1-2]

And in the meantime my songs will travel,
and the devirginated young ladies will enjoy them
    when they have got over the strangeness. [Section I]

> Cimbrorumque minas et benefacta Mari. [2. 1. 24]

Nor of Welsh mines and the profit Marus had out of them. [Section V. 2].

> tale facis carmen docta testudine quale
> Cynthius impositis temperat articulis. [2. 34. 79-80]

Like a trained and performing tortoise,
I would make verse in your fashion, if she should command it.
    [Section XII]

Sullivan, as usual, justifies Pound's technique which exploits casual resemblances between English and Latin words or possible but incorrect meanings of the Latin text.[59] Similarly, Kenner is lost in admiration when he contemplates the ironic bilingual puns at work in these and similar lines.[60]

I think I can pin down the process of Pound's word-play more exactly than has hitherto been the case simply by making a distinction between playing on the sense and playing on the sound. Were one to take, for example, a phrase like *pompa belli* and facetiously translate it as "stomach pump," it is clear that only the sounds of the words have been imitated. On the other hand, a

---

[59] *EPSP*, pp. 95-104. He gives a good explanation (p. 102) of the mechanism by which Pound arrived at the last of these translations.

[60] Hugh Kenner, *The Poetry of Ezra Pound* (London: Faber and Faber, and New York: New Directions, 1951), Ch. 17 ("Propertius").

word manipulator can also play with the meaning of the foreign words. Let us take, for example, the phrase in which T. S. Eliot gracefully honored Pound, *il miglior fabbro*. By rendering this as "the best smith," and by recalling then that Sydney Smith, the renowned wit, was called "the Smith of Smiths," one might in jest come to the admittedly far-fetched conclusion that Eliot's phrase was a reference to Sydney Smith.

But there is also a compromise method by which the jokester mainly uses sound associations while still translating some of the words, some correctly, others not. In the "fractured French" of some years ago, *honni soit qui mal y pense* was transmogrified into "Honey, your silk stocking is hanging down."[61] Similarly, if *il miglior fabbro*, my earlier example, were to be rendered "the best man at Faber & Faber," it has suddenly turned into a reference to Eliot himself in his publishing capacity. This is nearer to Pound's "Welsh mines"; and perhaps it would not be amiss to speak of this *modus operandi* as "fractured Latin."

Incidentally, I cannot agree with Sullivan when he attempts to discover "good philological grounds" for "the devirginated young ladies."[62] Propertius is not Martial; *tangere* sometimes bears a sexual connotation, but *tacta puella* is not contrasted with *virgo intacta* in any known context and would be peculiarly inept in this one.[63] Rather, one detects here the same impulse that led Pound to render "Itala per Graios orgia ferre choros" (3. 1. 4) by "Bringing the Grecian orgies into Italy, and the dance into Italy" (Section I), or even more obviously, to match "ut regnem mixtas inter conviva puellas" (2. 34. 57) against "I shall triumph among young ladies of indeterminate character" (Section XII). Despite Pound's protestations ("Good God! They say you are *risqué*, / o canzonetti"),[64] these overdrawn interpretations, like his epigrams in the classical style, merely betray a certain amiable weakness for ribald pleasantries.

---

[61] F. S. Pearson, 2nd., *Fractured French* (New York: Doubleday, 1950).

[62] *EPSP*, pp. 96-97.

[63] Camps prefers to read "gaudeat ut solito tacta puella sono," since the usual reading leaves *tacta* unsupported. See his note *ad loc.*

[64] See "Ancora" in *Selected Poems*.

IV

A comparison of *Homage* with the Propertian text leads us, in the language of a polyglot punner much defter than Pound, by a commodius vicus of recirculation, back to the nagging question of whether *Homage* is a translation. By this time, two conclusions are irresistible: first, *Homage* was compiled with little if any delving into the lexicon; and second, Pound could hardly have claimed to be much of a Latinist. Neither of these theses is particularly revolutionary. Robert Conquest in an abrasive article[65] accused Pound of having made his version *calamo currente*, without looking up words. This must have been the case. He was equally unconcerned about tracking down elusive mythological and historical topics; Ida and Cithaeron, for example, are both assumed to be persons rather than mountains, while "royal Aemilia drawn on the memorial raft" is a Cleopatra-like wraith, created *ex nihilo* when Pound failed to grasp a reference to the Roman general, L. Aemilius Paulus.

Pound's Latin turns out to be—it is hardly surprising—imperfectly learned and inaccurately utilized, like most of his other languages. A partisan witness, Pound himself, once wrote: "I do not imagine I am the sole creature who has been well taught his Latin and very ill taught his Greek."[66] In sober fact, on the evidence presented above, even if Pound had undergone fair school preparation in Latin, he never really mastered the language in detail. In any case, what he did know had become rusty by the time he came to compose *Homage*, and his limited grasp of a Latin text was further compromised by his notorious inclination to thumb his nose at scholarly niceties. A further clue is given in *How to Read*.[67] After nonchalantly rejecting all of Greek literature except for Homer and Sappho, Pound set the record straight about the Romans as well. "Catullus, Ovid, Propertius, all give us something we cannot find now in Greek authors. A specialist may

[65] *The London Magazine*, 3. 1. 33-49 (April, 1963).

[66] From the beginning of the essay, "Translators of Greek: Early Translators of Homer," contained in *Literary Essays of Ezra Pound* (above, n. 40), p. 249.

[67] Included in *Literary Essays of Ezra Pound*, pp. 15-40 (Roman authors are treated on pp. 27-28).

read Horace . . . I am chucking out . . . Virgil without the slightest
compunction . . . One can throw out at least one third of Ovid."
How very convenient, when all but a few pages of Roman poetry
can safely be consigned to the dung heap! It follows that one need
not read the rejected authors, and Pound probably never did, once
his formal schooling was at an end. But even a part time or Sunday
Latinist requires a more substantial reading list; to what authority
can such a reader lay claim, if he has dipped only into Catullus,
Ovid and Propertius while shunning Virgil and Horace and taking
no notice of Lucretius, Tibullus,[68] and the rest?

By way of parenthesis, if Pound's credentials as a Latinist are
as weak as I believe them to be, we can hardly take seriously his
brash assertion that Propertius habitually employed a peculiarly
sensitive form of irony (*logopoeia*), which by a striking coincidence
is closely akin to Pound's own. Sullivan may or may not be correct
—I am sceptical—in corroborating the presence of such Propertian
logopoeia (paradoxically, he finds faint traces of it even in the
aetiological poems of Book IV).[69] Even if this assertion were true,
how would Pound have known? Sullivan defers too much to
Pound's indubitable poetic flair. *Homage* shows that its author,
whose horizons in Latin literature were absurdly circumscribed,
was obtuse to numerous subtleties of his text. Surely then he is to
be trusted even less in his interpretation of Propertian attitudes
and moods.

Viewed solely as a translation, *Homage* suffers not only from the
major flaws I have tried to isolate. Some passages have been
rendered chaotically and impressionistically, where words are
picked up here and there out of the Latin and strung together in
an only remotely related paraphrase.[70] Naturally, this is intentional, as is another trait not so well documented. I refer to the same
tacit censorship of uncongenial moralizing which marked Pound's
Seafarer and *Cathay*. In Section I, "I who come first from the clear

[68] Tibullus is mentioned in "Impressions of François-Marie Arouet (de
Voltaire)," III, in *Lustra*.

[69] *EPSP*, pp. 64-76.

[70] Cf. in Section V.2 the lines beginning "Although Callimachus did without
them" or in Section XII "And you write of Acheloüs."

font . . ." leaves untranslated the word *sacerdos* which would have jarred with the sarcastic jauntiness of "We have kept our erasers in order" and "I shall have, doubtless, a boom after my funeral." (Incidentally, I read III. 1 as devoid of *logopoeia* in Pound's sense; other Roman poets—one thinks of Horace as *Musarum sacerdos*—advanced similar claims for their poetic achievement.)[71] Similarly, at the beginning of Section II, "I had been seen in the shade . . .," where the poet enumerates various famous events in Roman history, there is a significant omission of the phrase "et versos ad pia vota deos" (3. 3. 10); it would have been out of character for the sophisticated Propertius of *Homage* to say that the gods lend an ear to pious prayers, although the genuine Propertius could and did say this readily enough.

V

If *Homage*, considered on its merits as a translation, is full of egregious defects, and if its translator hardly ranked as another Bentley, what follows? According to Donald Davie, the simplest way out is to deny absolutely that *Homage* is a translation at all; he accuses T. S. Eliot, Hugh Kenner, John Espey, and J. P. Sullivan of being "every one of them determined to eat his cake and have it, to assert that *Homage* is not a translation and yet that somehow it is."[72] Unfortunately, although Davie comes closer to the truth than the critics he takes to task, not many things in life or literature can be reduced to *either/or*. I have been listing some of the more crucial weaknesses of *Homage* as a translation, where Pound missed or jostled the meaning through his limitations as a Latinist or through sheer carelessness or wilfulness. I have noted some places where he cut capers, others where he skipped or slurred or rejected. These are drawbacks which of themselves might have rendered *Homage* a poor translation but still a translation. Something more fundamental, a violation of the spirit of Propertius, is at stake. Pound has forced the tone; he has created a Propertius in his own image. He has exaggerated, for example, an ancient *topos*, dear to all the elegiacs or even to all writers of

[71] See Butler and Barber (above, n. 42), *ad loc.*
[72] *Ezra Pound: Poet as Sculptor* (above, n. 31), pp. 79-80.

love poetry, that the poet who serenades his mistress is unfitted to attempt martial poetry. Pseudo-Anacreon's lyre responds with love-strains when he wants it to play epic themes:

θέλω λέγειν Ἀτρείδας,
θέλω δὲ Κάδμον ᾄδειν,
ἁ βάρβιτος δὲ χορδαῖς
ἔρωτα μοῦνον ἠχεῖ.

Pound has compelled his Propertius to inveigh against Virgil in the savage way he himself lashed out at British imperialism ("Upon the Actian marshes Virgil is Phoebus' chief of police"). Above all, he has erratically imparted to many formal and traditional compositions a levity, an easygoing modern familiarity, that would be appropriate only occasionally.[73] I am not saying for a moment that Propertius does not sometimes exhibit irony, wit, and even humor.[74] But Pound compounded his crime by humorous anachronism ("frigidaire patent," "handkerchiefs," "chief of police") and by over-dramatization in the manner of today, so that the unexcited words, "non ego Titanas canerem, non Ossan Olympo / impositam" (2. 1. 19-20), emerge, inflated and hyperbolic, in Section V, 2 as "Neither would I *warble* of Titans, nor of Ossa *spiked onto* Olympus" (where the words I have italicized seem to bear out Mauberley's complaint that "The age demanded an image / Of its accelerated grimace").

Davie, as we have observed, sidesteps the whole troublesome issue by denying that *Homage* is a translation. To be quite fair, there are connected passages (Section III, for instance, based on 3. 16) which are not only translations but, despite the usual lapses, brilliantly successful ones. A great many shorter passages or single lines are magnificent. Who but Pound could have thought up "You are a very early inspector of mistresses" ("quo tu matutinus, ait, speculator amicae" 2. 29A. 31) or "She wept into uncombed

[73] Sullivan parries this, *EPSP*, pp. 61-64. He even argues that IV. 6, far from being a conventional tribute to Augustus, is a parody of such a tribute and is intended to demonstrate Propertius' incapacity to lend himself to propaganda. Pasoli (see above, n. 16), p. 53, calls this a "machiavellica soluzione."

[74] Eckard Lefèvre, *Propertius Ludibundus* (Heidelberg: Carl Winter, 1966), is a detailed study.

hair, And you saw it" ("incomptis vidisti flere capillis" 3. 6. 9),
even if, true to form, neither of these lines is completely accurate.
Had Pound deigned to consult a literal translation of Propertius,
as when composing *Cathay* he had followed the Fenellosa literal
version, he could easily have avoided a great many annoying
mistakes which, at least for Latinists, are bound to seem blemishes.
I cannot imagine that *Homage* would have suffered if Pound had
used a crib to correct his lesser errors (to echo Ben Jonson, would
that he had "trotted" a thousand!). Nevertheless, although
Homage bears all the unmistakable marks of an attempted translation (and I feel that *in petto* Pound continued to regard it so), its
apparent disloyalty to the shade of Propertius rather than its mere
inaccuracies, flagrant as these may be, make us hesitate to apply a
term which seems, oddly enough, to be both too loose and too tight.

Sullivan thinks he has found another way out of the hermetically
sealed chamber. He has reminded us of such works as Fitzgerald's
Rubaiyat or Johnson's *The Vanity of Human Wishes*, which form a
genre distinct from more formal translation,[75] the "paraphrase,"
"adaptation," "imitation" (a term to which Robert Lowell has
recently staked out a claim), or more insidiously, "creative translation." Whether *Homage* truly belongs under this rubric is less
certain. In the *Rubaiyat* the original text was manipulated with
great freedom by a poet who was no great expert in the language
and literature of Persia. All the same, Fitzgerald's prefaces and
annotations testify eloquently to a sincere effort to interpret Omar;
this was intended to be a translation. Johnson's poem, on the other
hand, like his *London*, "could count on a readership who knew
Juvenal's poem about as well as a bookish person of our time
knows, say, *Vanity Fair*."[76] The learned Latinist, by means of a
skilled and satiric allusiveness, delighted those of his readers, and
in those days they were proportionally numerous, who could
appreciate the interplay of ancient source and modern instance.
Homage was not designed for a comparable audience nor with the
same artistic purpose.

[75] *EPSP*, on *Rubaiyat*, pp. 14-16; on "creative translation" in general,
pp. 17-23.
[76] John Wain, "Dr. Johnson as Poet," *Encounter* 38 (1972), p. 56.

The only even partially satisfactory solution is to take *Homage* as an English poem on a par with *Mauberley*. This means sharing common ground with Davie, but at least I will have arrived there by a different route. One must first have tried earnestly to judge *Homage* as a translation; only after we see that it cannot properly be included under that heading are we entitled to treat *Homage* for convenience as simply another poem by Pound. Classical scholars may continue in secret and for their own naughty diversion to compare *Homage* with the Propertian text, rejoicing in their private knowledge. Otherwise, there will never be any agreement on a suitable designation for this sport among literary works: translation in the strict sense it is not, but still too much of a translation to be passed off as an "appreciation." *Cathay* and *The Seafarer* pass the test and qualify as translations, even if now and again Pound can be caught posing as disreputable old Li-po or identifying himself with the tempest-tossed wanderer (in his own *persona* he had said: "Take thought / I have weathered the storm, / I have beaten out my exile"). While composing *Homage*, Pound first wrapped himself in Roman garb, took up his position before the mirror, and began to recite in imitation of his famous model; before long, amused by the sound of his voice and his reflection in the glass, he forgot his assumed role, slipped imperceptibly into his own favorite attitudes, and soon was pronouncing his usual favorite themes. It sounded fine but had ceased to be Propertius in a toga; it was just Uncle Ez declaiming in a bed-sheet.

It is better in any case to avoid the obviously partisan coinage, "creative translation," which seems to require the protection of quotation marks. The term calls to mind one of those epithets which, as Lucretius tells us (4. 1160ff.), are adopted by a lover to mitigate the defects of his beloved. The girl with a sallow complexion is not improved by being called a nut-brown maid, and one shudders at the disfiguration which might be concealed behind a "creative translation." Whether translator or adapter, Pound needs no such dubious accolade. I should be tempted to place *Homage* slightly to one side of his other translations, but in a broad sense, as George Steiner writes in the introduction to *The Penguin Book of Modern Verse Translation*, these translations have "altered

the definition and ideals of verse translation in the twentieth
century as surely as Pound's poetry has renewed or subverted
English and American poetics."[77]

Many years ago, apropos of a discussion about *Homage*, one of
my teachers, the distinguished Latinist Arthur Stanley Pease,
informed me that Pound, many years before that, had written to
the publishers of the Loeb Library with an offer to do a version of
Propertius for them. Pease was the soul of truth, and it is possible
that he was passing along an apocryphal story. Perhaps there are
archives still available to confirm or refute this assertion; in any
case, I gladly turn it over for investigation to *Paideuma*, the new
magazine devoted to Poundian studies.[78] (The Loeb translation of
Propertius by H. E. Butler first appeared in 1912; Pound settled
in London in the fall of 1908 and might have expressed interest in
Propertius prior to 1912 even if he did not begin on *Homage* before
1916.) I sincerely hope that Pound really did submit such a
proposal, because I am enthralled by the contemplation of what
might have come to pass. Suppose, wildly improbable as it might
be, that the Loeb editors had given their consent. Would Pound
have handed them his *Homage* and had it politely rejected? Or
would he have sweated, no doubt in vain, to grind out a tame and
literal version couched in the customary translator's English?
Merely to think of either possibility is unsettling: I am glad that
we possess Pound's *Homage* just as it is, however we choose to
call it.

[77] Penguin Books, 1966, p. 33.
[78] University of Maine, Orono, Maine, 1972–.

The Urbana Anglo-Saxon Sylloge
of Latin Inscriptions

LUITPOLD WALLACH*

The manuscript collection of the University of Illinois Library at Urbana harbors the fragment of an Anglo-Saxon sylloge of inscriptions of unknown origin which is ascribed to the period from the late ninth to the early tenth centuries.[1] The bifolium which was removed from a bookbinding is written in a strongly and carefully executed Anglo-Saxon minuscule. It contains an interesting poem in hexameters ascribed to the Venerable Bede which is in all likelihood from his lost *Liber epigrammatum heroico metro* mentioned in his *Historia ecclesiastica gentis Anglorum* V. 24.[2] Traces of Bede's lost epigrammatic poetry which seem to survive have been listed by W. F. Bolton[3] and also by Günter Bernt.[4]

I

The bifolium in parchment, 375 × 230 millimeters, has 24 lines to the page. Large initials drawn in black and filled with red color begin each poem or inscription. The title lines and all the

* I am indebted to the Library of the University of Illinois at Urbana for permission to publish the *Urbanensis* and to the Rare Book Librarian, N. F. Nash, for kindly arranging the photographic reproduction of folio 2v of the manuscript.

[1] See H. P. Kraus, *Catalogue* 88: *Fifty Mediaeval and Renaissance Manuscripts* (New York, 1958), 8, item 4.

[2] Bertram Colgrave and R. A. B. Mynors, eds., *Bede's Ecclesiastical History of the English People* (Oxford, 1969), p. 570.

[3] *A History of Anglo-Latin Literature 597-1066* (Princeton, 1967), pp. 167 f.

[4] *Das lateinische Epigramm im Übergang von der Spätantike zum frühen Mittelalter* (Münchener Beiträge zur Mediävistik und Renaissance-Forschung 2 [München, 1968]), pp. 164–171.

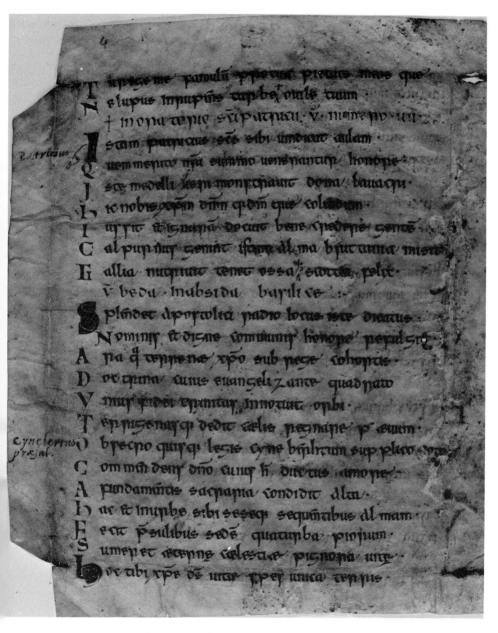

Fragment of an Anglo-Saxon sylloge.

initials of each line in all epigrams are written in red. Folio 1 recto
is reproduced in its natural size in H. P. Kraus' *Catalogue 88* (p. 9);
folio 1 verso and folio 2 recto are found in a reduced format (on
p. 124, No. 4). The facsimile of folio 2 verso is reproduced here; it
shows clearly the distinct Anglo-Saxon hand of the scribe. The
palaeographical description of the bifolium is quite revealing.

Of the sixteen metrical items of the manuscript, Nos. III–V and
XIV are preceded by crosses drawn in red ink. The one of No.
XIV on the facsimile of folio 2 verso can be seen here. Even the
Versus Vergilii (*Ecl.* 7. 65-66), No. IV, are introduced by a cross.
The titles of I–V, VII–IX, XIII and XV have at the very end a
red punctuation sign of three dots; it is visible on the facsimile at
the end of the title line of No. XV. The number of verses of the
individual poems is listed in the manuscript after the title heading
for Nos. I and X–XIV; II–VII and XV have no titular numbering. *Versus* is spelled out in Nos. IV and VIII; otherwise it is
always represented by the capital V with the abbreviation
stroke on top of the letter. For technical reasons, those strokes
above the V are not reproduced in the subsequent edition of the
inscriptions.

Abbreviations include the following: the often used enclitic q;
for *que*; the *Nomina sacra* ds, dns, xps, scs with horizontal strokes
over the second letters for *deus, dominus, Christus, sanctus* and cases.
Omitted *m* in accusative and genitive cases in the plural is
indicated by the horizontal stroke over the vowel preceding *m*.
Typically Anglo-Saxon signs of abbreviation are the symbol for
est in I. 1 and VII. 1; the *h* with the horizontal stroke above the
curved part of the letter for *haec* in III. 1, V. 10, XV. 8. In addition
to the usual abbreviation for *per*, that is the *p* with the horizontal
stroke through the lower shaft of the letter, as in VII. 1, we find
twice the typical Insular form for *per*, the *p* with tail or hook, as in
XV. 6 and in *perpes*, XI. 8; *p* with horizontal stroke above the
letter, designating *prae*, appears in I. 3, VIII. 3, XI. 5, and XV. 5:
praestent, praestas, praetioso, praesulibus; the *p* with a lower loop to the
left for *pro* occurs in *prolis* IX. 1, and in X. 1, *proelia*. The vowels *a*
and *i* suprascript above *q* appear in XV. 3 *qua* and VIII. 6 *qui*.
Also there are for *vel* the letter *l* with diagonal cross stroke in I. 5,

and the stroke above *r* in the three-lettered form *nri* for *nostri* in XIV. 2, and in the two-lettered form *mr* for *martyris* in the title line of No. VI.

For ligatures of curved elongated *e* with *n*, see, e.g., *colendum* XIV. 4, *Splendet* XV. 1; the same *e* in ligature with *r* in *germine* XI. 3, *suffert* XII. 1; *e* with *t* in *et* XI. 4 and XV. 2; *a* with *e* in *caelis* and *aevum* in XV. 6. The *e* caudatum at the end of words occurs in *aeterne . . . vite* XV. 2. Naturally, strict uniformity in the spelling of words is not to be expected; thus the spelling *pretiosa* occurs once in XII. 4, while XI. 5 spells *praetioso* with the abbreviation *p* for *prae*.

The bifolium under consideration, numbered folio 1 and 2 for convenient reference, certainly belonged at one time to a complete quire. Its sixteen texts prove that the bifolium cannot have formed the innermost sheet of parchment within the original quire for the following reasons.

The texts I–XVI are distributed on the four pages of the bifolium as follows: Folios 1r: Nos. I–V. 7; 1v: V. 8–IX. 1-4; Folios 2r: Nos. X–XIII. 4; 2v: XIII. 5–XVI. No. IX, the last inscription on folio 1 verso, is incompletely transmitted. It consists of four verses instead of six; verses 5 and 6 of the epitaph are missing, because they were written on the recto page of a subsequent, now lost folium. In addition, our folio 2 recto offers as title for No. X the inscription on an altar "Ab alia parte altaris." This obviously means that another inscription from the same altar preceded our No. X within the entire quire on a now lost folium, *in verso*. Thus it is evident that the preserved bifolium formed neither the first nor the innermost folium within the original quire which belonged to a larger, no longer extant Anglo-Saxon sylloge of inscriptions, which, for the most part, consisted of tituli on the walls and altars of church buildings, and of epitaphs on tombstones, in England, Gaul, and Italy, augmented by some epigrams drawn directly from manuscripts, such as No. XV, and probably also XVI. The latter may have formed the first verse of an epigram by Bede, in view of the parallel references listed for it below in the edition of the texts of the Urbanensis.

II

Syllogae inscriptionum in codice Urbanensi traditae cum similibus comparatio

The texts I–XVI of folios 1 and 2 of the Urbanensis are here edited with commentary in the notes that accompany the individual texts. The following abbreviations are used in the commentary:

Clavis—*Clavis patrum latinorum*, ed. E. Dekkers and Aemilius Gaar (*Sacris Erudiri* III, 2d ed.; Brugge and 's-Gravenhage, 1961)

Diehl—Ernestus Diehl, *Inscriptiones Latinae Christianae Veteres* I–III (Berlin, 1926–1931), IV: *Supplementum*, ed. J. Moreau and H. I. Marrou (Dublin, 1967)

Hesbert, *CAO*—René Hesbert, *Corpus Antiphonalium Officii* (*CAO*) III (Rome, 1968), IV (1970)

de Rossi—I. B. de Rossi, *Inscriptiones Christianae Urbis Romae septimo saeculo antiquiores* II, 1 (Rome, 1888)

Silvagni—Angelus Silvagni, *Inscriptiones Christianae Italiae saeculo XVI antiquiores* I, 2 (Rome, 1935)

[Folio 1r (Nos. I–V. 7)]

[I] Ad vincula sancti Petri. V(ersus) VII

His solidata fides, his est tibi, Roma, catenis
Perpetuata salus, harum circumdata nexu
Libera semper eris; quid enim non vincula praestent
Quae tetigit qui cuncta potest absolvere [?] cuius
5   Haec invicta manu vel relegiosa triumpho
Moenia non ullo poenitus quatientur ab hoste.
Claudit iter bellis qui portam pandit in astris.

I. 1-7 Arator, *De actibus apostolorum* I. 1070-1076, ed. A. P. McKinlay, *CSEL* 72 (Vienna, 1951), 75.

2 Perpetua MS   Perpetuata Arator
6 penitus Arator

This text is a wall inscription at St. Peter in Chains in Rome. The text appears in a sylloge of epigrams, s. IX, mistakenly ascribed to Alcuin, *MGH, Poetae* I, p. 345, No. 3, where v. 2 *Perpetuata salus* is replaced by Diehl 981. 4:

Simplicio nunc ipse dedit sacra iura tenere;

for the latter cf. Arator, I. 393-394:

> . . . Non, prodige, rerum
> Venditor ista facis, sed qui tua iura tenere.

On Alcuin's acquaintance with Arator see Wallach in *Speculum* 29 (1954), p. 146 f., and the reference in *Alcuin and Charlemagne* (Cornell Studies in Classical Philology, 32; 2nd printing, 1968), 284.

[II] Vincula Petri.

> Solve, iubente deo, terrarum Petre, catenas
> Qui facis ut pateant caelestia regna beatis.

II Title added by original scribe after *catenas* v. 1 1-2 epigram by Achilleus of Spoleto; cf. *Clavis* 1484; Migne, *PL, Supplementum* III, 1246; Hesbert, *CAO* III, 4981; IV, 7678, 8200.

> 1 iuvente MS., read correctly *iubente*, and not *iuvante* as in *Sylloge Laureshamensis*, de Rossi VIII. 82 (p. 114), and *Sylloge Centulensis*, de Rossi, VII. 12 (p. 80). Compare also Ludwig Bieler, *Scriptorium* 26 (1972), 79.

> 2 Cf. Arator, *de actibus apost.* I. 972 ut velit ad cunctos caelestia regna patere; Diehl 986, Epitaph of Felix IV: Certa fides iustis caelestia regna patere. Compare also *Sylloge of Cambridge*, ed. A. Silvagni, *Rivista di archeologia cristiana* 20 (1943), 100, and Silvagni 4139.

[III] Item ad vincula.

> Inlesas olim servant haec tecta catenas,
> Vincla sacrata Petri: ferrum pretiosior auro.

III. 1-2 Diehl 1781

> 2 pretiosius Diehl, but compare Isaiah 13. 12 pretiosior erit vir auro, and Ovid, *Ars amat.* 2. 299 tibi sit pretiosior auro

[IV] Versus Vergilii.

> Fraxinus in silvis pulcherrima, pinus in hortis,
> Populus in pluviis, abies in montibus altis.

IV. 1-2 Vergil, *Ecl.* VII. 65-66

> 1 ortis MS

[V] In absida sancti Laurenti(i).

Demovit dominus tenebras ut luce creata,
His quondam latebris sic modo fulgor inest.
Angustos aditus venerabile corpus habebat
Huc, ubi nunc populum largior aula capit.
5 Eruta planities patuit sub monte reciso
Estque remota gravi mole ruina minax.
Presule Pelagio martyr Laurentius olim

[Fol. 1 *verso* (Nos. V. 8–IX)]

Templa sibi [statuit tam pretiosa dari.]
Mira fides gladios hostiles inter et iras
10 Pontificem meritis haec celebrasse suis.
Tu modo sanctorum cui crescere constat honores
Fac sub pace coli templa dicata tibi.

V. 1-12 Diehl 1770

8 statuit . . . dari illegible in MS.
10 celerasse MS., celebrasse correctly *Sylloge Laureshamensis quarta*,
de Rossi VIII. 46, p. 106
12 templa MS., tecta Diehl

[VI] Ad [basilicam] sancti martyris Laurenti[i].

Martyrium flammis olim, levita, sub[isti].
Iure tuis remplis lux veneranda redit.

VI. 1-2 Diehl 1771 *basilicam* inserted in title on account of its
occurrence in the *Sylloge Laureshamensis quarta*, de Rossi VIII. 47,
p. 106, and in the *Sylloge Turonensis*, de Rossi VI. 9, p. 63.

1 leuita MS. leuuita Diehl sub MS. *isti* not legible in MS.
2 beneranda Diehl

[VII] In sancta Maria trans Tiberim.

Haec domus est Christi semper mansura pudori.
Iustitie cultrix plebi servabit honorem.

VII. 1-2 Diehl 1783

2 servavit Diehl

[VIII] Versus Damasi (de) sancto Felice.

> Corpore mente animo pariterque et nomine Felix,
> Sanctorum in numero Christi sociate triumphis,
> Qui ad te sollicite venientibus omnia praestas,
> Nec quemquam pateris tristem repedare viantem;
> 5 Te duce servatus mortis quod vincula rupi,
> Hostibus extinctis fuerant qui falsa locuti,
> Versibus his Damasus supplex tibi vota rependo.

VIII. 1-7 *Epigrammata Damasiana*, ed. Antonius Ferrua (Rome, 1942), No. 39, p. 214.

4 tristem pateris Ferrua cf. also Silvagni 4745.

[IX] In tumulo matris sancti Agustini.

> Hic posuit cineres genetrix castissima prolis,
> Agustine, tui(s)altera lux meriti(s),
> Qui servans pacis caelestia iura sacerdos
> Commissos populos moribus institutis.
> 5 [gloria vos maior gestorum laude coronat
> virtutum mater felicior subole.]

IX. 1-4 See Ernst Diehl, *Inscriptiones latinae christianae veteres* IV, *Supplementum*, ed. J. Moreau and H. I. Marrou (1967), No. 91; also Antonio Casamassa, *Scritti Patristici* I (Rome, 1955), 215 f. The MS offers only vv. 1-4, and reads in v. 2 *tui* and *meriti*, while vv. 5-6 are missing; cf. *Clavis* 1485. For the verse ending of v. 3 compare *PL, Supplementum* IV. 5 (Paris, 1971), 2112 No. 2, Epitaphium Vicecii:

> Ecce sacerdotis tenuit qui iura sacerdus;

Diehl 1689, 4 from the year 586:

> iura sacerdotii servans nomenque iugalis;

Venantius Fortunatus, *Carmina* IX, 9, 7 ed. F. Leo, *MGH, Auct. Ant.* VI, 1 (Berlin, 1881), 215:

> iura sacerdoti sacro moderamine servans.

Sven Blomgren, "Fortunatus cum elogiis collatus," *Eranos* 71 (1973), 109, is not aware of the earlier occurrence of the phrase in Monica's epitaph.

[Fol. 2 *recto* (Nos. X–XIII. 4)]

[X] Ab alia parte altaris. V. IIII.

> Qui cruce munitus superas fera proelia mundi
> Felicesque trahis victor ad astra choros,
> Serva, Paule, tui veneranda sacraria templi,
> Ne latro depopulans vastet ovile tuum.

X. 1-4 Printed among the poems of Alcuin, ed. Ernst Dümmler, *MGH, Poetae latini aevi carolini* I (Berlin, 1888), 345 No. CXIV. 5, but not by Alcuin, and therefore not listed by Josef Szöverffy, *Weltliche Dichtungen des lateinischen Mittelalters* I (Berlin, 1970), 450.

2 chorus MS., I read *choros* with de Rossi XXVII C. 4, p. 285.

[XI] Ad imaginem IIII animalium. V. VIII.

> Nascitur humana celsus de carne creator,
> Ut homo per hominem scandit ad astra deum.
> Ecce leo, Iude natus de germine, mundum
> Liberat, et loeti sceptra triumphat ovans.
> 5 Hostia summa patris praetioso sanguine Christus
> Permundans orbem regna sub alta vocat.
> Adsumptis aquilae Christus petit aethera pennis,
> Conregnatque poli perpes in arce patri.

XI. 1-8 Inscription attached to wall-painting depicting the animal symbols of the four evangelists, see *MGH, Poetae* I, pp. 346-347, No. CXVII (and note to text X. 1-4, above), where two more verses are listed: "Ostendis Christum populis, baptista Johannes, / Hic ecce agnus et hic, qui tollit crimina mundi," which are from the *Sylloge of Cambridge*, ed. A. Silvagni, *Rivista di archeologia cristiana* 20 (1943), 91 No. 12. 16-17; cf. also Silvagni 4147. 17-18. For XI. 3 cf. *Apoc.* 5. 5.

[XII] In porticu Stephani et Laurenti(i). V. IIII.

> En, Stephanus lapides suffert, Laurentius ignes,
> Perque iter angustum regna beata petunt.
> Iure micat rutilo levitarum aula colore,
> Quos vitae ad palmam mors pretiosa vocat.

XII. 1-4 See *MGH, Poetae latini aevi carolini* I, No. CXIV. 6 (p. 345), and the note to X. 1-4, above.

[XIII] Ad Lateranis. V. VI.

Virgo dei genetrix quem totus non capit orbis,
In tua se clausit viscera factus homo.
Vere fide genitus purgavit crimina mundi,
4   Et tibi virginitas inviolata manet.

[Fol. 2 *verso* (Nos. XIII. 5–XVI. 1)
See the facsimile reproduced here.]

5   Tu, rege me famulum pro tua pietate meosque,
Ne lupus inrupens turbe(t) ovile tuum.

XIII. 1-4 As antiphon see Hesbert, *CAO* III No. 5448; the first distich also Hesbert, *CAO* IV No. 6333, but not listed in index, p. 504. On both distichs see Henri Barré, "Antiennes et Répons de la Vierge," *Marianum* 29 (1967), 181-183.

Title Ad alteranis MS., I read *Ad Lateranis* for the reasons stated below in note 5.
3 fide genitus in our MS, and in MS L, Saint Loup de Bénévent, saec. XII fin., Hesbert, *CAO* III No. 5448, p. 542, otherwise *fides geniti*.
6 *turbe* our MS, *t* added by modern corrector 6 Cf. text X. 4, above, and the *Sylloge of Cambridge*, ed. Angelo Silvagni, *Rivista di archeologia cristiana* 20 (1943), 86.8, "ne lupus insidians vastet ovile dei," and Venantius Fortunatus, *Carm.* III. 15. 13. ed. Friedrich Leo (*MGH*, *Auctores Antiquissimi*), 68:
   nil lupus insidiis canto subducit ovili.
Cf. furthermore John 10. 1-16, *passim*. For the liturgical context see Georges Frénaud, "L'antienne mariale 'Virgo dei genitrix quem totus non capit orbis'," *Revue Grégorienne* 31 (1952), 201–209.

[XIV] In oratorio sancti Patricii. V. numero VII.

Istam Patricius sanctus sibi vindicat aulam,
Quem merito nostri summo venerantur honore.
Iste medelliferi monstravit dona lavacri.
Hic nobis Christum dominumque deumque colendum
5   Iussit et ignaram docuit bene credere gentem.
Calpurnus genuit istum, alma Brittania misit;
Gallia nutrivit, tenet ossa Scottia felix,
[Ambo stelligeri capientes praemia caeli.]

XIV. 1-8 Cellanus of Péronne, Epitaph of St. Patricius, ed. Ludwig Traube, "Perrona Scottorum" in Traube's *Vorlesungen und Abhandlungen* III, ed. Samuel Brandt (Munich, 1920), 107; reprinted in Migne, *PL, Supplementum* IV, 5 (Paris, 1971), 2191; *Clavis* 1127; Wilhelm Levison, "Zu den Versen des Abtes Cellanus von Péronne, "*Zeitschrift für Celtische Philologie* 20 (1936), 382–390, reprinted in Levison's *Aus rheinischer und fränkischer Frühzeit* (Düsseldorf, 1948).

> 3 medelli ueri with modern *f* above *u* in MS
> 4 etiam *om.* in MS and after *nobis, Christum* added
> 7 After *ossa* modern insertion
> 8 This verse is omitted in MS.

[XV] V. Beda(e). In absida basilice.

> Splendet apostolici radio locus iste dicatus
> Nominis, et digne communis honore refulget
> Ara, qua terrenae Christo sub rege cohortis
> Doctrina cuius evangelizante quadrato
> 5 Unius fidei trinitas innotuit orbi,
> Terrigenasque dedit caelis regnare per aevum.
> Obsecro, quisque legis, Cyneberhtum supplice voto,
> Commendans domino cuius haec ductus amore,
> A fundamentis sacraria condidit alta.
> 10 Hac et in urbe sibi seseque sequentibus almam
> Fecit praesulibus sedem, qua turba piorum
> Sumeret aeterne caelestia pignora vite.

XV. 1-12 Perhaps from Bede's lost *Liber epigrammatum*; cf. *Clavis* No. 1370 a; and Günter Bernt, (see above, 4.), p. 169.

> 7 After *supplice* the deleted letters *voto* became more visible through the photographic treatment, (see p. 151 n. 7)
> 8 Commendens MS, I read *Commendans* (see below the parallels cited under 8)
> 12 aeterne . . . vite with *e caudatum*; caelestiae MS, I read *caelestia* pignora

1 Cf. Venantius Fortunatus, *Carm.* VI, 2, 101 ed. Friedrich Leo, *MGH, Auctores antiquissimi* IV, 1 (Berlin, 1881), 133:

> *Splendet* in ore dies detersa fronte serenus;

Hesbert, *CAO* III, no. 5010 (p. 489): *Splendet* Bethleemiticus campus de candidata turba infantium, in MSS. *saec.* XI and XII; also *MGH*, *Epist.* V (Karolini Aevi 3; Berlin, 1899), 572. 45:

> *Splendet* enim verum vero de lumine lumen.

1 Werner Jaager, *Bedas metrische Vita S. Cuthberti* (Palaestra 198; Leipzig, 1935), 70 vv. 159 f.:

> Virtus sic una gemello
> Effulget *radio*: dictis qui tristibus ante

2 Bede, *VC*, p. 59, 19:

> Affrica Cypriani dictis meritisque *refulget*;

Bede, *De Psalmo XLI*, ed. J. Fraipont, *CCL* 122, p. 448. 29: "... sub nocte *refulget*."

2–3 Cf. Alcuin's inscription *MGH*, *Poetae* I, p. 337, no. XI. 14:

> Agmine apostolico quoniam haec *ara refulget*.

4 Cf. Bede, *Historia Ecclesiastica* (*HE*), ed. B. Colgrave and R. A. B. Mynors (Oxford, 1969), Bk. II. 17 (p. 194. 3), Paulino *evangelizante*; *HE* III. 3 (p. 220. 6), ut *evangelizante* antiste; *HE* III. 7 (p. 232. 12) Itaque *evangelizante* illo.

5 For Bede's use of *innotuit* in the *HE*, see P. F. Jones, *A Concordance to the Historia Ecclesiastica of Bede* (Cambridge, Mass., 1929), 262 f.

6 Cf. Bede, *De celebritate quattuor temporum*, ed. J. A. Giles, *The Complete Works* I (London, 1843), 57 v. 7:

> *Terrigenasque* monet Christo accusare piatos;

HE IV. 3 (p. 342, line 2 from below), ut terrigenas ad timendum se suscitet.

6 The same verse ending in Bede's *Vita Cuthberti* (*VC*), 213 (p. 74) ... qui pane per aevum; 436 (p. 91) ... durate per aevum; 793 (p. 119) luce per aevum; 979 (p. 133) ... salusque per aevum.

7 Cf. *VC* 933 (p. 130) *Obsecro* te supplex summi per sceptra tonantis, and the parallels listed by Jaager, pp. 57-58.

8 Cf. Bede, *De die judicii* 160 (p. 444, J. Fraipont, *CCL* 122 [1955]):

> *Commendans* precibus Christi modo meque canentem;
> Fortunatus VIII. 16. 5 (p. 198 Leo):

> *Commendans* humilem tibi me, sacer arce Gregori;

Carmina epigraphica 703. 7 (Buecheler):
Commendans sanctis animam corpusque fovendum;

Bede, prose *VC* IV, ed. Bertram Colgrave (Cambridge, 1940), 166:
. . . ac statim commendans;

Bede, *HE* V. 19 (p. 528 Colgrave-Mynors):

Hanc Domino qui aulam *ductus* pietatis *amore Fecit*, et eximio sacravit nomine Petri.
9 *HE* I. 33 (p. 114): *Fecit* autem et monasterium . . ., in quo Aedilberct ecclesiam . . . *a fundamentis* construxit; and similar often in *HE*; cf. Bede concordance cited above to v. 5 s.v. *Fecit* and *A fundamentis*; also often in inscriptions cf. Diehl III, Index s.v. *a fundamentis*.
10-11 See *HE* I. 33 cited to v. 9 above; cf. also *HE* III. 25 (p. 294) Qui [*sc.* Finan] in insula Lindisfarnensi *fecit* ecclesiam episcopali sedi congruam; often in a similar fashion in the *HE*.
11 Cf. Damasus, *Epigrammata* ed. A. Ferrua (Rome, 1942), 16. 1, p. 120:

Hic congesta iacet quaeris si *turba piorum*;

the same verse ending Diehl 3433, 8; also Eugenius of Toledo, *Carm.* IX. 1 ed. F. Vollmer (*MGH, AA* XIV; Berlin, 1905), 239:

Incolit hoc templum sed felix *turba piorum*;

also in *Conflictus veris et hiemis*, ed. *MGH, Poetae* I, 204, v. 44: Et Dafnis pariter, pastorum et *turba piorum*.
12 *HE* V. 7 (p. 470), in Epitaph of Caedwalla, v. 6:

Cuius fonte meras *sumeret* almus aquas;

HE III. 22 (p. 284) . . . vitae caelestis institutio cotidianum *sumeret* augmentum.

[XVI No title, perhaps by Bede]:

Hoc tibi Christe, deus *vitae spes unica* terris.

XVI. The single line certainly forms the beginning of an epigram, since it displays, like the preceding items I–XV, a large initial drawn in black and filled with red color.

The text may well be by Bede; cf. Bede, *Oratio Bedae*, ed. J. Fraipont, *CCL* 122 (1955), 445. 1: O Deus aeternae mundo *spes unica vitae*; Bede, *De Psalmo XLI* (p. 448. 31): Deprecor implorans tete, *spes unica vitae*.

Cf. also Bernowinus, *Carmen XIII.* 4 ed. Ernst Dümmler, *MGH,*
Poetae I, p. 417: Sis pius et clemens mihi, sis *spes unica vitae*; Sedulius,
Carmen paschale I, 60, ed. I. Huemer (*CSEL* 10 [1885]), 20: omnipotens
aeterne Deus, spes unica mundi.

III

The preceding texts I–XVI are for the most part presented as
tituli, that is, as inscriptions on the walls of churches in Rome, in
Gaul (such as XIV), and in Anglo-Saxon England (e.g., XV). In
a few instances the inscription is located in a certain part of the
building, be it *in oratorio* (XIV), *in porticu* (XII), in the *apse* (V,
XV), or on an *altar* (X). No. IX is listed as the epitaph of Monica,
the mother of Augustine. No. XI "On the image of the four
animals" may well represent the inscription attached to a wall
painting, probably depicting some of the animal symbols (lamb,
lion, ox, eagle) of the four evangelists (cf. de Rossi V. 10, p. 55).

The critical evaluation of our texts in relation to other extant
collections of inscriptions will reveal the historical tradition to
which the *Urbanensis* belongs. I am using for this purpose the
following collections edited (with the exception of Ca) by I. B.
de Rossi, *Inscriptiones Christianae Urbis Romae septimo saeculo anti-*
quiores II, 1 (Rome, 1888):

Ca—*Sylloge of Cambridge,* ed. Angelo Silvagni, in *Rivista di*
archeologia cristiana 20 (1943)

C—*Sylloge Centulensis,* cod. Leningrad F, XIV. 1, ed. de Rossi
No. VII, p. 72

L 1—*Sylloge Laureshamensis prima,* de Rossi XIII, p. 151

L 4—*Sylloge Laureshamensis quarta,* cod. Vaticanus Palat. lat. 833,
de Rossi VIII, p. 98

P—*Sylloge Parisina,* cod. Paris, B.N. lat. 8071, de Rossi XXI, p. 244

P 1—*Sylloge Parisina,* cod. Paris, B.N. lat. 8093, de Rossi XXVI,
p. 273

T—*Sylloge Turensis,* cod. Klosterneuburg 729 and Göttweig 64,
de Rossi VI, p. 58

V—*Sylloge Virdunensis,* cod. Verdun 45, de Rossi XII, p. 131

W—*Sylloge Wirceburgensis,* cod. Würzburg Mp. m. f. 2, de Rossi
XIV, p. 154

A few of our texts, namely I–III, V–VIII, are found also in L4. But this correspondence between the Urbanensis and L4 does not vouch for any direct interdependence; textual differences between otherwise corresponding texts exclude the assumption of any direct interrelationship. Thus our No. 1, v. 4 reads *cuius* with the critical edition of Arator, while L4, de Rossi VIII No. 64 (p. 110), reads *vincta*. No. II reads *Solve iuvente*, while L4 (p. 114) has the incorrect *Solve iuvante*, which also occurs in C, de Rossi VII No. 12 (p. 80). No. III reads *pretiosior auro*, while V, de Rossi XII No. 1 (p. 134), and W, de Rossi XIV No. 10 (p. 157), have *pretiosius auro*. No. V reads *celerasse*, also W, de Rossi XIV No. 9 (p. 157), while L4 (p. 106) offers correctly *celebrasse*, and T, de Rossi VI No. 10 (p. 63), has *cebrasse*. No. VI occurs also in L4 (p. 106). Our No. VII seems to constitute the only other extant transmission of the inscription, which until now seems to have been represented only by L1, saec. IX, de Rossi XIII No. 10 (p. 151): "Romae . . . in S. Mariae Transtiberinae basilica super portam maiorem." No. VIII appears in P, de Rossi XXI No. 9 (p. 247), and the latter's v. 4 reads, like our text in v. 4, *pateris tristem*, whereas P v. 5 has *mortis quam hostibus*, while our VIII has the genuine text "mortis quod vincula rupi." No. IX is found in P1, de Rossi XXVI A, No. 2 (p. 273) and reads like IX *Agustine*, but in contrast to our poem has all six verses of the epitaph, which are found also in Paris, B.N. lat. 2832, de Rossi XXV No. 16 (p. 267).

The results of the preceding investigation can be summarized as follows. The *Urbanensis* mirrors in a number of its inscriptions the undeniable fact that they are connected with an obviously continental tradition, to which also the *Sylloge Laureshamensis quarta* belongs. Otherwise the *Urbanensis* represents palaeographically and by provenience as well as by composition an Anglo-Saxon product. This is emphasized in addition by the inclusion of the Bede text (XV) and perhaps also No. XVI.

The occurrence of I and X–XII in a ninth-century sylloge of inscriptions transmitted in MSS together with certain poems by Alcuin (edited by Ernst Dümmler, *MGH*, *Poetae* I No. CXIV, pp. 344 f., and No. CXVII, pp. 346 f.) should lead us to renew the investigation begun long ago by de Rossi XXVII C (p. 285 f.).

My comments on No. XI point out a newly recognized connection between that still unknown sylloge, saec. IX, and the *Sylloge of Cambridge*.

The actual authors of some of the inscriptions are not always unknown. The verses of No. I constitute the famous hexameters by Arator promising the Romans deliverance from the sufferings of the Gothic Wars through the help of St. Peter's chains. No. II is an older epigram on Peter by Achilles of Spoleto (about 419), whose hexameters are included as antiphon, *responsorium*, and *versus* in the Frankish Antiphonary of Compiègne from the second half of the ninth century, and in manuscripts related to it. The epigram is one of the twenty hexameter texts in this service book. Damasus' *elogium* of Felix (No. VIII) and Cellanus of Péronne's epitaph of St. Patrick (XIV) are well known inscriptions. The Vergil verses of No. IV, which do not occur in any other sylloge, probably adorned some wall picture. The inscription on the tombstone of Monica, the mother of Augustine, written by Anicius Auchenius Bassus filius, a Roman magistrate and a member of the important family of the Anicii at Ostia, was known for a long time only through its transmission in MSS. Only in 1945 was the right section of the epitaph's original marble slab accidentally discovered at Ostia.

No. XIII, "Virgo dei genetrix", requires special attention, since H. P. Kraus, *Catalogue* 88, 10 lists the distichs as "an unpublished six line poem on the Lateran Basilica" (p. 10). On the contrary, it is the often published text of an antiphon, consisting of two distichs[5] and one of the fifteen distichs in the Frankish Antiphonary of Compiègne. Paschasius Radbertus of

[5] See Hesbert, *CAO* III, p. X, *Preface*; Ulysse Chevalier, *Repertorium Hymnologicum* II (Louvain, 1897), No. 21767; III (1904), No. 34587; G. M. Dreves, *Hymni inediti* (Analecta hymnica medii aevi XI [Leipzig, 1891]), p. 54, No. 83.

For text XIII, and the reading of the MS. *Ad alteranis* changed to *Ad Lateranis* see, e.g., the "Roman Stations" listed by G. G. Willis, *Further Essays in Early Roman Liturgy* (Alcuin Club Collections, 50 [London, 1968]), pp. 28 f.; also *Le Sacramentaire Grégorien*, ed. Jean Deshusses (Spicilegium Friburgense: Textes XVI [Fribourg, Switzerland, 1971]), p. 134, No 166, *app. crit.* to Tit. 38 *Ad Lateranis*, and p. 619 No. XXXIV: In Quadragesima. *Ad Lateranis*.

Corbie may have cited the first distich already about the year 830 in a sermon probably written by him (*PL* 96. 243A).

Bede is named in the title of No. XV as the author of the twelve hexameters. According to this title, the text was written on the wall in the apse of some church building erected in honor of one of the apostles, since we read in vv. 1–3:

> That consecrated site glitters in the sheen of the apostolic Name, and in beauty fittingly shines bright the public Altar.

One Cyneberhtus established the lofty oratorium from the very foundations and everybody who reads the inscription on the wall is asked by Bede to pray for the founder. The latter has built for himself and his successors a lofty episcopal see. Bede's *Ecclesiastical History of the English People*[6] provides in the *Preface* (p. 6), in IV. 12, and in V. 23 the key to the proper identification of Cyneberhtus. He was the fourth bishop of Lindsey, and supplied Bede with historical information about his own missionary activities; he was active about 731. The reports by Bede and our poem supplement each other. The poem contains elements of the foundation narrative style of church buildings used again and again in Bede's *Historia ecclesiastica* (listed in my comments on XV to vv. 4-5, 8-12). Traces of Bede's style and habits, as they appear especially in his metrical *Vita Cuthberti* (*VC*), are recorded for vv. 1-2, 6-8, and 12. Additional traces of certain deviations from classical Latin prosody which, according to Werner Jaager's investigations, occur in the *Vita Cuthberti*, are found also in XV. *Unius* in v. 5 does not have the old length; its *i* is shortened, since it forms the first dactyl of the verse:

> Unius fidei trinitas innotuit orbi.

The same is true, e.g., for *VC* 58:

> Unius incertos satagant abstergere fletus,

and in *VC* 488:

> Unius et solum superat sententia verbi.

[6] See Colgrave and Mynors, eds., pp. 6, 370, 558.

Also the *o* of the first person singular of the present tense is always long, while our text reads it with a short *o* in the first dactyl of verse 7: Obsecro quisque legis . . . The *VC* has ten instances in which *o* is short, and always in the first dactyl of the hexameter, as for instance in *VC* 35:

> Tu, rogo, summe, juva, donorum spiritus auctor.

Bede was certainly fully aware of his own deviations from classical prosody. In his treatise *De arte metrica* (ed. H. Keil, *Grammatici latini* VII [Leipzig, 1880], 247 f.), he refers to the long *i* in Paulinus of Nola's *Carmen* 27, 72 (ed. W. von Hartel [*CSEL* 30; 1894], 265):

> ut citharis modulans unius verbere plectri,

and simultaneously points to the occurrence of a shortened *i* in Sedulius, *Hymnus* I. 5 (ed. I. Huemer [*CSEL* 10; 1885], 155):

> unius ob meritum cuncti periere minores.

The various results of our critical investigation permit us to ascribe the wall inscription XV on good grounds to Bede, and more specifically, as has been suggested recently, to Bede's lost *Liber epigrammatum heroico metro*.

The fragment of the Anglo-Saxon sylloge of inscriptions preserved in the *Urbanensis* is related to the continental *Sylloge Laureshamensis quarta*[7] as well as to a sylloge of inscriptions from the ninth and tenth centuries, which needs to be investigated more thoroughly and is somehow connected with certain manuscripts of Alcuin's poems. On these grounds the date of the *Urbanensis* is not the late ninth century or the early tenth, as assumed in the Kraus *Catalogue* 88, but more likely a somewhat later date, that is to say, the latter part of the tenth century, if not the beginning of the eleventh.

[7] Transmitted in codex Vaticanus Palat. 833. Heinrich Fichtenau, *Karl der Grosse und das Kaisertum* (Darmstadt, 1971), pp. 300 f., has convincingly shown that the unknown author of this sylloge was in all probability Richbod of Lorsch and Trèves, one of Alcuin's friends. No. XV occurs among epigrams to be edited in the *English Historical Review* by Michael Lapidge, who discovered that half of XV is published by John Leland, *Collectanea* III (2 ed. Thomas Hearne; London, 1774), p. 115.

The Marriage of Poetry and Music in France : Ronsard's Predecessors and Contemporaries

ISIDORE SILVER

I. *Trouvères* and *Troubadours*

When Ronsard wrote in 1550 ". . . & ferai encores revenir (si je puis) l'usage de la lire aujourdui resuscitée en Italie" (I, 48), without any doubt he was thinking of the intimate association of the lyre with poetry in Hellenic antiquity.[1] The entire context of the preface *Au lecteur* of the *Quatre premiers livres des Odes*, largely a

---

Abbreviations: L.—*Pierre de Ronsard: Œuvres complètes*, édition critique avec introduction et commentaire, by Paul Laumonier, in progress since 1914 under the auspices of the Société des Textes Français Modernes; *BHR—Bibliothèque d'Humanisme et Renaissance*; Boul.—André Boulanger, ed., *L'Art Poëtique de Jacques Peletier du Mans (1555)* (Paris, 1930); Cham.—Henri Chamard, ed., *Joachim du Bellay: Œuvres poétiques*, 6 vols. (Paris, 1908-1931); *Def.*—Henri Chamard, ed., *La Deffence et Illustration de la Langue Francoyse* (Paris, 1904; 2d ed. 1948; notes give first the pagination of the 1904 edition followed in square brackets by that of 1948; the 1904 text is reproduced); *DLF:MA*—Cardinal Georges Grente *et al.*, eds., *Dictionnaire des Lettres Françaises: Le Moyen Age*; *MPSS*—Jean Jacquot, ed., *Musique et poésie au XVIe siecle* (Paris, 1954); *RHLF—Revue d'Histoire littéraire de la France*; *RM—Ronsard et la Musique*, numéro spécial de *La Revue Musicale*, III (May 1, 1924), No. 7; *RPL*—Paul Laumonier, *Ronsard poète lyrique* (2d ed., Paris, 1923).

In the references the place of publication is Paris unless otherwise indicated.

[1] See Charles Comte and Paul Laumonier, "Ronsard et les musiciens du XVIe siècle," *RHLF* VII (1900), 343-344; cf. Mathieu Augé-Chiquet, *La Vie, les idées et l'œuvre de Jean-Antoine de Baïf* (Paris and Toulouse, 1909), pp. 303-305. Paul-Marie Masson discusses the influence of Greek lyric theory and poetry on Ronsard and his colleagues in "Le mouvement humaniste," in *Encyclopédie de la Musique et Dictionnaire du Conservatoire*, eds. Albert Lavignac and Lionel de La Laurencie (1913), III, 1298. Apart from this first page, however, Masson's purpose is to study French music of the sixteenth century "mesurée à l'antique" in the manner of Baïf's *Académie de Poésie et Musique* founded in 1570.

manifesto in favor of the naturalization of the Greek ode in France,
corroborates this in the strongest terms. But the word *revenir* would
imply that Ronsard was perhaps aware that an earlier alliance of
music and poetry similar to that in ancient Greece had existed in
France. He had written in the *Hymne de France* (1549):

> La Poesie & la Musique seurs,
> Qui noz ennuiz charment de leurs doulceurs,
> Y [en France] ont aquis leurs louanges antiques. [I, 32]

But in the *Bocage* of 1554 *aquis* became *raquis*, and the variant was
maintained until the suppression of the poem in 1578.

Nothing is inherently improbable in this conjecture. In the
eighth chapter, "Qui furent les Trouverres, Chanterres, Jugleor &
Jongleor," of the first book of his *Recueil de l'origine de la langue et
poesie françoise* (1581), Claude Fauchet writes: "Ces Trouveurs
donc & Chantres, ayans affaire l'un de l'autre s'accompagnoyent
volontiers. Et à fin de rendre leurs inventions & melodies plus
plaisantes & agreables, venoyent aux grandes assemblees & festins,
donner plaisir aux princes: . . .

> "Quand les tables ostees furent,
> "Cil Jugleur en piés esturent,[2]
> "S'ont vielles & harpes prises,
> "Chansons, sons, lais, vers & reprises,
> "Et de geste chanté nos ont.

Ce qu'anciennement ont fait les Poetes Grecs, chantans les
louanges des Dieux & des Roys."[3] In his *Art Poëtique François*,
begun about 1574 but not published until 1605, Jean Vauquelin
de la Fresnaye likewise alluded to what he regarded as the revival
by the *trouvères* of the Greek and Roman alliance of poetry, music,
and the dance:

> Ces Trouverres alloient par toutes les Provinces
> Sonner, chanter, danser leurs Rimes chez les Princes.

[2] "C'est *steterunt*" (footnote by Fauchet).
[3] Janet G. Espiner-Scott, ed., *Claude Fauchet: Recueil de l'origine de la langue et
poesie françoise, Rymes et Romans*, I (1938), p. 118.

> Des Grecs et des Romains cet Art renouvelé,
> Aux François les premiers ainsi fut revelé.[4]

Hints of a possible relation with Greek poetry are mentioned also in connection with the *troubadours*. Their most original contribution was lyric poetry, especially the *canson*, in which words and music, *los mots* and *lo so*, were closely associated.[5] For the *troubadours*, as for Ronsard, lyric poetry meant song. They sometimes arranged their verses in tripartite strophes of identical structure, since they were sung to the same melody.[6] "La strophe avec sa tripartition est peut-être un écho de la division grecque de l'ode."[7]

Claude Fauchet's assertion that *trouvères* and singers traveled together, "ayans affaire l'un de l'autre," implies a natural division of function which occurred if the composer lacked a good singing voice. If the poet was untrained in composition, he sought out a skilled musician to provide the setting for his verses.[8] It was the fortunate individual who possessed adequately all three arts of

---

[4] Georges Pellissier, ed., *L'Art poétique de Vauquelin de la Fresnaye* (1885), pp. 32-33, I, vv. 555-558. Cf. Frances Yates, *The French Academies of the Sixteenth Century* (London, 1947), p. 44.

[5] Joseph Salvat, "Les Troubadours," *DLF:MA*, p. 725, col. 1.

"En effet, à cette époque, c'est la chanson qui représente le mieux l'union de la poésie et de la musique. Ce qui est moins connu, c'est que cette coutume s'est maintenue pendant le XIVᵉ et le XVᵉ siècle et qu'il n'y a pas eu de solution de continuité entre l'art des jongleurs et celui de la Renaissance" (E. Droz and G. Thibault, *Poètes et Musiciens du XVᵉ siecle* [1924], p. 5).

[6] "La nature véritable de ces chansons nous est attestée par les manuscrits, qui nous en ont conservé le trésor infiniment riche: une quinzaine de manuscrits au moins, tant pour les trouvères que pour les troubadours, nous mettent en présence d'une évidence matérielle: ces témoins, du XIIIᵉ siècle et des premières années du siècle suivant, portent la première strophe de chaque chanson transcrite au-dessous de la mélodie sur laquelle on répétait toutes les autres" (Pierre Aubry, *Trouvères et troubadours* [3d ed., n. d.], pp. 5-6). But note a significant reservation by Théodore Gérold, *La Musique au Moyen Age* (1932), p. 165: "On a parfois l'impression que le musicien-poète a composé sa mélodie sur le texte de la première strophe sans grandement se soucier du contenu des suivantes."

[7] Joseph Salvat, *DLF:MA*, p. 725, col. 2.

[8] "There is no certainty that the poets always wrote their own tunes. Some of the poems in fact appear with different tunes in different manuscripts" (J. A. Westrup, "Medieval Song," in *New Oxford History of Music*, II [2d ed., 1961], 225).

poetry, composition, and voice.[9] The poet-composer was less rare
a phenomenon.[10] "En France, depuis les trouvères, le poète et le
musicien n'avaient souvent fait qu'un, et l'union traditionnelle des
deux éléments constitutifs de l'art lyrique français existait encore
à l'époque de la Renaissance."[11] G. Thibault, referring to the
early predecessors of the Pléiade, says that it was the *trouvères* and
troubadours "qui avaient réalisé l'union la plus intime qui se puisse
rêver entre les deux arts puisque l'auteur du poème était celui de
la mélodie; c'est bien en cet âge d'or que l'on[12] pouvait écrire:
'. . . la strophe sans la musique est comme un moulin sans eau.' "[13]

II. From Adam de la Halle to Jean Molinet

The union of poetry and music is illustrated in the work of
Adam de la Halle (c. 1235–c. 1285). He has left a number of songs
and motets for which he composed both words and music. Certain
critics assert that his greater accomplishment was as a musician.[14]
He was not merely a composer of songs but wonderfully inventive
in polyphony. Especially in his *rondeaux* the polyphonic technique
of the ancient descant applied to French texts reached its highest
level.[15]

Guillaume de Machaut (130?–1377) was not simply a poet who
happened to have enough instruction in music to compose settings
for his verses. Nor did he always write his poems with a view to the

---

[9] Such highly endowed artists were occasionally found both among the
nobility and persons of humbler station. See Jacques Chailley, "La musique
post-grégorienne," in *Histoire de la musique*, Roland-Manuel, ed., I (1960), 736.

[10] According to Aubry, p. 5, these poets, "le plus souvent, composèrent eux-
mêmes les mélodies de leurs chansons."

[11] *RPL*, p. 86.

[12] Aubry, p. 215, attributes the following aphorism to Folquet de Marseille.

[13] "Musique et poésie en France au XVIe siècle avant les 'Amours' de
Ronsard," *MPSS*, p. 80. Cf. Aubry, p. 9: "D'autres . . . écrivent à la fois les
paroles et la mélodie de leurs chansons: cette genèse est la forme la plus haute
et la plus parfaite de la composition lyrique. Déjà, l'antiquité grecque l'avait
compris ainsi." But see below, beginning of sec. III, for the comments by
François Lesure on the difference between the Middle Age and Renaissance
concepts of the alliance between poetry and music.

[14] Jacques Chailley, "Adam de la Halle," *DLF:MA*, p. 27, col. 2.

[15] Chailley, "La musique post-grégorienne," I, 765.

music that might accompany them. Neither faculty, poetic or musical, was subordinate to the other. "Il était poète *et* musicien, et non vraiment poète-musicien."[16]

According to Ernest Hoepffner, the editor of Machaut's works, the poet greatly contributed to the triumph of the *ballade*, the *chant royal*, the *virelai*, the *rondeau*, and the *lai*, which were to maintain their popularity until the sixteenth century.[17] As to his music, "Le côté architectural, combinatoire, cérébral, quasi mathématique de ces savantes mosaïques réalisées pour le plaisir de l'esprit et celui de l'oreille . . . nous captive et nous fait découvrir un aspect à peine soupçonné de la conception artistique du moyen âge, dominé par l'intelligence, la méditation, le symbolisme."[18]

The polyphonic complexity of Machaut's vocal music, resulting from the intricate musical rhythms and the interweaving of four, five, and possibly six voices, sometimes led to a de-emphasis of the text.[19] But it would be an error to imagine that the composer abandoned his commitment to the union of poetry and music, of sense and sound. As Jacques Chailley comments Machaut's *Mass* reveals the depth of that commitment: "Au centre du *Credo* . . . la déclamation jusque-là rapide et heurtée, s'interrompt par un ralentissement soudain sur les mots *Ex Maria Virgine* pour traduire la dédicace à la Vierge de son titre, et, en doubles longues, se transforme à l'approche de l'Incarnation en une admirable méditation d'une intensité expressive bouleversante.[20] Même artifice au début du *Gloria* pour évoquer la paix réservée sur terre aux hommes de bonne volonté."[21]

Machaut may be considered the last of the *trouveurs*. After him

[16] Jacques Chailley, *Histoire musicale du Moyen Age* (1969), p. 249; emphasis in text. Cf. Robert Bossuat, *Le Moyen Age* (1962), p. 239.

[17] *Œuvres de Guillaume de Machaut*, I (1908), i.

[18] Armand Machabey, *Guillaume de Machaut, 130?-1377: La vie et l'œuvre musical*, II (1955), 169.

[19] Marie Naudin, *Evolution parallèle de la poésie et de la musique en France* (1968), p. 76. See below, n. 45, E. E. Lowinsky's observation on the loose connection between word and tone in Machaut's compositions.

[20] "Ce fragment a été enregistré en 1939 par la *Psallette Notre-Dame*, dir. J. Chailley, disque *Gramophone*, DB 5118" (footnote by Chailley).

[21] Chailley, *Hist. mus. du Moyen Age*, p. 255.

the musical and poetic faculties are not often found united in the same individual.[22] In the fifteenth century the composer will limit himself to selecting the poems to be set to music. With some exceptions[23] the period in which the poet-musician flourished has come to an end. Music and poetry will henceforth be the specialties of different artists.[24]

Eustache Deschamps (c. 1346–c. 1406) exemplifies this development. He was a disciple and admirer of Machaut, a prolific poet, but not a composer. The music for his two *Lamentations* on the death of Machaut is the work of F. Andrieu.[25] Nevertheless, in the section "De Musique" of his *Art de Dictier*, Deschamps appears to have had a quasi-professional understanding of the music of his period and an enlightened appreciation of the relationship between the arts of poetry and music.

When reading the *Art de Dictier*, one receives the impression of witnessing the separation of the two disciplines,[26] for although

---

[22] Naudin, p. 76.

"Guillaume de Machault, au XIVe siècle, reste fidèle à cette tradition [de l'union intime entre les deux arts]. Mais déjà la musique avait développé l'art de combiner les parties différentes, ou contrepoint, de telle manière qu'il devenait difficile au même homme de passer maître à la fois dans la technique de la ballade, du lai, du virelai, du chant royal, du rondeau, et dans celle du déchant ou du motet. Au XVe siècle, et dans la première moitié du XVIe, le musicien n'a cure de poésie" (Louis Laloy, "Ronsard musicien," *RM*, p.108 [12]).

[23] See Nigel Wilkins, "The Post-Machaut Generation of Poet-Musicians," *Nottingham Medieval Studies*, XII (1968), 40-84.

[24] G. Thibault, "La chanson française au XVe siècle de Dufay à Josquin des Prés (1420 à 1480)," in *Hist. de la musique*, I, 895-896. On the close relationship between composers and poets from the death of Machaut until 1520, see Naudin, pp. 78-80.

[25] The words and music may be found in Droz and Thibault (see above, n. 5), pp. 13-20.

[26] In this field of inquiry absolutes must be carefully avoided and even generalizations must be advanced cautiously. The evolution of the relationship between poetry and music did not proceed in discrete leaps. In the generation following that of Deschamps, poetry, music, and the dance were still found in close alliance. "Au temps de Me Alain [Chartier], il ne faut pas s'imaginer un poète autrement que comme une sorte de musicien de cour. La poésie et la musique, la danse même, étaient étroitement associées. Jusqu'au temps de Mme Christine [de Pisan] (Charles d'Orléans conservera encore cette tradition),

Deschamps applies the term *musique* to both, he clearly expresses the distinction between them: "Et est a sçavoir que nous avons deux musiques, dont l'une est *artificiele* et l'autre est *naturele*. *L'artificiele* est celle dont dessus est faicte mencion; et est appellée artificiele de son art, car par ses .vi. notes, qui sont appellées *us, ré, my, fa, sol, la*, l'en puet aprandre a chanter . . . le plus rude homme du monde. . . . L'autre musique est appellée *naturele* pour ce qu'elle ne puet estre aprinse a nul, se son propre couraige naturelment ne s'i applique, et est une musique de bouche en proferant paroules metrifiées, aucunefoiz en *laiz*, autrefoiz en *balades*, autrefoiz en *rondeaulx cengles* et *doubles*, et en *chançons baladées*."[27]

His observations on the aesthetic superiority created by the union of the two arts reveal how deeply and personally he experienced that union in the works of his predecessors, especially Machaut; one senses his regret at not being sufficiently gifted to continue in so great a tradition. One detects also a conviction that was to be renewed some two centuries later in the thought and feeling of Ronsard:

Et aussi ces deux musiques sont si consonans l'une avecques l'autre, que chascune puet bien estre appellée musique, pour la douceur tant du chant comme des paroles qui toutes sont prononcées et pointoyées[28] par douçour de voix et ouverture de bouche; et est de ces deux ainsi comme un mariage en conjunction de science, par les chans qui sont plus anobliz et mieulx seans par la parole et faconde des diz qu'elle ne seroit seule de soy. Et semblablement les chançons natureles sont delectables et embellies par la melodie et les teneurs, trebles et contre-teneurs du chant de la musique artificiele.[29]

---

le poète doit être aussi bien chantant que disant. Complaintes et rondeaux sont encore chantés" (Pierre Champion, *Histoire poétique du quinzième siècle*, I [1923], 74-75).

[27] Gaston Raynaud, ed., *Œuvres complètes d'Eustache Deschamps*, VII (1891), 269-270. (The edition was begun by the Marquis de Queux de Saint-Hilaire.) Cf. my *Intellectual Evolution of Ronsard*, vol. II, *Ronsard's General Theory of Poetry* (St. Louis, 1973) pp. 152-153.

[28] "Accentuées" (footnote by Raynaud).

[29] VII, 271-272. Cf. L., XIV, 9.

Charles d'Orléans (1394–1465) was a born poet. He grew up in a circle of minstrels, musicians, and rhymesters who found a protector in his father, Louis d'Orléans.[30] From his youth Charles was a good musician who, like his mother Valentine, played the harp.[31] His passion for poetry and music (or was it youthful princely ostentation?) is revealed by the fact that at the age of twenty he ordered a magnificent robe embroidered with 960 pearls of which 568, sewn on both sleeves, reproduced the words and music of the song *Ma dame je suis plus joyeulx*.[32]

From the disposition of Charles d'Orléans' autograph manuscript of his poetry,[33] it is clear that ideally, at any rate, he conceived of verse and music as arts which entered into a very natural alliance and that he had intended to provide his poems with a musical setting. At the top of the pages of this autograph he had left blank spaces for the inscription of the musical notation; the words occupied the lower half of the page. But the project was never carried out.[34] A recent student of the subject believes that "At least for the greater part of his verse, and most likely for all of it, it seems reasonable to infer that music was at the most incidental and never an integral part of the work as it had been in the past. Despite his love of music, there is no evidence to suggest that Charles, like the troubadours of the twelfth and thirteenth centuries, composed a musical setting for his own verses."[35]

Jean Molinet (1435–1507) is one of the exceptions who, during the period of decline of the alliance of poetry and music after the death of Machaut, still continues, though on a greatly reduced scale, the tradition of the poet-composer. He seems aware that he

[30] Pierre Champion, ed., *Charles d'Orléans: Poésies*, I (1923), xxii–xxiii.

[31] Champion, *Hist. poét. du quinz. siecle*, II (1923), 41; cf. by the same author, *La Vie de Charles d'Orléans (1394-1465)* (1911), p. 477. In his edition of Charles' poetry (I, xxxiv), Champion mentions "la connaissance singulière qu'il avait de la musique."

[32] Droz and Thibault, p. 8; see pp. 32-37 for the words and hitherto unpublished music by an unknown composer of Charles d'Orléans' *Je ne prise point tels baysiers* and *Va tost mon amoureux desir*.

[33] Fonds fr. 25458.

[34] Champion, ed., I, xv.

[35] John Fox, *The Lyric Poetry of Charles d'Orléans* (Oxford, 1969), p. viii.

has not done much to arrest that decline, for in his *Response a Guillaume Cretin* he says: "En toy flourissent par excellence trois redolentes fleurs qui en moy perissent par viellesse. l'une est Gramaire, qui en moy decline, Musicque qui diminue et Rethoricque[36] dont je ne suis de riens trop ricque."[37] We possess at least one song for which he wrote the words and music: *Tart ara mon cueur sa plaisance.*[38] The Library of Munich owns a manuscript (88,7) containing a *Salve Regina* in five voices by Molinet.[39] He knew the composers of his time and was a good judge of their merits. He wrote two epitaphs of Ockeghem, one of which, *Nymphes des bois, déesses des fontaines*, was set to music by Josquin des Prés.[40] References to musical instruments and to the theory of music may be found in all parts of his work.[41] In his *Chroniques* there is a passage in praise of music which seems to contain a reminiscence of the Pythagorean belief in the harmony of the spheres deepened with many Christian overtones: "Car musique est la resonance des cieulx, la voix des angeles, la joye de paradis, l'esperit de l'aer, l'organe de l'église, le chant des oyselets, la recreation de tous cœurs tristes et désolés, la persecution et enchassement des diables."[42]

III. Jean Lemaire de Belges

The alliance of poetry and music that characterized the Middle Ages in France became even more an aesthetic concern in the Renaissance, particularly during the period in which Ronsard and his group were coming to prominence. According to François Lesure, "Les années autour de 1550 . . . marquent une période de transition . . . où le goût poétique des musiciens se transformait, où prenait surtout naissance un véritable concept de l'union de la

---

[36] That is, poetry; see below n. 48.

[37] Noël Dupire, *Jean Molinet: La Vie, les œuvres* (1932), p. 23.

[38] It is reproduced with the music in Droz and Thibault, pp. 60-64.

[39] Dupire, p. 23, citing R. Eitner, *Biographisch-Bibliographisches Quellen-Lexicon der Musiker*, VII, 20. See Dupire, pp. 23-24, for several other examples of Molinet's ability as a composer.

[40] See D. Yabsley, *Jean Lemaire de Belges: La Plainte du Désiré* (1932), p. 38.

[41] G. Thibault, "La chanson française," in I, 911; cf. Dupire, p. 354.

[42] Quoted by Naudin, pp. 82-83.

poésie avec la musique."[43] Thereafter, says the same author, it is the literary text which dictates its laws to the musical form. The composer seeks out a poem that will become his principal source of inspiration; he will follow it step by step, instead of using it as the point of departure for a principally musical creation.[44] There was considerable difference between this concept of the marriage of poetry and music and the one prevailing during the preceding centuries:

Throughout the Middle Ages the musical form was not constricted by the poetic framework. If we are to trust the testomony of manuscripts which preserve their works, the musicians arranged the words under the notes slightly at random and translated only the general sense of the poem.[45] The Renaissance . . . brought about one of the most radical innovations in the music domain. . . . Henceforth all parts are written to be sung and all words are accurately placed under the notes by the publishers . . . The question so dear to Debussy: "Music dominating words or dominated by words?" was answered by the musicians of the French Renaissance in but one way, and without compromise.[46]

Jean Lemaire de Belges (c. 1473–c. 1515) did not, so far as I am aware, address himself to this precise problem—it lay in the

---

[43] François Lesure, "La chanson française au XVIe siècle," in *Hist. de la musique*, I, 1057; cf. Naudin, p. 80.

[44] Art. cit., pp. 1046-1047.

[45] "Magister Aegidius of Murino, who speaks for the fourteenth century . . . writes: 'After the composition is finished, take the words of the motet and divide them into four sections. Then divide the music into four sections too, and set the first part of the text to the first part of the music as best you can and thus proceed to the end. And sometimes it is necessary to extend many notes over few words . . . until they are all used up.' In this wonderful formula music is the Procrustean bed into which the text has to fit itself as best it can. . . Even Guillaume de Machaut, composer and poet, did not concern himself with bringing about a correspondence between the rhythmic groupings of his composition and the groups of verses in his poem. It is not unusual for the music of a medieval *virelai* or *ballata* to tear apart the different stanzas of a poem . . . Here the Renaissance caused a veritable revolution" (E. E. Lowinsky, "Music in the Culture of the Renaissance," *Journal of the History of Ideas* 15 (1954), 535-536.

[46] François Lesure, *Musicians and Poets of the French Renaissance*, trans. Elio Gianturco and Hans Rosenwald (New York, 1955).

domain of the professional composer, now that the divorce of the musical and poetic disciplines had advanced so far. But he was eager to promote the cooperation of the two arts. On the occasion of the death in 1503 of his protector, Louis de Luxembourg, Jean Lemaire in *La Plainte du Désiré* called upon Josquin des Prés and other composers[47] to unite their talents with those of poets who lamented the death of the prince:

> Poetes bons, et bons musiciens,
> Doibvent icy, par bonne et meure audace,
> Prester du sucre ung chascun de sa casse,
> Pour adoulcir ce dueil qui autre passe,
> Et pour aider mes rhetoriciens.[48]
>
> Or meslez doncq telle armonie ensemble . . .
> Que tout le monde en sa machine tremble,
> Et que maint fleuve et maint rochier s'assemble
> Pour de voz chantz en grant pitie jouyr.[49]

In an article on "Jean Lemaire de Belges et les Beaux-Arts," Jean Frappier describes the period in which Lemaire lived as one of renewal and creative élan in music and painting. The poet's notion of an alliance among the different arts was not an abstraction—it was based on personal knowledge. "Sa connaissance de la musique, de la peinture, de la sculpture, de l'architecture, était directe et active."[50] Certain verses, however, appear to Frappier to repudiate the principle of imitation of the music of ancient Greece:[51]

> D'un viel Terpandre ou d'un viel Amphïon
> D'un Appollo harpant en sa quoquille,
> On n'a plus cure, et si les deffie on.

---

[47] Yabsley, pp. 81-82, vv. 158-175 of the speech of Rhétoricque.

[48] "*Rhetoricque* . . . poésie *ou* art de s'exprimer, soit en prose, soit en vers" (Jean Frappier, *Glossaire* of his edition of *Jean Lemaire de Belges: La Concorde des deux Langages* [1947]).

[49] Yabsley, vv. 192-203.

[50] *Atti del Quinto Congresso Internazionale di Lingue e Letterature Moderne* (Florence, 1955), pp. 107-108.

[51] *Art. cit.*, p. 110.

Lemaire could have had only the vaguest conception of this music. What we have here is, perhaps, nothing but a rhetorical device to express his pride in the great flowering of musicians of his own time:

> Pour ung Lynus chantant de voix tranquille,
> Ung Thamiras, Thubal ou Putagore,
> Il en est cent, et pour cent en est mille![52]

Those he mentions are few in number, but two of them, Josquin and Ockeghem, are among the very great who, together with Loÿset Compere:

> Font melodie aux cieulx mesmes cousine.
> Les neuf beau cieulx que Dieu tourne et tempere
> Rendent tel bruit en leurs spheres diffuses
> Que le son vient jusqu'en nostre hemisphere.[53]

Jean Lemaire must have shared to the end the conviction of Folquet de Marseilles that "la strophe sans la musique est comme un moulin sans eau," for in 1513, in a letter to François le Rouge, he wrote, "Rhetorique [read Poesie] et Musique sont une mesme chose."[54]

IV. Maurice Scève

> Leuth resonnant, & le doulx son des cordes,
> Et le concent de mon affection,
> Comment ensemble unyment tu accordes
> Ton harmonie avec ma passion!
>   Lors que je suis sans occupation
> Si vivement l'esprit tu m'exercites,
> Qu'ores a joye, ore a dueil tu m'incites

---

[52] Frappier, ed., vv. 238-243.

[53] Vv. 261-264, an allusion to the harmony of the spheres no doubt suggested by the mention of "Putagore" in v. 242. See below, n. 68. For Lemaire's knowledge of musical terms, see Jean Frappier, ed., *Jean Lemaire de Belges: Les Epîtres de l'Amant Vert* (1948), p. 32, vv. 415-426 of the second *épître*. The words and music of *L'epitaphe de l'Amant Vert* were published by Droz and Thibault, pp. 70–76. The composer is unknown.

[54] Quoted in *RPL*, p. 647, n. 4; *Hist. de la Pléiade*, 4 vols. (1939-1940), I, 136-137 and 137, n. 1.

Par tes accordz, non aux miens ressemblantz.
Car plus que moy mes maulx tu luy recites,
Correspondant a mes souspirs tremblantz.[55]

In these verses, as in a number of others, Maurice Scève (c. 1500–
1560) represents Délie as singing to the accompaniment of her
lute.[56] We can infer from these passages that he took for granted
the alliance of poetry and music in his time and deeply appreciated
its aesthetic value. But from none of them is it possible to deduce
that he had any personal knowledge of music as a discipline, or
that he would have welcomed a musical setting for the *Délie*
(1544). In fact, "tout permet de croire qu'un dessein de faciliter
la mise en musique, ou d'inviter le lecteur à chanter plusieurs
poèmes sur une même musique, est étranger à l'auteur, car la
répartition des masculines et féminines est capricieuse."[57]

Verdun Saulnier no doubt is right when he says that "A la
musique instrumentale, la décoration d'*Arion* [1536] et de la
Saulsaye [1547][58] doivent beaucoup."[59] The references to the lyre
and other musical instruments in *Arion* and to the *musette* and
chalumeau in *Saulsaye* are indeed purely decorative and conventional and imply neither knowledge nor ignorance of music.

In the encyclopedic poem *Microcosme* (1562), toward the end of
the second book where he analyzes the elements constituting the
trivium and *quadrivium*, Scève discusses music at length. The introductory verses coincidentally are similar in tonality to Ronsard's
contemporaneous prose preface (L., XVIII, 480–488) to the *Livre
de Meslanges contenant six vingtz chansons* (1560):

---

[55] I. D. McFarlane, ed., *The 'Délie' of Maurice Scève* (Cambridge, 1966),
pp. 306-307, *dizain* 344. Here and below in *dizain* 196, I have slightly modified
the orthography and punctuation.

[56] V. L. Saulnier, "Maurice Scève et la Musique," *MPSS*, p. 91, n. 11,
mentions *dizains* 157, 158, 160, 196, 344, and 345 as invoking "le thème du
chant et du luth."

[57] *Art. cit.*, p. 94. Nevertheless, a number of poems by Scève were set to
music in the sixteenth and twentieth centuries; see pp. 95-96, and the notes.

[58] Bernard Guégan, ed., *Œuvres poétiques complètes de Maurice Scève* (1927),
pp. 157-163, 167-187.

[59] *Art. cit.*, p. 93.

Musique, accent des cieux, plaisante symfonie
Par contraires aspects formant son harmonie:
Don de Nature amie à soulager à maints
Voire à tous, nos labeurs, et nos travaux humains.
Qui par l'esprit de l'air, nœu du corps, et de l'ame,
Le sens à soy ravit, et le courage enflamme:
Et par son doux concent non seulement vocale,
Mais les Demons encor appaise instrumentale,
Comme au Prophete saint l'esprit divin excite
Par le Harpeur sonnant le futur, qu'il recite,
Promettant s'accointer par melodieux sons
Terrestres animaux, et marineux poissons:
En guerre s'animer, et obtenant victoire
Par hymnes, et chansons rendre au Toutpuissant gloire.[60]

We need not follow Scève too closely in the complex details, the "cascade . . . de termes techniques [grecques]",[61] with which he he develops the theme. To do this adequately he appears to have versified the relevant pages of the *Margarita Philosophica* of Gregor Reisch.[62] After referring to the Biblical and Hellenic accounts of the invention of music, he distinguishes, with Reisch, "les diverses sortes de voix et de sons . . . les trois sortes de chants . . . les huit clefs . . . les calculs de tons et demi-tons, avec la terminologie classique . . . les quatre modes principaux . . . les trois genres de modulation."[63]

It is possible that Scève made available to Pontus de Tyard his copy of the *Margarita Philosophica*, for in the *Solitaire second*,[64] after describing the notational system of ancient Greek music, Tyard replies thus to a question by Pasithée: "Vous ne trouverez hors de propos que j'ajoute une autre mode de marques, laquelle j'ay recueillie d'un fort vieil exemplaire[65] venu en mes mains par la

---

[60] Guégan, ed., p. 244.

[61] V. L. Saulnier, *Maurice Scève*, I (1948), 481.

[62] Numerous editions of this work appeared in 1504 and following years. See below, n. 65.

[63] See Saulnier, *Maurice Scève*, I, 480-481 and the notes in II, 230-231, as well as his article in *MPSS*, p. 92.

[64] An erudite attempt to reconstitute the theory of ancient Greek music.

[65] Cf. Saulnier, *Maurice Scève*, I, 389: "Ce vieux livre pourrait bien n'être autre que la *Margarita Philosophica* de Gregor Reisch, que nous rencontrerons

grace de mon extremement aymé ami non jamais assez honoré de moy le Signeur Maurice Scève."[66]

"Quant à la communauté de curiosité entre Tyard et Scève touchant les problèmes musicaux," commented Saulnier, "j'en suis tout à fait convaincu. Il serait absurde, étant donné notre peu de documentation, de parler d'une collaboration de Scève aux *Discours philosophiques*."[67] But the sympathy with which Scève viewed the *Solitaire second* is evident from the fact that its one liminary poem bears the title and signature "En grace de si docte Solitaire [,] M. SC."

The second quatrain of this sonnet alludes to the Pythagorean theory of the music of the spheres;

> N'ignorant l'Ame avec les Cieus conmere
> De l'union de l'harmonial Chœur,
> Ha pu sentir se soulager le cœur,
> Voire & ravir hors sa cure ephimere.[68]

à propos de *Microcosme*: cette étude des modes, des tons, de l'harmonie, se retrouve chez Reisch comme chez Tyard et Scève."

[66] *Solitaire second, ou Prose de la musique* (A Lion, M.D.LV), p. 28. Harvard University Library, *FC5/T9532/555s2. The flyleaf of this copy bears the following comment: "Please note that in this copy [most of] the punctuation, signatures and catchwords have been scraped out." [Signed] W[illiam] A. J[ackson]. The correct punctuation has been restored in sec. viii below from the Mazarine copy, A. 11477, prem. pièce, Réserve.

A. Baur's observation, *Maurice Scève et la Renaissance lyonnaise* (1906), p. 108, n. 1, on this passage in the *Solitaire second*, "Il s'agit d'une nouvelle notation de la musique," is too ambiguous to be useful, and his assertion (p. 108) that the passage in question and the verses on music in the *Microcosme* "nous montrent l'auteur de la *Délie* très fort en théorie musicale," must be taken with caution. According to Saulnier, "Scève suit ici à grands pas le développement de Reisch" (I, 480). M. Augé-Chiquet, *Vie de Baïf*, (Paris and Toulouse, 1909), p. 316, on the faith of Baur's statements, went so far as to say that "Scève recherchait curieusement les partitions anciennes [!], était fort instruit dans la technique de l'art musical."

[67] *MPSS*, pp. 101-102. The *Solitaire second* was republished in the *Discours philosophiques* of 1587.

[68] *Solitaire second* (1555), p. 3.—In the *Microcosme* (ed. Guégan, p. 244), Scève assigns the invention of the theory to Tubal (Gen., 4. 22), but the accompanying account of Tubal's observation of the musical intervals produced by hammers of different weights is based on Greek legends of the discovery of the principle of the musical scale by Pythagoras. See Saulnier, *Maurice Scève*, II, 230, n. 425.

This theme had already made its appearance in *Délie* 196, in which the poet's lady is described as drawing celestial harmonies of great moral power from the cosmic diapason:

> Tes doigtz tirantz non le doulx son des cordes,
> Mais des haultz cieulx l'Angelique harmonie,
> Tiennent encor en telle symphonie,
> Et tellement les oreilles concordes,
> Que paix, & guerre ensemble tu accordes
> En ce concent, que lors je concevoys:
>   Car du plaisir, qu'avecques toy j'avoys,
> Comme le vent se joue avec la flamme,
> L'esprit divin de ta celeste voix
> Soubdain m'estainct, & plus soubdain m'enflamme.[69]

V. Clément Marot

Jean Rollin begins the Introduction of his book on Clément Marot's songs with this enthusiastic assertion: "Clément Marot poète et musicien! Le poète se met à l'épinette[70] et devant un Maurice Scève admirateur passionné [!] ... il chante!"[71] Rollin came to this conclusion about Marot's musicianship and Scève's intense admiration of it on the strength of the following epigram of 1536:

> *A Maurice Seve, Lyonnoys*
>   En m'oyant chanter quelcque foys
> Tu te plainds qu'estre je ne daigne
> Musicien, et que ma voix
> Merite bien que l'on m'enseigne,
> Voyre que la peine je preigne
> D'apprendre ut, re, my, fa, sol, la.
> Que Diable veulx tu que j'appreigne?
> Je ne boy que trop sans cela.[72]

About three-quarters of a century before Rollin this epigram

---

[69] McFarlane, ed., p. 227.

[70] "A paire of Virginals" (Randle Cotgrave, *A Dictionarie of the French and English Tongues* [London, 1611]).

[71] *Les Chansons de Clément Marot* (1951).

[72] C. A. Mayer, ed., *Clément Marot: Les Epigrammes* (London, 1970), p. 201.

had been used somewhat to the same purpose, though far more
cautiously, by O. Douen: "Il [Marot] était doué d'une belle voix
et chantait, bien qu'il paraisse n'avoir pas eu des connaissances
musicales très-approfondies."[73] Unlike Rollin, Douen does not
place Marot at the virginals, which are not mentioned in the
epigram, nor does he make a musician of him. The awkward thing
about Rollin's thesis, according to François Lesure, is not so much
what the epigram of 1536 says, as what the contemporaries of
Marot fail to say: "Comment concevoir qu'un personnage aussi
'public' que Marot . . . auquel on a adressé de nombreux hom-
mages poétiques, n'ait pas été célébré de son vivant comme
musicien, s'il l'avait vraiment été? . . . Marot musicien? Ronsard
musicien? Probablement ni l'un ni l'autre."[74] For C. A. Mayer the
silence of Marot himself is equally conclusive: "Marot était-il
musicien? A-t-il composé lui-même la musique de ses chansons?
Les a-t-il chantées lui-même? Aucun témoignage, aucun fait ne
nous permet de l'affirmer. Non seulement lui-même ne s'est-il
jamais vanté d'avoir composé des airs ou d'avoir chanté autrement
que de façon toute métaphorique, mais aucun contemporain ne
lui attribue une connaissance de la musique."[75]

Mayer's question, "A-t-il composé lui-même la musique de ses
chansons?" is not rhetorical. In a section entitled "Clément Marot
compositeur (?)," Rollin (pp. 117-119) seeks to establish the poet's
qualifications as a composer[76] on the basis of a single musical
setting dubiously attributed to Marot, of a poem, *Doulce mémoire*,
which he had not written. Perhaps the weakest part of Rollin's
study is the attempt (pp. 120-135) to demonstrate the reality of
Marot's musical endowment by quoting many poems in which the

---

[73] *Clément Marot et le Psautier huguenot*, I (1878), 38.

[74] "Autour de Clément Marot et ses musiciens," *Revue de musicologie*, XXXIII
(1951), 111. See also the masterly review of Rollin's book by V. L. Saulnier,
BHR, XV (1953), 130-136, which corroborates the position taken by Lesure.

[75] *Clément Marot: Œuvres lyriques* (London, 1964), pp. 15-16.

[76] Douen (above, n. 73), I, 39, had implied as much in 1878. See Saulnier's
review, pp. 131 and 133, which refutes the positions of Douen and Rollin.
Douen's assertations, that Marot "jouait sans doute de l'épinette" and that
"Il a composé les airs de plusieurs de ses chansons," rest on no documentary
evidence.

sole evidence adduced is an abundance of references to murmuring waters, bird songs, and the like. Rollin's failure to distinguish between passages of this nature and those containing specifically musical allusions, his unwillingness to recognize that the frequent mentions of musical instruments (*lyre, flageol, trompette bellique*) or activities ("Arriere ceste lyre / Dont je chantais l'amour . . .")[77] have a merely metaphorical intention, does nothing to illuminate the question of Marot's relationship to the music of his time.

That relationship probably was close because Marot's *chansons* were ideally adaptable to the requirements of the composers and public taste. The distinguishing qualities of his poems were "le ton populaire, la simplicité, la parfaite aisance."[78] He thus became a favorite with musicians long before their infatuation with Ronsard. "His jesting philosophy corresponded ideally to the genre of the *chanson parisienne.* Composers showed themselves eager to circulate it . . . at court Marot rubbed elbows with musicians of renown; and it is not coincidence that we find over twenty-five of his texts in the *chansons* of Claudin de Sermisy, master of the royal chapel."[79] Before 1532 he had written thirty-two *chansons*; they appeared in the collections of Attaignant and enjoyed great popularity.[80]

But Marot anticipated Ronsard in a far more important association of poetry with music. This was first pointed out by Jacques Peletier in his *Art poëtique* of 1555:

Ce nom d'Ode a esté introduit de notre temps, par Pierre de Ronsard: auquel ne faillirai de temoignage, que lui estant ancor en grand' jeunesse, m'en monstra quelques unes de sa façon, en notre ville du Mans:[81] et me dit deslors, qu'il se proposoit ce genre d'escrire, à

---

[77] Abel Grenier, ed., *Clément Marot: Œuvres complètes,* I (1938), 274.

[78] Mayer, *Marot: Œuvres lyriques,* pp. 14-15.

[79] Lesure, *Musicians and Poets,* p. 24. Because of their elegance, wit, clarity, and brevity, Marot's epigrams shared with his *chansons* the favor of composers. "On a recensé 118 poèmes ou fragments de poèmes attribués à Marot et mis en musique au XVIᵉ s. . . . : 44 chansons (ou fragments), 48 épigrammes, 12 rondeaux, 2 ballades, 3 élégies (fragments), 2 estrennes, 1 épître (fragment), 2 sonnets" (Lesure, "Autour de Clément Marot," p. 114).

[80] Pierre Jourda, *Marot* (1956), p. 62.

[81] An allusion to the first meeting between Ronsard and Peletier, 6 March 1543.

l'imitation d'Horace: comme depuis il a monstré à tous les François: et encor plus par sus sa premiere intention, à l'imitation du premier des Liriques, Pindare. Combien toutesfois, que de ce temps là, *il ne les fit pas mesurées à la Lire*: comme il a bien su faire depuis . . . Pource, cette nouveauté se trouva rude au premier:[82] et quasi n'i avoit que le nom inventé. Mais quant à la chose, *si nous regardons les Pseaumes de Clement Marot*: *ce sont vraies Odes*, sinon qu'il leur defailloit le nom, comme aux autres la chose.[83]

Peletier is too generous in assigning to Ronsard the priority in introducing the word *ode* into the French language. The word occurs in 1511 in v. 296 of Jean Lemaire's *Temple de Venus*, but as Jean Frappier points out in a note, the word was gallicized for the first time in 1488.[84] Ronsard was no doubt as unaware as Peletier of these facts when he wrote in 1550 in the preface *Au lecteur* of the *Quatre premiers livres des Odes*:

Donques desirant . . . m'approprier quelque louange, encores non connue, ni atrapée par mes devanciers, & ne voiant en nos Poëtes François, chose qui fust suffisante d'imiter: j'allai voir les étrangers, & me rendi familier d'Horace, contrefaisant sa naive douceur, des le méme tens que Clement Marot (seulle lumiere en ses ans de la vulgaire poësie) se travailloit à la poursuite de son Psautier, & osai le premier des nostres, enrichir ma langue de ce nom Ode,[85] comme l'on peut voir par le titre d'une imprimée sous mon nom dedans le livre de Jaques Peletier du Mans.[86]

Ronsard in 1550 and Peletier in 1555 covered very much the same general ground: Ronsard's imitations of Horace, his supposed priority in the use of the term *ode*, and references to Marot's

---

[82] "Tout d'abord cette nouveauté (l'ode) était encore informe" (footnote by Boulanger).

[83] Boul., pp. 172-176; my emphasis. Peletier's orthography has been modified to conform to normal sixteenth-century usage.

[84] See Frappier's edition of *La Concorde des deux Langages*, p. 19 and p. 67, n. 93. Cf. *RPL*, pp. xxxi–xxxiii.

[85] Ronsard first used the word in 1547 and was thus claiming priority by about a year over Sebillet, who employed it a number of times in 1548 in his *Art Poétique françoys*, ed. F. Gaiffe (1932), pp. 37, 141, 146-148, 150-152.

[86] L., I, 44; see also, I, 3 and crit. app.

translation of the Psalms. But in this last respect the difference between the two statements is marked. Ronsard was not satisfied with claiming precedence in the use of the word *ode*—he demanded recognition as the creator of lyric poetry in France. In the same preface to the reader he says: "Quand tu m'appelleras le premier auteur Lirique François, & celui qui a guidé les autres au chemin de si honneste labeur, lors tu me rendras ce que tu me dois" (L., I, 43). Thus Ronsard passes over in silence the fact that Marot's *Pseaumes*, because they were "mesurés à la lyre," were genuine odes, as Peletier reminded him five years later.

There is some truth in the following comments of Paul Laumonier: "Admettons que les chefs de la nouvelle école aient été de bonne foi en proclamant que nul n'avait composé avant eux ni odes badines ni odes sérieuses. C'était une illusion assez naturelle chez des auditeurs enthousiastes de Dorat, et chez des révolutionnaires qui achevaient une évolution préparée de longue main par d'autres et déjà presque arrivée à son terme."[87] Yet Ronsard and his colleagues must have known that to be "mesurées à la lyre" the strophes of Marot's *Pseaumes* had to be "superposables en tous leurs éléments . . . afin que le musicien . . . pût adapter la même mélodie à toutes les strophes de la pièce: l'unité métrique rendant possible l'unité musicale, la pièce méritait vraiment alors d'être appelée *lyrique*; ce qualificatif se justifiait à nouveau, comme chez les anciens poètes grecs, par l'alliance intime de la poésie et de la musique."[88] Given the wide popularity of the psalms of Marot in the various strata of French society, Ronsard must have been acquainted with collections such as the *Trente et un psaumes* by Marot set to music by Pierre Certon and published in Paris in 1546, the *Cinquante psaumes* published by the composer Loys Bourgeoys in Lyons in 1547, or the *Vingt-huit psaumes* arranged by Clément Jannequin and published in Paris in 1549[89] Laumonier was therefore entirely justified in concluding

---

[87] *RPL*, p. xlvii.

[88] *RPL*, p. 652; Laumonier's emphasis. Cf. L., I, xxxviii–xxxix.

[89] See C. A. Mayer, *Bibliographie des Œuvres de Clément Marot*, vol. II, *Editions* (Geneva, 1954), nos. 153, 157, and 171.

that "c'est Clément Marot qui a instauré le premier dans la poésie française l'ode 'mesurée à la lyre.' "[90]

Ronsard's insistence on his priority could therefore not be maintained insofar as it applied to the marriage of music and lyric verse, but it could be vindicated, as the poet did to the very end of his life, if it were restricted to the field of Greek poetry. During Ronsard's early period that field was largely dominated by his effort to naturalize the Pindaric ode in France. The preface of the odes of 1550 inextricably confuses Ronsard's inaccurate claim to priority in the alliance of music and the ode in general with his just assertion of precedence in an attempt to restore the union of music and the Greek ode.

VI. Mellin de Saint-Gelais

When Du Bellay wrote in the *Deffence*: "Chante moy d'une musette bien resonnante et d'une fluste bien jointe ces plaisantes ecclogues rustiques," he brought a long, irascible, sarcastic, sometimes uninformed, but not entirely unreasonable reply from Barthélemy Aneau whose purpose was to show that the divorce between music and poetry had already been consummated in antiquity:

Quel langage est ce, chanter d'une musette et d'une fluste? Tu nous as proposé le langage françois: puis tu fais [de nous][91] des menestriers, tabourineurs et violeurs. Comme ton Ronsard trop et tresarrogamment se glorifie avoir amené la lyre greque et latine en France, pource qu'il nous fait bien esbahyr de ces gros et estranges motz *strophe* et *antistrophe*.[92] Car jamais (paraventure) nous n'en ouysmes parler. Jamais nous n'avons leu Pindar. . . . Pource n'abaissez point la poësie à la menestrerie, violerie et flageolerie. Car les poëtes lyriques du passé, ne ceux du present, ne chantoient, ne sonnoient, ne chantent, ne sonnent leurs vers . . . mais les composoient et composent en beaux

---

[90] *RPL*, p. 652, and see n. 2: "Marot appelle les *Pseaumes* des 'chansons mesurées' (éd. Jannet, IV, 61)."

[91] The words in brackets are Chamard's emendation.

[92] L., I, 46.

vers mesurez, qui puys apres par les musiciens estoient et sont mis en musique, et de la musique és instrumens.[93]

Aneau admits, however, a contemporary exception to the general rule, an exception whose exemplary modesty, he strongly implies, might well be imitated by Ronsard and his fellows: "Et si vous autres me mettez en avant un Mellin, Monsieur de Saint Gelais, qui compose, voire bien sur tous autres, vers lyriques, les met en musique, les chante, les joüe et sonne sur les instrumens, je confesse et say ce qu'il sait faire, mais c'est pour luy. Et en cela il soustient diverses personnes, et est poëte, musicien, vocal et instrumental . . . Mais de telz que luy ne s'en trouve pas treize en la grand douzaine, et si ne se arrogue rien et ne derogue à nul."[94]

These assertions concerning Saint-Gelais' abilities as a musician and his unassuming contributions to the alliance of poetry and music are several times corroborated in the verses he has left us. His *Complainte du loyal et malheureux amant à sa dame mal pitoyable* is preceded by the mention "Pour dire au luth en chant italien."[95] On the poem entitled *Sur une guitterre espaignolle rompue et puis faicte rabiller* [réparer] *par Monseigneur d'Orléans*, Blanchemain has the following note: "Sainct-Gelays étoit un habile joueur de luth. Il est probable qu'il en donnoit des leçons au petit duc."[96]

His biographer H. J. Molinier refers to the popularity of Saint-Gelais' *chansons*: "Il était . . . à même de les mettre en musique lui-même, et de les chanter."[97] More recently François Lesure has expressed the hope that Saint-Gelais might be given due credit for his accomplishments in the field of music and poetry

---

[93] *Def.*, II, IV, pp. 225-226 [122-123]; in the same chapter see also p. 208, n. 3 [112, n. 4].

[94] *Ibid.*, pp. 226-227 [p. 123].

[95] Prosper Blanchemain, ed., *Œuvres complètes de Melin de Sainct-Gelays*, I (1873), 69. The editor's *Notice* refers three times (pp. 7, 10, 15) to Saint-Gelais' musical talent and reports Guillaume Colletet's assertion that this talent was known to "tous les autheurs de son siècle" (p. 26).

[96] *Ibid.*, I, 234-236; cf. pp. 239-240, *Sur un luth* and the note by Bernard de La Monnoye; II, 78-79, also entitled *Sur un luth*, and La Monnoye's note.

[97] *Mellin de Saint-Gelays (1490?-1558): Etude sur sa vie et ses œuvres* (Rodez, 1910), p. 430; cf. pp. 89, n. 1, and 395.

"because . . . he composed music to his own poems, sang them and played them on instruments."[98]

The most persuasive assertion, more convincing even than that of Aneau, is the quite disinterested eulogy which Ronsard, Saint-Gelais' successor as poet laureate of France, wrote three years after his rival's death in 1558:

> Sainct Gelais qui estoit l'ornement de nostre aage,
> Qui le premier en France a ramené l'usage
> De scavoir chastouiller les aureilles des Rois
> Par un luth marié[99] aux doulceurs de la voix,
> Qui au ciel demenoit sa divine armonie,
> Veid, mal-heureux mestier! une turbe infinie
> Advancez devant luy, & peu luy profitoit
> Son luth, qui le premier des mieux appris estoit. [L., XIII,
> 25-26; cf. VIII, 157]

Extraordinary tribute from a poet, notoriously sensitive on the subject of his priority in lyric poetry, who in these verses not only recognizes Saint-Gelais "pour son précurseur dans l'ode,"[100] but also as the one who had resuscitated the alliance of poetry and music in France![101]

VII. Thomas Sebillet

Had Ronsard and Du Bellay not been so deeply concerned to establish their poetic hegemony, they might have realized that Thomas Sebillet, in spite of his attachment to the forms of the Rhétoriqueurs and the Marotiques, had anticipated some of their theoretical positions in his *Art poétique françoys* of 1548, just as Saint-Gelais had in part anticipated their practice. For example, in the chapter entitled "De l'antiquité de la Poësie, et de son excellence," Sebillet points to an alliance of poetry and music in

---

[98] *Musicians and Poets*, p. 22.

[99] The variant of 1584 reads: "Par sa Lyre accordante . . ."

[100] L., XIII, 26, n. 2. In spite of Peletier's prompting, Ronsard never paid a comparable tribute to Clément Marot, who, though not a musician or composer himself, had notably advanced the alliance of poetry and music.

[101] This was not, however, the alliance which Ronsard had advocated in the preface to the *Odes*; see end of preceding section.

the sacred rites of all the ancient peoples: "Moïse . . . premier divin Pöéte . . . *chanta-il* grace et louenge a dieu autrement qu'en *vers pöétiquement mesuréz*? Et . . . les responses que rendoient aussi entre les Grecz Apollo Pythien et Delphique . . . *estoient en vers* . . . Lés Romains mesmes dés le commencement de leur ville . . . *feirent chanter* à leurs Salies prestres de Mars louenges et supplications auz dieuz *mesurées* en carmes pöétiques: lesquelz . . . ont esté toujours *harmonieusement chantéz* en leurs temples." This tradition of the ancients has been continued into modern times: "Nous aussi . . . *chantons* la pluspart des louenges et priéres que nous dressons a Dieu et ses saintz, *en vers et carmes mesuréz*." But, says Sebillet, the practice eventually spread from the sacred to the profane: "Les monarques . . . voians et oians dire qu'un . . . Apollo . . . par la douceur de ses vers chantéz avoit illustré la gloire des plus hauts et plus puissans dieuz, prirent ensemble envie de s'égaler auz dieuz, et estre comme euz louéz et congnuz a la postérité par le carme des Pöétes. De la Homére, de la Hesiode, de la Pindare resentirent entre les Grecz admiration et louenge de leur divine versification."[102]

In the chapter "Du Cantique, Chant Lyrique ou Ode et Chanson,"[103] on the other hand, Sebillet addressed himself to the marriage of lyric poetry and music in a manner which considerably confused the issue:

"Le chant Lyrique, ou Ode . . . se façonne . . . variablement et inconstamment . . . lés plus cours et petis vers y sont plussouvent usités et mieus séans, a cause du Luth ou autre instrument semblable sur lequel l'Ode se doit chanter.[104] Aussy la matiére suyt l'effet de l'instrument, qui comme le chant Lyrique, et l'Ode comme l'instrument exprime tant du son comme de la vois lés affections et passions ou

[102] Gaiffe, ed., pp. 11-13. Taken together, the words I have emphasized show that Sebillet was not writing metaphorically.

[103] See *RPL*, pp. xv and xix-xx, where Laumonier has carefully analyzed Sebillet's treatment of these forms.

[104] "Cette déclaration très catégorique est à noter, puisqu'elle devance de deux ans celle de Ronsard dans la *Préface des Odes*" (footnote by Gaiffe). In reality, Sebillet and Ronsard were discussing two very different kinds of poetry, and consequently two very dissimilar kinds of alliance between poetry and music.

tristes, ou joieuses, ou creintives, ou esperantes,[105] desquéles ce petit
Dieu (le premier et principal suget de Pöésie, singuliérement aus Odes
et Chansons) tourmente et augmente lés esperis[106] dés Amoureus. Ainsy
est le chant Lyrique aussy peu constant qu'ilz sont, et autant prompt
a changer de son, de vers, et de Ryme, comme eus de visages et d'acou-
tremens. Pource n'en atten de moy aucune régle autre, fors que
choisisses le patron dés Odes en Pindarus Pöéte Grec, et en Horace
Latin, et que tu imites a pied levé Saingelais és Françoises, qui en est
Autheur tant dous que divin."[107]

As he read this passage, Ronsard must have experienced a sense
of total frustration, certainly shared by Du Bellay.[108] He accepted
without question Sebillet's description of lyric poetry as variable
and inconstant, but in the period under discussion Ronsard
assigned an entirely different meaning to these terms. For Sebillet
the inconstancy and variability of the moods of lyric poetry,
alternating between joy and sorrow, fear and hope, arose from its
almost exclusive preoccupation with Eros, "ce petit Dieu (le
premier et principal suget de Pöésie, singuliérement aus Odes et
Chansons)." Ronsard was to worship at the altar of this divinity
more assiduously than any of his contemporaries, but in the years
that saw the publication of Sebillet's *Art poétique*, Du Bellay's
Deffence, and his own preface to the *Odes*, his concept of the
variability of lyric poetry was inspired in part by Aristotle's theory
of mimesis, and in part by the endless diversity of Pindar's style.
He says in 1550:

Nulle Pöësie se doit louer pour acomplie, si elle ne ressemble la
nature, laquelle ne fut estimée belle des anciens, que pour estre in-
constante, & variable en ses perfections. . . . Je ne fai point de doute
que ma Pöësie tant varie ne semble facheuse aus oreilles de nos
rimeurs, & principalement des courtizans, qui n'admirent qu'un petit
sonnet petrarquizé, ou quelque mignardise d'amour . . . pour le
moins, je m'assure qu'ils ne me sçauroient accuser, sans condamner

---

[105] The intention of this bewildering sentence seems to be to assure as nearly
perfect a marriage as possible between poetry and music, voice and instrument.
[106] "Exalte les passions" (footnote by Gaiffe).
[107] Gaiffe, ed., pp. 146-148.
[108] Cf. Gaiffe, p. 148, n. 2; *Def.* (1904), pp. 213-214.

premierement Pindare auteur de telle copieuse diversité . . . Dans mes autres livres . . . tu pourras . . . contempler de plus prés les saintes conceptions de Pindare, & ses admirables inconstances. [L., I, 47-48].

Appearing at a time when Ronsard had probably already written his Pindaric odes to Henri II and Catherine de Médicis, as well as those which celebrated the victories of François de Bourbon and Guy de Chabot, when he was no doubt contemplating the Pindaric odes for Dorat, Du Bellay, Baïf, and above all, Michel de l'Hospital, Sebillet's absurd assimilation of Pindar with Saint-Gelais must have seemed inexpressibly shallow. Though the great majority of Ronsard's musicians preferred eventually to provide settings for his erotic poetry, his intense commitment to Pindar led him to say "& ferai encores revenir (si je puis) l'usage de la lire aujourdui resuscitée en Italie, laquelle lire seule doit & peut animer les vers, & leur donner le juste poix de leur gravité" (L., I, 48). The ancient alliance of poetry and music, which Ronsard then dreamed of reconstituting, responded to an ideal of which neither Sebillet nor Saint-Gelais seemed able to form a conception.[109]

VIII. Pontus de Tyard

Literary and intellectual activity in the transition period from the dominance of Marot to the rise of the Pléiade was so great that the four years separating Sebillet's *Art poétique* from Tyard's dialogues, the *Solitaire premier ou Prose des Muses, et de la fureur Poëtique* and the *Solitaire second ou Prose de la musique,*[110] transformed the understanding of what the alliance between poetry and music ought to be.

When he entered Pasithée's house, Solitaire tells us, "Je la trouvay assise, et tenant un Leut en ses mains, accordant au son des cordes, que divinement elle touchoit[,] sa voix douce et

---

[109] Cf. Gustave Cohen, *Ronsard, sa vie et son œuvre* (1956), p. 78: "Où il est visible que Sebillet n'a pas compris ces idées . . . c'est que, tout en proposant Pindare comme modèle, il fait de l'amour . . . le sujet pricipal de l'Ode."

[110] Both were published in 1552. A copy of the *Solitaire second* of that date is in Milan, according to *Hist. de la Pl.*, III, 147, n. 3. I have used the edition of 1555 (see above, n. 66).

facile: avec laquelle tant gracieusement elle mesuroit une Ode
Françoise."[111] The dialogue ends immediately after Solitaire has
performed a Pindaric ode to his own accompaniment on the
lute.[112] It may not be too fanciful to regard these incidents as
symbolizing the tendency of Tyard's thinking. The *Solitaire
premier*, as the subtitle indicates, examines, among other things, the
theory of poetic fury. But the musical performances with which
the work begins and ends represent Tyard's deep interest in
furthering the alliance of poetry and music[113] and of emphasizing
its remote Hellenic origins. "Comment," says Pasithée toward the
end of the *Solitaire premier* as her friend is preparing to leave,
". . . voulez-vous icy fermer le pas? Vrayement l'entreprinse de
ceste journée n'est achevée: Oubliez-vous l'accointance, laquelle
(bien que tacitement) vous avez fait[e] de la Poësie et de la
Musique,[114] comme de deux ruisseaux qui procedent d'une mesme
sourse, et rentrent en une mesme mer?"[115]

Indeed Solitaire has not forgotten. He will devote the following
day to another dialogue, the *Solitaire second*, essentially an effort to
recreate the Hellenic theory of music[116] in which the close relationship with poetry occupies so central a position. It is on this point
that Pasithée first seeks clarification, "puis que sa connoissance est
de si excellente eficace en l'elevacion de l'ame par aliance avec la
fureur Poëtique."[117] Solitaire replies that while poetry is at present
in a flourishing state in France, music is in a serious decline,
"comme si nous en estions incapables, ou si les Grecs & les Latins
devoient defendre cete partie de Filozofie, à ceus qui ne seroient
adoptez en leur famille."[118]

Solitaire is acutely aware of the difficulties which must impede

[111] Silvio F. Baridon, ed., *Pontus de Tyard: Œuvres, Le Solitaire premier* (Lille
and Geneva, 1950), p. 5.

[112] Baridon, ed., pp. 75-77.

[113] Cf. Yates, *The French Academies*, p. 79.

[114] Baridon, ed., p. 19.

[115] Baridon, ed., p. 74.

[116] See above, n. 64. A suggestion of this development is already present in
the *Solitaire premier*, Baridon, ed., pp. 29-30.

[117] *Sol. sec.* (1555), p. 10.

[118] *Ibid.*, pp. 10-11. See above, n. 66.

the rebirth of the intimate union of music and poetry which flourished in Hellenic times. That "ravissante energie des anciens Poëtes lyriques . . . mariant la Musique à la Poësie" was possible because those poets were masters of both disciplines: "ils estoient nez à l'une & à l'autre."[119] This is no longer the case—the divorce between the two arts has proceeded too far: "Les Musiciens . . . tous, ou la plus part, sont sans lettres, & connoissance de Poësie: comme aussi le plus grand nombre des Poëtes mesprise &, si j'ose dire, ne connoit la Musique."[120]

Yet Solitaire is not ready to abandon the ideal vision. He hopes that someone bolder and more capable than he will undertake to write an "art Poëtique aproprié aus façons Françoises." Of this theorist he would demand that "à l'image des Anciens . . . noz chans ussent quelques manieres ordonnees de longueur de vers, de suite ou entremellement de Rimes,[121] & de Mode de chanter, *selon le merite de la matiere entreprise par le Poëte*, qui . . . seroit dine Poëte-musicien, & témoigneroit que la harmonie & les Rimes sont presque d'une mesme essence: & que sans le mariage de ces deus, le Poëte & le Musicien demeurent moins jouissans de la grace qu'ils cherchent aquerir."[122]

In this concluding passage of the *Solitaire second*, where the formal elements, both metrical and musical, seem to play so preponderant a role, the governing principle is the primacy of the word, for everything must be ordered "selon le merite de la matiere entreprise par le Poëte." Tyard has not waited until the end of his dialogue to establish this principle. When asked whether he prefers monody to choral music, Solitaire replies: "Le premier . . . est à mon jugement beaucoup estimable: *car si l'intencion de Musique semble estre, de donner tel air à la parole, que tout escoutant se sente passionné, & se laisse tirer à l'afeccion du Poëte*: celui qui scet

---

[119] *Ibid.*, p. 132.

[120] *Ibid.*, p. 133; cf. John C. Lapp, ed., *The Universe of Pontus de Tyard: A Critical Edition of* L'Univers (Ithaca, N.Y., 1950), p. xxx.

[121] I.e., *rythmes*; see Cotgrave (above, n. 70), s. vv. *rime, rithme, ryme*; cf. *Def.*, II, viii, pp. 270-272 [150-152].

[122] *Sol. sec.*, pp. 155-156; my emphasis. Cf. *Hist. de la Pl.*, IV, 136.

proprement acommoder une voix seule, me semble mieus ateindre
à la fin aspiree: vù que la Musique figuree[123] le plus souvent ne
raporte aus oreilles autre chose qu'un grand bruit, duquel vous ne
sentez aucune vive eficace: Mais la simple & unique voix, coulee
doucement, & continuee *selon le devoir de sa Mode choisie pour le
merite des vers*, vous ravit la part qu'elle veut."[124]

Although purely instrumental music has considerable ethical
influence, it attains its greatest power when it has recognized the
primacy of the word and is joined with the word in indissoluble
union. Early in the second dialogue Solitaire reminds Pasithée
"Pourquoy la Poësie & la Musique sont compagnes":[125] just as
physical exercises were considered necessary in ancient Greece
for the maintenance of bodily health, so "la Musique servoit
d'exercice pour reduire l'ame en une parfette temperie de bonnes,
louables, & vertueuses meurs, emouvant & apaisant par une naïve
puissance & secrette energie, les passions & afeccions . . . qui fut
ocasion prestee aus premiers Poëtes & Theologiens de l'acom-
pagner de Poësie, au nom de fureur sous la charge des Muses."[126]
Between ethics and music there is, in Solitaire's view, so intimate
a relationship, that "les accions guidees à bonne fin, & les
passions, temperees par les vertus, sont dites la vreye Musique de
l'homme."[127] These reflections lead him naturally to the prayer
which, he says, Pythagoras uttered to invoke the Muses as he was
about to play the lyre, "à fin que par leur ayde soient rassemblees
en un mes parties plus celestes, égarees quelquefois loin de leur
immortelle sourse, pour le soutenement de cete humanité: Et ce
entendant non seulement de la Musique harmonieuse de voix &

---

[123] *Musique figuree* is thus defined in *Sol. sec.*, p. 132: "L'industrie de savoir
contre un suget raporter deus, trois, ou plusieurs voix harmonieusement."
[124] *Ibid.*, p. 132; my emphasis. Cf. Henri Weber, *La Création poétique en
France au seizieme siecle*, 2 vols. (1956), I, 149.
[125] *Ibid.*, p. 11, margin.
[126] *Ibid.*, p. 11; Tyard gives a number of striking examples, drawn from
ancient and modern times, of the power of music over the body and soul of the
listener (pp. 8, 154, and 113-117); see also Kathleen M. Hall, *Pontus de Tyard
and his* Discours philosophiques (Oxford, 1963), pp. 86-87.
[127] *Sol. sec.*, p. 150.

d'instrument, mais encores de celle harmonie des vertuz qui guide l'Ame à son bien souverein."[128]

In one respect, however, Solitaire refuses to follow Pythagoras and rejects the theory of the harmony of the celestial spheres as a "legere & frivole . . . opinion." It is Le Curieus, a third interlocutor in the dialogue, who takes it upon himself to present and defend this theory: "Il semble estre assez impertinent de nier, que ces Cieus, tournans d'un ordre tant certein, eslongnez en tant justes proporcions: ces Elemens, conjoins ensemble tant convenamment: & les Saisons, rechangees par une tant constante inconstance, ne soient simmetriez en quelque juste & raisonnable proporcion. Peut il estre, que des corps si grans, & si violens en leurs cours que les Cieus, fissent un continuel mouvement sans aucun son?"[129] But Solitaire will not be persuaded against the testimony of the senses: "Toute l'Academie ne pourroit, sans plus vives raisons, me faire croire, que les Cieus rendent aucun son, & que l'opinion ne soit moins que de bon jugement, de penser que nous soyons sours[130] aus plus grans sons, & aus moindres ayons l'ouïe si pronte."[131]

IX. Joachim du Bellay

When Du Bellay wrote in the *Deffence*, "Chante moy ces odes, incongnues encor' de la Muse francoyse, d'un luc bien accordé au son de la lyre greque et romaine,"[132] he was not thinking primarily about the desirability of an alliance of music and poetry, although his choice of words would seem to indicate this. As one may guess from the title of the chapter where this recommendation occurs, "Quelz genres de poëmes doit elire le poëte francoys," he was thinking about the kind of poetry which, in his view, ought to displace the genres that had hitherto prevailed. In his note on this

---

[128] *Ibid.*, p. 154.

[129] *Ibid.*, p. 135; pp. 139, 142, 145, 147 have other references to the harmony of the spheres. See *Hist. de la Pl.*, IV, 147 and n. 7; Hall, p. 85; Lapp, pp. 49-50.

[130] Believers in the theory of the harmony of the spheres held that habituation from birth to so constant a sound made it inaudible. See Aristotle's refutation in *De Caelo*, 290 b 12-291 a 26.

[131] *Sol. sec.*, p. 146.

[132] *Def.*, II, IV, pp. 208-209 [112-113].

passage Chamard clarifies Du Bellay's meaning: "Entendez: sur un luth qui s'accorde harmonieusement avec la lyre des anciens. Ce n'est qu'une simple figure, et du Bellay veut dire qu'il faut concevoir l'ode à la manière antique, comme une imitation de Pindare et d'Horace." As Kenneth J. Levy has explained: "[Du Bellay] ne cherchait pas querelle à l'air en tant que forme d'écriture musicale, mais à la poésie qu'il servait. Il proposait des fins plus nobles à cette écriture."[133] But the nobler ends of musical composition could be realized only in association with a nobler poetry.

Du Bellay must have thought highly of the value of such an association, as may be inferred from a sonnet to Nicolas Denisot:

> De trois fureurs la doulce poincte éveille
> La saincte erreur des plus divins esprits,
> Le docte vers, le pinçeau bien appris,
> Et des accords la doulceur nompareille.
>
> Chacun des trois d'une egale merveille
> Se faict sentir: l'esprit sent les escripts,
> Par le tableau le regard est surpris,
> Et par la voix est surprise l'oreille.
>
> Par ces deux la tu ravis jusq'aux cieulx,
> O Denisot, les espris & les yeulx,
> Mais si le tiers, que Musique lon nomme,
>
> Egal aux deux encores tu avois,
> Tu ravirois, non l'oreille de l'homme,
> Mais les lyons, les pierres & les boys.   [Cham., II, 287]

Du Bellay leaves no doubt that if Denisot's musical abilities equalled his talents as a poet and painter,[134] he would rival Orpheus himself. But as Chamard said of the exhortation in the *Deffence*, "Ce n'est qu'une simple figure," which tells us little about Du Bellay's interest in furthering the union of poetry and music. The same may be said of the many apostrophes to the lyre and other references to music scattered through the *Vers lyriques* and

[133] "Vaudeville, vers mesurés et airs de Cour," *MPSS*, p. 194.
[134] See Verdun L. Saulnier, *Du Bellay, l'homme et l'œuvre* (1951), p. 129.

the *Recueil de Poesie*,[135] both published in 1549 when the alliance of the two arts must have been one of the warmest subjects of discussion at Coqueret. Even when Du Bellay writes to Catherine de Médicis:

> Royne donques, ne refuse
> De l'humble & petite Muse
> Les vers que j'ay mariez
> A ma Lyre, qui accorde
> Leurs sons divers sur sa chorde
> A ta grandeur dediez.   [Cham., III, 87]

he almost certainly intends nothing more than a conventional metaphor.

One must interpret with caution the vows that Du Bellay made in the euphoric anticipation of the Italian voyage:

> Je me feray sçavant en la philosophie,
> En la mathematique & medicine aussi:
> Je me feray legiste, & d'un plus hault souci
> Apprendray les secrets de la theologie:
>
> Du lut & du pinceau j'esbateray ma vie,
> De l'escrime & du bal.

It is not easy to know how well the lute may have fared in competition with so many other disciplines, or indeed, how well any of them prospered. Not too well, if we may judge by the remaining verses of this sonnet:

> Je discourois ainsi,
> Et me vantois en moy d'apprendre tout cecy,
> Quand je changeay la France au sejour d'Italie.
>
> O beau discours humains! je suis venu si loing,
> Pour m'enrichir d'ennuy, de vieillesse & de soing,
> Et perdre en voyageant le meilleur de mon aage.
>
> Ainsi le marinier souvant pour tout tresor
> Rapporte des harencs en lieu de lingots d'or,
> Ayant fait, comme moy, un malheureux voyage. [Cham., II, 77]

---

[135] Cham., ed., III, 21, 46, 51, 60, 83, 93.

If it was true, as Claude Fauchet and others seemed to think, that poetry and music in the French Middle Ages enjoyed a relationship not entirely dissimilar to the one that flourished in ancient Greece, it would seem to follow from a study of the texts presented in the preceding pages that, after a period of several centuries in which Hellenic influence was in virtual eclipse, the rich aesthetic possibilities of the Greek alliance of the two arts began to be understood once again. The general movement toward this understanding did not follow a simple ascending line and could not result in anything that genuinely resembled the Hellenic prototype. But the two arts moved toward closer union in response to the increasing desire of a generation of humanist poets to reinstate the alliance as it had existed in ancient Greece. In the assessment of this movement it would be as unjust to underestimate the importance of the practical contribution made by Clément Marot and the musicians who composed the settings of his *Pseaumes,* as to overlook the significance of the theoretical contribution made by Pontus de Tyard in his effort to revitalize the Hellenic conception of the essential unity of these arts.

The Latin Poems of Giovanni Pico della Mirandola: A Supplementary Note

Giovanni Pico occupies an illustrious place in the civilization of Renaissance Italy, as has been recognized by his contemporaries and by subsequent centuries. His work spans a number of different fields and hence has attracted scholars of varied interests: literature and the humanistic studies, philosophy and theology, the sciences and Oriental studies.[1] We know from his correspondence and from other testimonies,[2] that he wrote also Italian and Latin poetry but he destroyed most of his verse, himself, and what remains is neither extensive nor very important. It certainly is not sufficient to secure for Pico an outstanding place in the history of Renaissance poetry; it merely adds an interesting facet to the

---

[1] *L'Opera e il pensiero di Giovanni Pico della Mirandola nella Storia dell' Umanesimo*, Convegno Internazionale (Mirandola, 15-18 Sept. 1963), ed. A. Rotondò, 2 vols. (Florence, 1965). My contribution to this congress, "Giovanni Pico della Mirandola and his Sources" (I, 35-133), contains a tentative list of manuscripts of Pico's writings (107-123) and a bibliography of editions (124-125) and of previous literature (125-133). Fundamental are the studies by E. Garin, *Giovanni Pico della Mirandola* (Florence, 1937); *La culture filosofica del Rinascimento italiano* (Florence, 1961); Pico, *De hominis dignitate, Heptaplus, De ente et uno, e Scritti vari* (ed. E. Garin, [Florence, 1942]), with a bibliography of editions and translations (pp. 89-99). See also G. Di Napoli, *Giovanni Pico della Mirandola e la problematica dottrinale del suo tempo* (Rome, 1965); S. da Valsanzibio "Le componenti dell'animo di Giovanni Pico della Mirandola," *Miscellanea Francescana* 65 (1965), 34-106; B. Kieszkowski, "Les rapports entre Elie del Medigo et Pic de la Mirandole," *Rinascimento* 15 (1964), 41-91; Ch. Wirszubski, "Giovanni Pico's Companion to Kabbalistic Symbolism," in *Studies in Mysticism and Religion, Presented to Gershom G. Scholem* (Jerusalem, 1967), pp. 353-362; and, "Giovanni Pico's Book of Job," *Journal of the Warburg and Courtauld Institutes* 32 (1969), 171-199.

[2] Giovanni Pico della Mirandola, *Carmina latina*, ed. W. Speyer (Leyden, 1964), pp. 12-19.

physiognomy of a man who attracts our attention for a number of other reasons.

Pico's Italian poems are scattered in a number of miscellaneous manuscripts, and most of them were published in the same year (1894)[3] by Ceretti and Dorez. The present state of our knowledge of Pico's Italian poems was summed up recently by Goldbrunner who was able to add another poem.[4] The sonnets must have circulated rather widely; I found one of them, without the author's name, in the commonplace book kept by Willibald Pirckheimer when he was a student at the University of Padua.[5]

Pico's Latin poems seem to have circulated less widely. One religious poem, entitled *Deprecatoria ad Deum*, was included in the printed edition published shortly after Pico's death by his nephew Giovanni Francesco,[6] and another written in praise of Girolamo Benivieni's poems was printed with the writings of Benivieni and eventually found its way into the Basel edition of Pico's works.[7] Bottiglioni added in 1913 three poems from a manuscript in the Laurenziana.[8] Then the fifth centenary of Pico's birth in 1963 brought unexpected additions. Wolfgang Speyer published in 1964 ten poems from a Vatican manuscript, which he tracked down with the help of a seventeenth-century copy now in Münster.[9] Without knowing of Speyer's work, I presented in 1963 to the Pico Congress in Mirandola the text of fifteen poems, including the same ten that were to be edited by Speyer, based on a

[3] Giovanni Pico della Mirandola, *Sonetti inediti*, ed. F. Ceretti (Mirandola, 1894); L. Dorez, "I sonnetti di Giovanni Pico della Mirandola," *Nuova Rassegna* II 2 (1894), 97-114.

[4] H. Goldbrunner, "Zu den Gedichten des jungen Pico della Mirandola," *Archiv für Kulturgeschichte* 49 (1967), 105-110. On pp. 109-110, he publishes a poem in Sestine from Vat. lat. 5225, vol. IV, f. 809v-810.

[5] British Museum, ms. Egerton 1926, f. 20. The first sonnet (inc. Quando nascesti amor) is usually attributed to Pico and appears in Ceretti's edition (p. 48).

[6] See Pico, ed. Garin, pp. 93-95, and the list of the poems below. Garin (ed., p. 7) and Bottiglioni (pp. 228-229) give only a part of this long poem.

[7] See the list of the poems below.

[8] G. Bottiglioni, *La lirica latina in Firenze nella 2.a metà del secolo XV* (Pisa, 1913), pp. 215 and 229-230, after Laur. 90 sup. 37.

[9] See above, n. 2. Speyer followed Vat. lat. 5225, vol. IV, f. 797-809 and Münster, Nordkirchen 29, f. 269-276v.

manuscript in Munich. Among the other five which I presented, the most important ones were two long poems preserved in a miscellaneous manuscript of the Folger Library. My edition was printed in the proceedings of the Congress in 1965.[10] I subsequently found one more poem which I am dedicating to James Hutton and which will appear at the end of this article (Appendix V). This brings the total number of Pico's Latin poems known today to nineteen.[11] Among them are two distichs (one has two versions), one tetrastich, one poem of six lines and one of ten. This leaves fourteen varying in length from eighteen to one hundred and twenty lines.

The fact that no less than ten poems have been published almost simultaneously by Speyer and myself from different manuscript sources makes it necessary to compare the two editions and to recollate the three chief manuscripts, to which for one poem (no. 5 in Speyer's edition) a fourth manuscript and Bottiglioni's text must be added. In doing so, I have utilized Leonard Grant's review of Speyer's edition, which contains several good conjectures,[12] and Agostino Sottili's review of both Speyer's and my editions, where a number of valuable observations and comparisons are made.[13] The appendices provide a description of all manuscripts known to contain Pico's Latin poems (Appendix II) and a collation of the ten poems as found in the manuscripts and modern editions (Appendix IV). The results of that collation may be summarized for our purpose as follows.

N (see Appendix II for descriptions and letter designation) is

---

[10] See *L'opera e il pensiero di Giovanni Pico della Mirandola* I (1965), 85-107. Poems 5-14 (pp. 90-104) correspond to the poems edited by Speyer. They are given from München CLM 485, f. 53v–66. Poems 1 and 2 (pp. 85-88) are given after Folger ms. V a 23, f. 300-301. I had seen Vat. lat. 5225 before I wrote my study (cf. *Iter Italicum* II [Leyden, 1967], p. 373), but my note was buried in my files.

[11] See the list of the poems below in Appendix III. One of the three poems given by Bottiglioni is substantially identical to one of the ten poems published by Speyer and myself. Not included in my count is the Parma poem, which I consider to be apocryphal, nor the Iesi distich, which is but a variant of a poem included in the collections edited by Speyer and me.

[12] W. Leonard Grant, *Renaissance News* XVIII (1965), 218-220.

[13] A. Sottili, *Romanische Forschungen* 78 (1966), 165-169.

clearly a copy of V and differs from it only in a number of errors. This relationship is attested by the marginal note in N as compared with the introductory note in V, as Speyer has shown. The testimony of N is valuable since it links its source (V) with Paulus Manutius; Speyer assures us that V is actually in the hand of this famous scholar, an assertion which I am in no position to doubt. The introductory note in V, substantially repeated in the margin of N, tells us that V was copied in Rome in 1562 from an older manuscript made available by Costanzo Landi. M is a collection of Latin poems by various writers put together by Lodovico Domenichi, at the request of Duke Cosimo, for Friedrich Fugger (who died as bishop of Regensburg in 1600) during the latter's visit to Florence. It contains a preface by Domenichi dated from Florence, 1560.[14] Since Domenichi was from Piacenza as was Costanzo Landi, I am glad to accept the suggestion made by Sottili and Goldbrunner[15] that M and V are derived from the same manuscript then belonging to Landi. This conclusion is confirmed by the condition of the text. In poem 5 (I follow Speyer's serial numbers) an entirely different tradition of the text is represented by L and followed in Bottiglioni's edition (b). I note numerous errors in L (lines 7, 8, 10, 11, 15, 27, 32, 37, 38, 39), and at least two author's variants distinguishing L from both M and V (the title, and line 12). Yet there are at least two passages, the second of them rightly noted by Speyer and Sottili, where a common error of M and V may be corrected with the help of L (lines 9 and 18). In at least two more passages the reading of M and V must be emended, although in this case no other manuscript source such as L has been available (1. 69 and 9. 63).

Given the relationship between M and V, none of their variants should go back to the author. There are notable variants in the titles, but it is conceivable that Manutius or Domenichi tampered with the titles in the way of additions or omissions. This means that in a few cases where none of the variants is obviously wrong (1. 92;

---

[14] Domenichi's letter was published by me in full (*L'opera e il Pensiero* I, 104-105).

[15] Sottili, p. 166; Goldbrunner, p. 106.

4. 22; 9. 73), we must decide in favor of one as the likely reading of the archetype.

A tabulation of the errors of the manuscripts leads to the following picture. N has fifteen individual errors, not counting the cases where it follows V: 1. 34, 56, 63, 94 (misled by a marginal note in V), 111, 115; 2. 18, 19, 27, 28; 3. 20; 5. 12, 16, 21; 8. 39. Not included are the cases where in N previous mistakes have been corrected.

V seems to be seven times in error when compared with M: 1. 53, 73, 85, 109; 4. 22; 6. 2; 9. 60. M has sixteen errors: 1. 30, 32, 42, 45, 58, 92, 112; 2. 13; 3. 10, 15; 4. 11; 7. 25, 28; 8. 58; 9. 62, 73. Thus V is the better manuscript, as might have been expected from its provenance, but in at least seven instances, M allows us to correct the text of V, without our recurring to other manuscripts or to conjecture.

These conclusions may now be applied to the actual text as it appears in the two editions by Speyer (s) and myself (k).

Both editions should be corrected in the following places:

> 1. 68 dissolvisse: *read* dissoluisse (suggested by Grant and Prete).
> 1. 76 dissolvenda: *read* dissoluenda (suggested by Grant and Prete).
> 3. 12 polo: *read* solo (suggested by Grant).
> 5. 9 autumni: *read* autumnus (Lb).
> 9. 52 illi: *read* illic (suggested by Grant).
> 9. 87 erat: *read* erit (suggested by Grant).

The text of s should be changed in the following instances:

> 1. 53 horroribus: *read* sororibus (M)
> 1. 73 in: *read* an (M)
> 1. 85 illa: *read* ullo (M)
> 1. 94 Tisyphone (V in marg., N): *read* Persephone (MV)
> 2. 27 haerebat (N): *read* haerebas (MV)
> 2. 28 sua (N): *read* tua (MV)
> 4. 22 fessa: *read* fusa (M)
> 6. 2 vehet: *read* vehat (M)
> 9. 60 schemate: *read* stemmate (M)

The text of k should be corrected as follows:

1 (5). 30 tenuis: *read* tenerae (V)
1 (5). 42 nexus: *read* carcer (V)
2 (6). 13 asse: *read* axe (V)
2 (6). 33 diis: *read* dis (V)
2 (6). 35 hisdem: *read* isdem (V)
3 (7). 10 insomnem: *read* insomni (V)
3 (7). 15 tunc: *read* dum (V)
4 (8). 11 illis: *read* illi (V)
5 (9). 18 furiat: *read* furiet (Lbs)
7 (11). 25 aversatur: *read* adversatur (V)
7 (11). 28 quot quassata: *read* quot quot quassa (V; M has quot
        quot quassata)
8 (12). 58 sunt: *read* sint (V)
9 (13). 62 amatae: *read* hamatae (V)
9 (13). 63 quam saepe: *read* qua saepe (MV)

After the completion of my previous study, I found one more
poem by Pico which will be given in Appendix V.[16] This poem
appears in two different manuscripts, one of which is the same
Vatican manuscript from which Speyer drew his ten poems.[17] The
poem escaped his attention since it appears in a different section
of a large miscellany, separated by nearly 200 folios from the other
ten poems, which are copied together as a group. The entire
manuscript including the later section presumably belonged to
Paulus Manutius, although I am not sure that the new poem was
copied by the same hand, considered to be that of Manutius
himself, that transcribed the other ten. The fact that the poem
appears in a different section of the manuscript suggests that it was
not copied from the same archetype as the other ten. Also the new

[16] I wish to thank Augusto Campana and Hermann Goldbrunner, who both
had seen the poem in the Vatican manuscript, and Wolfgang Speyer to whom
I had turned over the information, for leaving the publication of this poem to
me; I am also grateful to Eugenio Garin, to whom I had promised the poem
for *Rinascimento*, and who kindly released me from my promise, thus making
it possible for me to dedicate the edition to James Hutton.

[17] Vat. lat. 5225, vol. IV. The ten poems edited by Speyer appear on f. 798-
809 (with the introductory note on f. 797), and the new poem on f. 982-982v.

poem is not in the Munich manuscript of Domenichi, who presumably obtained the text of the other ten poems from the same
source as did Manutius. The new poem appears also in another
manuscript, which contains no other work of Pico, Treviso
Comunale 41. It is a collection of Latin poems by different authors,
and it probably was copied earlier in the sixteenth century.[18] The
two manuscripts of the new poem are clearly independent of each
other, but they may have a common archetype that was not an
autograph, for they have at least one common error (line 7
relictam). There are four errors in V (lines 10, 19 sime, 20, 21)
and two errors in T (lines 19 and 26). The text is thus in reasonably
good condition. Line 22 (fiunt) is somewhat harsh but I am not
sure it calls for an emendation.

I find Pico's Latin poems rather elegant and agreeable; they
can stand comparison with most of the better Latin verse of his
time, if not with that of Pontano or Poliziano or the most celebrated writers of the sixteenth century. Much of this poetry was a
conscious imitation of classical models, and the extent to which
Pico used metaphors, phrases, or entire lines from the Roman
poets would require much further study. It is not the duty of an
editor, I think, to exhaust this subject. However, the contribution
made to it by Speyer in his edition is useful; he certainly has
pointed out many lines reminiscent of Vergil (1. 43, 65, 96, 108;
4. 39; 6. 3, 4; 7. 7, 19), Propertius (1. 90; 3. title, 34; 4. 1, 50;
8. 60; 9. 8, 82), Ovid (1. 71; 3. 1, 30; 8. 4, 22, 30), Tibullus (8. 17,
and 52), Horace (5. 3; 9. 5), Lucan (2. 29; 7. 9-10), Maximianus
(1. 100; 4. 23-24), Lucretius (1. 107), Manilius (7. 2), Valerius
Flaccus (2. 35). Goldbrunner has pointed out an echo of Propertius
in the new poem (line 8),[19] and I am inclined to think that
Propertius was Pico's favorite model.[20]

A few conclusions may be drawn from the modest body of Latin

---

[18] Treviso, Biblioteca Comunale, cod. 41, f. 66-66v. I am indebted to
Roberto Zamprogna for a photostat of the two pages.

[19] Goldbrunner, p. 108.

[20] L'Opera e il Pensiero I, 50, where I cite a testimony of Beroaldus (Pico,
Opera [1572], p. 410):"hic [sc. Picus] post severiora studia in Propertii lec-
tione tanquam amœnissimo diversorio requiescere consuevit."

poems by Pico that has so far come to light. Pico does occupy a respectable place in the history of Neolatin poetry, and this place would probably be more conspicuous had he not destroyed the remainder of his poems. On account of his Latin poems, he occupies a more important place in the humanist movement to which he also belonged through his letters, his personal connections, his books and scholarly interests. The Latin poems, though mostly written during the early years of Pico's life and career, increase the share of humanist activities within his work, as compared with scholastic philosophy and theology and the other intellectual interests for which he is much better known. On the other hand, I should like to restate what I have said many times, that humanism, although an especially famous and distinguished element, constitutes nevertheless only one element in the broad area of Renaissance learning and literature. This view is not contradicted by the fact that Pico as well as many other scholars and writers of his time was active both in the *Studia humanitatis* and in other intellectual pursuits not normally thought to belong to the humanities.

APPENDICES

Appendix I.   Principal Editions

OPERA: Johannes Picus Mirandulanus, *Opera* (Basel, 1572), pp. 339-340. Joannis Pici Mirandulae deprecatoria ad Deum, inc. Alme Deus summa qui maiestate verendus.

BENIVIENI: *Opere di Hierony* [*mo*] *Benivieni* (Florence: Giunta, 1519), f. 69v–70. Elegia Johannis Pici Mirandulae adolescentis egregii ad Florentiam in laudem Hieronymi Benivenii eius civis, qui nuper adolescens et ipse Buccolicum carmen ediderat, inc. Laetor io Tyrrhena tibi Florentia, laetor. Cf. Garin, ed., p. 6, n. 2.

BOTTIGLIONI (b): Gino Bottiglioni, *La lirica latina in Firenze nella 2. a metà del secolo XV* (Pisa, 1913). P. 215: In Pygmeum, inc. Ingentes parvo versas sub pectore fastus. From Laur. 90 sup. 37, f. 62v. Pp. 228-229: In laudem Dei et pro oratione ad Deum facienda carmina domini Jo. Mirandulae, inc. Alme Deus summa qui maiestate verendus (gives only the first 10 and the last 10 lines of this long poem). From Naz. Pal. 52, pp. 178-180. Pp. 229-230: Ad

Petrum Medicem ode Pici qua et ipsum et iuvenes omnes ex temporum instabili vicissitudine ad virtutem exhortatur, inc. Nunc cancri octipedis brachia Cynthius. From Laur. 90 sup. 37, f. 129v–130. P. 230: Tetrastichon Pici ad Angelum Politianum, inc. Saepe tuas versu tentavi scribere laudes. From Laur. 90 sup. 37, f. 130v.

GARIN: G. Pico della Mirandola, *De hominis dignitate, Heptaplus, De ente et uno, e scritti vari,* ed. E. Garin (Florence, 1942), p. 7. Elegiaco carmine ad Deum deprecatoria, inc. Alme Deus, summa qui maiestate verendus (gives only the first 16 lines of this long poem).

SPEYER (s): Giovanni Pico della Mirandola, *Carmina Latina,* ed. W. Speyer (Leyden, 1964). Pp. 35-39, no. 1: Joannis Pici Mirandulae comitis carmina, inc. Si qua meis, ut lector erunt, errata libellis. Pp. 40-41, no. 2: Ad amicum excusatio quod amet, elegia secunda, inc. Quid me nequitiae damnas? quid dicis inertem. Pp. 42-43, no. 3: Conqueritur adversos sibi in amore deos, elegia tertia, inc. Ut furit Ogygii resonans trieterica Bacchi. Pp. 44-45, no. 4: De somniis ei amicam referentibus, inc. Nox est grata viris et nox est grata puellis. Pp. 46-47, no. 5: Ex temporum vicissitudine iuvenes ad virtutem adhortatur, inc. Nunc Cancri octipedis brachia Cynthius. P. 48, no. 6: Ad Jo. Franciscum nepotem, inc. Iam veluti e specula video, tua quale per aequor. Pp. 49-50, no. 7: Ad Deum deprecatio, ut bella tollat, quae per totam fremunt Italiam, inc. O pater, aeterno qui saecula volvis ab aevo. Pp. 51-53, no. 8: Ad Galeotum fratrem militantem quod, ut ille sub Marte, ita ipse sub Cupidine mereat, elegia quinta, inc. Castra licet teneant pictis fulgentia signis. Pp. 54-57, no. 9. Detestatur amores illustrium feminarum, elegia sexta, inc. O quisquis teneros, iuvenis, sectaris amores. P. 58, no. 10. Distichon, inc. Me vatem, si sum, fecit me Pleona: plectrum. The edition is based on Vat. lat. 5225, vol. IV, f. 797-809, and on its copy, ms. Nordkirchen 29, f. 269-276v of the Universitätsbibliothek in Münster.

KRISTELLER (k): P. O. Kristeller, "Giovanni Pico della Mirandola and his Sources," in *L'Opera e il Pensiero di Giovanni Pico della Mirandola nella Storia dell' Umanesimo,* Convegno Internazionale (Mirandola, 15-18 Settembre 1963), vol. I, *Relazioni* (Florence,

1965), 35-133. Pp. 85-87, no. 1: Joannis Pici Mirandulae, Martia conqueritur Pici discessum, qui ad exteras gentes ire parabat et studiis incumbere, inc. Ergo sollicito moriar confecta dolore. From ms. Folger V a 23, f. 300-300v. P. 88, no. 2: Joannes Picus ad Phyllida ut tandem ei facilem se praebeat, inc. Quid tibi saevitiae mecum est mea vita? Quid istam. From ms. Folger V a 23, f. 301. P. 89, no. 3: Joannes Mirandolensis prothonotarius Lodovico Pictorio, inc. Carmina Phoebee dictant tibi culta sorores. From Ferrara ms. I 396, f. 13v. P. 89, no. 4: Picus, inc. Tres uno servas, tres uno in corpore perdis. From Vat. lat. 2836, f. 7 and 11. Pp. 90-93, no. 5: Joannis Pici Mirandulae Concordiaeque Comotis carmina, inc. Si qua meis, ut lector erunt, errata libellis. From München, CLM 485, f. 53v-56. Pp. 93-94, no. 6: Ad amicum excusatio quod amet, inc. Quid me nequitiae damnas, quid dicis inertem. From München CLM 485, f. 56v-57v. P. 95, no. 7: Conqueritur adversos sibi in amore deos, inc. Ut furit Ogygii resonans trieterica Bacchi. From München CLM 485, f. 58-58v. Pp. 96-97, no. 8: De somniis ei amicam referentibus, inc. Nox est grata viris, et nox est grata puellis. From München CLM 485, f. 59-60. Pp. 97-98, no. 9: Ex temporis vicissitudine iuvenes ad virtutem cohortatur, inc. Nunc Cancri octipedis brachia Cynthius. From München CLM 485, f. 60-61. P. 98, no. 10: Ad Jo. Franciscum eius nepotem, inc. Iam veluti e specula video tua quale per aequor. From München CLM 485, f. 61v. P. 99, no. 11: Ad Deum deprecatio, inc. O pater, aeterno qui saecula volvis ab aevo. From München CLM 485, f. 61v–62v. Pp. 100-101, no. 12: Ad fratrem militantem, inc. Castra licet teneant pictis fulgentia signis. From München CLM 485, f. 62v–64. Pp. 101-104, no. 13: Detestatur amores illustrium foeminarum, inc. O quisquis teneros iuvenis sectaris amores. From München CLM 485, f. 64-66. P. 104, no. 14: Disticon, inc. Me vatem, si sum, fecit me Pleona: plectrum. From München CLM 485, f. 66. P. 104, no. 14 bis: (Distichon, variant version), inc. Me fecit vatem, si sum, Phillis mea, plectrum. From Iesi, Biblioteca Comunale, ms. Planetti s.n., formerly Annibaldi 274, f. 26. Pp. 106-107, no. 15: Versi di Giovanni Pico nell'origine sua, Come Manfredo sposo segretamente Euride, inc. Cesaris Euride Constanti filia furtim. From

Parma, Biblioteca Palatina, cod. Parm. 1198, f. 200. Probably apocryphal.

Appendix II.   Manuscripts

CHANTILLY, Musée Condé, cod. 102 (1938), cart. misc. s. XVI, f. 62v. Deprecatoria ad Deum, inc. Alme Deus. The volume was written in Rome in 1544 for Cardinal Georges d'Armagnac by F. Vidonius Britan(nus). Kristeller, *Pico*, p. 109. Institut de France, Musée Condé, Chantilly, *Le Cabinet des Livres, Manuscrits* I (Paris, 1900), 101-103. *Catalogue Général des Manuscrits des Bibliothèques Publiques de France, Bibliothèque de l'Institut, Musée Condé à Chantilly* (Paris, 1928), p. 19.

FERRARA, Biblioteca Comunale Ariostea, cod. I 396, cart. misc. s. XVI in., f. 13v. Lodovico Pictorio, inc. Carmina Phoebee. Kristeller, *Pico*, p. 110. Kristeller, *Iter Italicum* I (Leyden, 1963), p. 56. G. Antonelli, *Indice dei manoscritti della Civica Biblioteca di Ferrara* I (Ferrara, 1884), p. 191.

FIRENZE, Archivio di Stato, Carte Gianni, cod. 47, cart. misc. s. XV, f. 2v–3v. Elegy in praise of Girolamo Benivieni. Kristeller, *Pico*, p. 111. Kristeller, *Iter* I, p. 64.

FIRENZE, Biblioteca Marucelliana, cod. A 184, cart. misc., f. 8-9v (s. XV). Elegia ad Deum, inc. Alme Deus (damaged). Kristeller, *Pico*, p. 111. Kristeller, *Iter* I, p. 108.

FIRENZE (L), Biblioteca Medicea Laurenziana, cod. 90 sup. 37, cart. misc. s. XV ex., f. 62v (65v). In Pygmeum, inc. Ingentes parvo. f. 129v (132v)–130v (133v). Ad Petrum Med[icem] ode Pici que et ipsum et iuvenes omnes ex temporum instabili vicissitudine ad virtutem exortatur, inc. Nunc Cancri octipedis. f. 130v (133v). Tetrast[ichon] Pici ad Angelum Polit[ianum], inc. Saepe tuas versu. A. M. Bandinius, *Catalogus Codicum Latinorum Bibliothecae Mediceae Laurentianae* III (Florence, 1776), col. 537 and 546. Kristeller, *Pico*, p. 111. Garin, p. 6, n. 2. Photostats kindly supplied by Dott. Berta Maracchi.

FIRENZE, Biblioteca Medicea Laurenziana, cod. Acquisti e Doni 288, cart. misc. s. XV-XVI in., f. 1-2. Elegia ad Florentiam in laudem Hieronymi Benivenii. Kristeller, *Pico*, p. 111. Kristeller, *Iter* I, p. 102.

FIRENZE, Biblioteca Nazionale Centrale, cod. Pal. 52, cart. misc. s. XVI–XVII, pp. 178-180. In laudem Dei et pro oratione ad Deum facienda carmen, inc. Alme Deus. Kristeller, *Pico*, p. 112. *I codici palatini della R. Biblioteca Nazionale Centrale di Firenze* I (Rome, 1889), pp. 59-61. Garin, p. 6, n. 2; p. 54, n. 1.

FIRENZE, Biblioteca Riccardiana, cod. 2726, cart. misc. s. XVI in., f. 9-9v. Deprecatoria ad Deum, inc. Alme Deus. Kristeller, *Pico*, p. 113. Kristeller, *Iter* I, p. 222.

IESI, Biblioteca Comunale, Fondo Planettiano, cod. s.n. (formerly Annibaldi 274), cart. misc. s. XVI ex., f. 26. Epigram, inc. Me fecit vatem. Kristeller, *Pico*, p. 114. Kristeller, *Iter* I, p. 249.

LONDON, British Museum, ms. Additional 19050, cart. misc. s. XVI, f. 43-44v. Deprecatoria ad Deum, inc. Alme Deus. Kristeller, *Pico*, pp. 114-115. Garin, p. 54, n. 1. *Catalogue of Additions to the Manuscripts in the British Museum, 1848-53* (London, 1868), pp. 191-192.

MÜNCHEN (M), Bayerische Staatsbibliothek, Cod. Lat. Monac. 485, cart. misc. s. XVI (1560), f. 53v–56. Carmina, inc. Si qua meis. 56v–57v: Ad amicum excusatio quod amet, inc. Quid me nequitiae. 58-58v: Conqueritur adversos sibi in amore deos, inc. Ut fugit Ogygii. 59-60: De somniis ei amicam referentibus, inc. Nox est grata viris. 60-61: Ex tempor[um] vicissitudine iuvenes ad virtutem cohortatur, inc. Nunc Cancri octipedis. 61v: Ad Jo. Franciscum eius nepotem, inc. Iam veluti e specula. 61v–62v: Ad Deum deprecatio, inc. O pater aeterno. 62v–64: Ad fratrem militantem, inc. Castra licet. 64-66: Detestatur amores illustrium foeminarum, inc. O quisquis teneros. 66: Distichon, inc. Me vatem si sum. The manuscript was put together by Ludovico Domenichi for Friedrich Fugger, later bishop of Regensburg, as appears from the preface dated Florence, Quarto idus Julii MDLX. Kristeller, *Pico*, p. 116 (cf. pp. 90-105). *Catalogus codicum latinorum Bibliothecae Regiae Monacensis*, by C. Halm and others, vol. I, pt. 1 (Munich, 1868), pp. 100-101. 2d ed. (1892), pp. 136-137.

MÜNSTER (N), Universitätsbibliothek, cod. Nordkirchen 29, cart. misc. s. XVI–XVII, f. 269-276v (s. XVII). Joannis Pici Mirandulae Comitis Carmina. In the margin: Paulus Manutius ex vetusto exemplari Constantii Landi Complani comitis anno

MDLXII Romae descripta, cum caeteris suis miscellaneis manu exaratis Bibliothecae Vaticanae intulit. F. 269-270v: (first poem), inc. Si qua meis. 270v–271v: Ad amicum excusatio quod amet, Eleg. 2 da, inc. Quid me nequitiae damnas. 271v–272: Conqueritur adversos sibi in amore deos, Eleg. 3 tia, inc. Ut furit Ogygii. 272-272v: De somniis ei amicam referentibus, Elegia 4 ta, inc. Nox est grata viris. 273-273v: Ex temporum vicissitudine iuvenes ad virtutem adhortatur, Eleg. [sic], inc. Nunc Cancri octipedis. 273v: Ad Jo. Franciscum nepotem, inc. Jam veluti e specula. 273v-274: Ad Deum deprecatio ut bella tollat quae per totam fremunt Italiam, inc. O pater aeterno. 274-275: Ad Galeottum fratrem militantem quod ut ille sub Marte, ita ipse sub Cupidine mereat, Elegia 5 ta, inc. Castra licet teneant. 275-276v: Detestatur amores illustrium foeminarum, Elegia 6 ta, inc. O quisquis teneros. 276v. Distichon, inc. Me vatem, si sum. Speyer, p. 8. Bömer, "Handschriftenschätze Westfälischer Bibliotheken," *Zentralblatt für Bibliothekswesen* 26 (1909), 338-359, at p. 353.

NAPOLI, Biblioteca Nazionale, cod. XIII H 65, mbr. misc. s. XV, at the end. Elegy in praise of Girolamo Benivieni. Kristeller, *Pico*, p. 117. Kristeller, *Iter* I, p. 433.

OXFORD, Bodleian Library, cod. Rawlinson C 209 (Western ms. 12071), mbr. misc. s. XV, f. 30. Deprecatoria ad Deum, inc. Alme deus. Cf. Kristeller, *Pico*, p. 117. *Catalogi codicum manuscriptorum Bibliothecae Bodleianae Partis quintae fasciculus secundus* (Oxford, 1878), col. 96.

PARIS, Bibliothèque Nationale, cod. lat. 7858, mbr. misc. s. XV, f. 62-63. Deprecatoria ad Deum, inc. Alme Deus. With the coat of arms of Bishop Guillaume Briçonnet. Kristeller, *Pico*, p. 117. *Catalogus codicum manuscriptorum Bibliothecae Regiae* IV (Paris, 1744), p. 406. Information supplied by Emilie Boer and Tristano Bolelli.

PARMA, Biblioteca Palatina, cod. Parm. 1198, cart. misc. s. XVI ex.–XVII in., f. 200–200v. Versi di Giovanni Pico nell'origine sua come Manfredo sposo segretamente Euride, inc. Cesaris Euride Constanti filia furtim. The poem is of doubtful authenticity. Kristeller, *Pico*, p. 118. Kristeller, *Iter* II (1967), p. 48.

TREVISO (T), Biblioteca Comunale, cod. 41, cart. misc. s. XVI,

f. 66-66v. Jo. P. Mi., inc. Cur sic assiduo. Kristeller, *Iter* II, p. 196.
VATICANO, Città del, Biblioteca Apostolica Vaticana, cod. Vat.
lat. 2836, cart. misc. s. XVI in., f. 3 and 11. Pico, epigram, inc.
Tres uno servas. Kristeller, *Pico*, p. 119. Kristeller, *Iter* II, p. 353.
The ms. belonged to Angelo Colocci; cf. S. Lattès, "Recherches
sur la bibliothèque d'Angelo Colocci," *Mélanges d'archéologie et
d'histoire* 48 (1931), p. 342.
VATICANO (V), Città del, Biblioteca Apostolica Vaticana, cod.
Vat. lat. 5225, cart. misc. s. XVI, vol. IV, f. 797: Joannis Pici
Mirandulae Comitis Carmina. Ex vetusto exemplari descripta
cuius vir summo splendore ac summa virtute praeditus Constantius Landus Complani Comes mihi Romae benigne potestatem fecit.
MDLXII. f. 798-800v: Joannis Pici Mirandulae Comitis Carmina,
inc. Si qua meis. 800v–802: Ad amicum excusatio quod amet,
Eleg. 2 a, inc. Quid me nequitiae. 802-802v: Conqueritur adversos
sibi in amore deos, Eleg. 3 a, inc. Ut furit Ogygii. 802v–804: De
somniis ei amicam referentibus, Eleg. 4 a, inc. Nox est grata viris.
804-805: Ex temporum vicissitudine iuvenes ad virtutem adhortatur, inc. Nunc Cancri octipedis. 805: Ad Jo. Franciscum
nepotem, inc. Iam veluti e specula. 805-805v. Ad Deum deprecatio, ut bella tollat, quae per totam fremunt Italiam, inc. O pater
aeterno. 805v–807. Ad Galeotum fratrem militantem, quod ut ille
sub Marte, ita ipse sub Cupidine mereat, Eleg. 5 a, inc. Castra
licet teneant. 807-809: Detestatur amores illustrium foeminarum,
Eleg. 6 a, inc. O quisquis teneros. 809: Distichon, inc. Me vatem,
si sum. f. 982-982v: Joannis Pici Mirandule, inc. Cur sic assiduo.
Speyer, p. 9. Kristeller, *Iter* II, pp. 373 and 587.
VATICANO, Città del, Biblioteca Apostolica Vaticana, cod. Chigi
J IV 148, cart. misc. s. XV–XVI, f. 45-46v. Deprecatoria ad
Deum, inc. Alme Deus. Kristeller, *Iter* II, p. 482.
WASHINGTON, The Folger Shakespeare Library, ms. V a 23, cart.
misc. s. XVI, f. 300-300v. Joannis Pici Mirandulae, Martia
conqueritur Pici discessum, qui ad exteras gentes ire parabat et
studiis incumbere, inc. Ergo sollicito moriar. f. 301: Joannes Picus
ad Phyllida ut tandem ei facilem se praebeat, inc. Quid tibi
saevitiae. Kristeller, *Pico*, pp. 122-123.
WOLFENBÜTTEL, Herzog-August-Bibliothek, cod. 37.24 Aug. fol.,

cart. misc. s. XVI, f. 14v: Deprecatoria ad Deum, inc. Alme Deus. Kristeller, *Pico*, p. 123. Garin, p. 54, n. 1. O. von Heinemann, *Die Handschriften der Herzoglichen Bibliothek zu Wolfenbüttel*, Zweite Abtheilung, III (1898), 151, no. 2434.

Appendix III.   List of Pico's Latin Poems

1.   Alme Deus summa qui maiestate verendus. Deprecatoria ad Deum. Mss.: Chantilly 102; Firenze Maruc. A 184; Naz. Pal. 52 (In laudem Dei et pro oratione ad Deum facienda); Ricc. 2726; London British Museum Add. 19050; Oxford Rawlinson C 209; Paris Lat. 7858; Vat. Chigi J IV 148; Wolfenbüttel 37.24. Aug. fol. Editions: Pico, *Opera* (Venice, 1498), f. E IV–E IV verso; *Opera* (Basel, 1572), pp. 339-340. Probably in all other editions of Pico's *Opera* (as listed by Garin, pp. 89-90). With Baptista Pallavicinus, *De flenda cruce* (Vienna, 1511), cf. Panzer, IX 7.38. *Carmina illustrium poetarum Italorum* VII (Florence, 1720), 192–193. Many other editions listed by Garin, pp. 93-94. Garin, p. 7 (incomplete). Bottiglioni, pp. 228-229 (incomplete). 62 lines.

1*. Caesaris Euride Constanti filia furtim. Versi . . . nell'origine sua come Manfredo sposo segretamente Euride. Parma, Palatina, Parm. 1198. Kristeller, pp. 106-107, no. 15. 28 lines. Probably not authentic.

2.   Carmina Phoebee dictant tibi culta sorores. Lodovico Pictorio. Ferrara I 396. Kristeller, p. 89, no. 3. 10 lines.

3.   Castra licet teneant pictis fulgentia signis. Ad (Galeottum) fratrem militantem (quod, ut ille sub Marte, ita ipse sub Cupidine mereat). Mss.: München, CLM 485. Münster, Nordkirchen 29. Vat. lat. 5225 IV. Editions: Speyer, pp. 51-53, no. 8. Kristeller, pp. 100-101, no. 12. 60 lines.

4.   Cur sic assiduo corrumpis lumina fletu. Treviso 41. Vat. lat. 5225 IV. Unpublished (see below). 28 lines.

5.   Ergo sollicito moriar confecta dolore. Martia conqueritur Pici discessum, qui ad exteras gentes ire parabat et studiis incumbere. Washington, Folger V a 23. Kristeller, pp. 85-87, no. 1. 82 lines.

6.   Iam veluti e specula video tua quale per aequor. Ad Jo.

Franciscum [eius] nepotem. Mss.: München CLM 485. Münster, Nordkirchen 29. Vat. lat. 5225 IV. Editions: Speyer, p. 48, no. 6. Kristeller, p. 98, no. 10. 6 lines.

7. Ingentes parvo versas sub pectore fastus. In Pygmeum. Laur. 90 sup. 37. Bottiglioni, p. 215. 18 lines.

8. Laetor io Tyrrhena tibi Florentia, laetor. Elegia ad Florentiam in laudem Hieronymi Benivenii eius civis, qui nuper adolescens et ipse Buccolicum carmen ediderat. Mss.: Firenze, Archivio di Stato, Carte Gianni 47. Laur. Acquisti e Doni 288. Napoli, Biblioteca Nazionale, cod. XIII H 65. Editions: Benivieni, *Opere*, f. 69v-70. Pico, *Opera* (Basel, 1572), pp. 758-759. *Carmina illustrium poetarum Italorum* VII (Florence, 1720), 190-192. Other editions listed by Garin, p. 96. 54 lines.

9a Me fecit vatem, si sum, Phillis mea, plectrum. Iesi, ms. Planetti. Kristeller, p. 104, no. 14 bis. 2 lines.

9b Me vatem, si sum, fecit mea Pleona, plectrum. Distichon. München CLM 485; Münster Nordkirchen 29; Vat. lat. 5225 IV. Editions: Speyer, p. 58, no. 10. Kristeller, p. 104, no. 14. 2 lines.

10. Nox est grata viris, et nox est grata puellis. De somniis ei amicam referentibus. München CLM 485; Münster Nordkirchen 29; Vat. lat. 5225 IV. Speyer, pp. 44-45, no. 4. Kristeller, pp. 96-97, no. 8. 50 lines.

11. Nunc Cancri octipedis brachia Cynthius. Firenze, Laur. 90 sup. 37 (Ad Petrum Medicem Ode qua et ipsum et iuvenes omnes ex temporum instabili vicissitudine ad virtutem exhortatur). Ed. Bottiglioni, pp. 229-230. München CLM 485. Münster Nordkirchen 29; Vat. lat. 5225 IV. (Ex temporis vicissitudine iuvenes ad virtutem adhortatur). Speyer, pp. 46-47, no. 5. Kristeller, pp. 97-98, no. 9. 41 lines.

12. O pater, aeterno qui saecula volvis ab aevo. Ad Deum deprecatio (ut bella tollat, qiae per totam fremunt Italiam). München CLM 485; Münster Nordkirchen 29; Vat. lat. 5225 IV. Speyer, pp. 49-50, no. 7. Kristeller, p. 99, no. 11. 32 lines.

13. O quisquis teneros iuvenis sectaris amores. Detestatur amores

illustrium foeminarum. München CLM 485; Münster Nordkirchen 29; Vat. lat. 5225 IV. Speyer, pp. 54-57, no. 9.
Kristeller, pp. 101-104, no. 13. 90 lines.

14. Quid me nequitiae damnas, quid dicis inertem. Ad amicum
excusatio quod amet. München CLM 485; Münster Nordkirchen 29; Vat. lat. 5225 IV. Speyer, pp. 40-41, no. 2.
Kristeller, pp. 93-94, no. 6. 54 lines.

15. Quid tibi saevitiae mecum est mea vita, quid istam. Ad
Phyllida ut tandem ei facilem se praebeat. Washington
Folger V a 23. Kristeller, p. 88, no. 2. 34 lines.

16. Saepe tuas versu tentavi scribere laudes. Tetrastichon ad
Angelum Politianum. Laur. 90 sup. 37. Bottiglioni, p. 230.
4 lines.

17. Si qua meis, ut lector erunt, errata libellis. München CLM
485; Münster Nordkirchen 29; Vat. lat. 5225 IV. Speyer,
pp. 35-39, no. 1. Kristeller, pp. 90-93, no. 5. 120 lines.

18. Tres uno servas, tres uno in corpore perdis. Vat. lat. 2836.
Kristeller, p. 89, no. 4. 2 lines.

19. Ut furit Ogygii resonans trieterica Bacchi. Conqueritur
adversos sibi in amore deos. München CLM 485; Münster
Nordkirchen 29; Vat. lat. 5225 IV. Speyer, pp. 42-43, no. 3.
Kristeller, p. 95, no. 7. 34 lines.

Appendix IV. New Collation of the Ten Poems Published Independently by Speyer and Kristeller

(The numbering of the poems follows Speyer's edition)

L: Laur. 90 sup. 37, f. 129v–130 (as reported by Bottiglioni and
collated in photostat), containing only no. 5

M: München, CLM 485, f. 53v–66 (used by Kristeller, but
recollated in photostat)

N: Münster, ms. Nordkirchen 29, f. 269-276v (used by Speyer, but
recollated in microfilm)

V: Vat. lat. 5225, vol. IV, f. 797-809 (used by Speyer, but
recollated in microfilm)

b: Bottiglioni, pp. 229-230 (for no. 5 only)

s: ed. Speyer, pp. 35-58 (following N and V)

k: Kristeller, I, pp. 35-133, at pp. 90-104 (following M)

Grant: W. Leonard Grant, *Renaissance News* 18 (1965), 218-220 (reviewing Speyer)

Sottili: A. Sottili, *Romanische Forschungen* 78 (1966), 165-169 (reviewing Speyer and Kristeller)

Goldbrunner: H. Goldbrunner, "Zu den Gedichten des jungen Pico della Mirandola," *Archiv für Kulturgeschichte* 49 (1967), 105-110.

For the origin of M, see the letter of Lodovico Domenichi to Friedrich Fugger, dated Florence, Quarto idus Julii MDLX, in M, f. II (ed. k, pp. 104-105). V has the following note on f. 797: Joannis Pici Mirandulae Comitis. Ex vetusto exemplari descripta cuius vir summo splendore ac summa virtute praeditus Constantius Landus Complani Comes mihi Romae benigne potestatem fecit. MDLXII. Marginal note in N: Paulus Manutius ex vetusto exemplari Constantii Landi Complani Comitis anno MDLXII Romae descripta cum ceteris suis miscellaneis manu exaratis Bibliothecae Vaticanae intulit.

1. title	Joannis Pici Mirandulae Concordiaeque Comitis Carmina Mk: Concordiaeque *om.* NVs	
1. 30	tenerae NVs: tenue M: tenuis *male coniecit* k (*quam correctionem codici M attr.* Sottili)	
1. 32	inexperto NVsk: in experto M	
1. 34	mens MVsk: mons N	
1. 42	carcer NVs: nexus M (*quam lectionem debiliter defendit Sottili*): corpus coniecit k	
1. 45	contigerat NVsk: contingerat M	
1. 53	sororibus Mk: horroribus NVs	
1. 56	faticato MVsk: fatigato N	
1. 58	dicta NVsk: docta M	
1. 63	semper nobis MVsk: nobis semper N	

1. 68   dissolvisse: dissoluisse *proponunt Grant et Sesto Prete*

1. 69   quicquam MNV: quisquam *corr.* sk

1. 73   an Mk: in NVs

1. 76   dissolvenda: dissoluenda *proponunt Grant et Sesto Prete*

1. 83   possit ex possint *corr.* N

1. 85   ullo Mk: illa NVs

1. 91   regnum MVks: regnam N

1. 92   sitne NVs: sitve Mk

1. 94   Persephone MVk: Tisiphone *in marg.* V: Tisiphone Ns

1. 109   metitur MNks: meatur (?) V

1. 111   morsu Mks: morsu *ex* motu *corr.* V: motu N

1. 112   rodit NVsk: rodi M

1. 115   unquam MVsk: unque N

2. title   elegia 2a *add.* NVs

2. 5   fortia *ex* grandia *corr.* N

2. 13   axe NVs: asse Mk

2. 18   sanxerunt MVsk: sanxerant N

2. 19   sequor MVsk: sequar N

2. 27   haerebas MVk: haerebat Ns (*quam lectionem codici V attribuunt s et Sottili*)

2. 28   tua MVk: sua *ex* tua *corr.* N: sua s (*quam lectionem codici V attribuunt s et Sottili*)

2. 33   dis Vs: diis MNk

2. 35   isdem s: isdem *ex* eisdem *vel* hisdem *corr.* V: eisdem N: hisdem Mk

2. 48   tinxit *ex* finxit *corr.* N

3. title   elegia 3 a *add.* NVs

3. 1   furit *ex* fugit *corr.* M

3. 10   insomni NVs: insomnem Mk

3. 12   polo: solo *coni. Grant, quem sequitur Sottili*

3. 15   dum NVs: tunc Mk

3. 20   fuget MVsk: fugat N

3. 25   cera *ex* cara *corr.* N

4. title   elegia 4 a *add.* NVs

4. 11   illi NVs: illis Mk

4. 22   fusa Mk: fessa NVs

4. 35-38   *ordinem distichorum primo mutavit deinde correxit* N

5. title   adhortatur NVs: cohortatur Mk — elegia *del.* V, *add.* N.
           Ad Petrum Med[icem] ode Pici qua et ipsum et iuvenes
           omnes ex temporum instabili vicissitudine ad virtutem
           exortatur Lb

5. 2   flammifera *ex* flammiferam *corr.* N

5. 7   ocior MNVsk: ocio Lb

5. 8   pomiferum MNVsk: pro miserum Lb — frugiferam
           MNVskb: frugiferum L

5. 9   autumnus Lb: autumni MNVsk

5. 10   innumero MNVsk: *lac. exh.* Lb — sustinent MNVLsk:
           sustinet b

5. 11   musta MNVsk: musia Lb

5. 12   madidis MNVsk: madido Lb—quem MVLskb: quam
           N—pedibus parit MNVsk: pede parturit Lb

5. 15   gelu MNVsk: genu Lb

5. 16   silvas et Mk: Sylvas et VLsb: sylvascet N

5. 18   furiet Lbs: furiat MNVk

5. 19   Thressas s: tressas MNVLb: pressas *coni.* k

5. 21   tristior MVLskb: tristrior N

5. 22   fronte *in marg. add.* N

5. 27   dissimili vice MNVsk: dissimila voce Lb

5. 29   queis MNVsk: quis Lb—legibus MNVLsk: in legibus b

5. 32   fugit MNVskb: fugut [sic] L

5. 35   curvatasque MNVskb: curvatas que L

5. 37   in genis MNVsk: ingeniis Lb

5. 38   agite MNVsk: agre [?] L

5. 39   intereant MNVsk: *lac. exh.* Lb

5. 41   vere *ex* fore *corr.* N

6. title   eius *om.* NVs

6. 2   vehat Mk: vehet NVs

7. title   ut bella tollat, quae per totam fremunt Italiam, *add.* NVs

7. 8   *Emendatione opus esse putant Grant et Sottili.*

7. 25   adversatur NVs: aversatur Mk

7. 28   quot quot quassa NVs: quot quot quassata M: quot quassata *coni.* k

8. title   ad fratrem militantem Mk: ad Galeotum [Galeottum N] fratrem militantem quod, ut ille sub Marte, ita ipse sub Cupidine mereat, Elegia 5 a NVs

8. 2   Galeote Msk: Galeote *ex* Galeotte *corr.* V: Galeotte N

8. 21   fusus *ex* funus *corr.* N

8. 39   frater premit MVsk: frateremit (?) *ex correctione* N

8. 41   lambro *codd.*: Lambro s: ferro *coni.* k

8. 43   harundo MVsk: arundo N

8. 47   galeatus: Galeatus *ex* Galeattus *corr.* N

8. 49   quotiens: quoties N

8. 58   sint NVs: sunt Mk

9. title   elegia 6 a *add.* NVs

9. 17   rupit *ex* rumpit *corr.* M

9. 35   quotiens: quoties N

9. 41   percitus MN (*ex correctione*) Vsk: parcitus (?) *in V scriptum asserit* s

9. 52   illi: illic *coni.* Grant

9. 60   stemmate Mk: schemate NVs

9. 62   hamatae NVs: amatae Mk

9. 63   quae ... qua MNVs: quae ... quae in *M scriptum esse asserit* k: quae ... quam *coni.* k (*quam lectionem codici M attribuit Sottili*)

9. 64   placidis *corr.* k: placitis MNVs

9. 73   pavore Ns: *ex* pudore *corr.* V: timore Mk

9. 79   illus *post* primum ite *del.* M

9. 87   erat: erit *proponunt Grant et Sottili*

Appendix V. A new Poem

Joannis Pici Mirandule

Cur sic assiduo corrumpis lumina fletu?
   Cur furis in roseas ungue rigente genas?
Cur ita sollicitas vano tua corda dolore,
   O nunc et semper cura futura mei?

5 Me ne aura credis leviorem Pleona, me ne
      Vincere populeas mobilitate comas?
   Vivere tu credis me te potuisse relicta?
      Tu nostram credis iam cecidisse fidem?
   Falleris ah nimium mea spes, mea sola voluptas.
10   Exuvias nostri pectoris una tenes.
   Soli cessit honos, soli tibi nostra voluntas,
      Cor, animus, nostri quicquid et ante fuit.
   Non amor incerto noster pede vita vagatur:
      Quo cepit semper navigat ille freto.
15 Quin etiam crescit nostris crescentibus annis
      Cumque ipso augetur tempore nostra fides.
   Hanc tibi nympha dedi, tibi semper serviet uni
      Et cupio tantum posse placere tibi.
   Velat Agenoreo si me toga picta colore,
20   Si levis incessus, si mihi pexa coma est,
   Si nostri Assyriis sparguntur odoribus artus,
      Hec fiunt ut me Pleona sola probes.
   Tristia nec seve curo iam stamina Parce:
      Et tu Parca mea es et mea fila tenes.
25 Sola potes longos vitam producere in annos,
      Sola potes media fila secare via.
   Quare pone metus: nostri mea nympha fuisti
      Principium, nostri finis amoris eris.

Apparatus for the New Poem

T: Treviso, cod. 41, f. 66-66v
V: Vatican, Vat. lat. 5225, vol. IV, f. 982-982v

Title Joannis Pici Mirandule V: Jo.P.Mi. T
   7 te *ex* ne *corr.* V — relictam TV: *correxi*
   8 Cf. Prop. II 20. 4 (*Goldbrunner*)
  10 nostri T: num V
  11 Voluntas *ex* volumptas *corr.* V
  14 *lacunam cum rasura post* semper *exh.* T
  19 velat V: valeat T — si me T: sime V
  20 incessus T: in census V
  21 nostri T: nostris V
  22 fiunt: faciunt *mavult Sesto Prete*
  26 media . . . via V: mediam . . . viam T

On Two English Metamorphoses

WALTER MacKELLAR

In England in the late seventeenth and early eighteenth centuries, poems describing parks and estates, gardens and picturesque "prospects" from hill-tops, whatever pleasing scenes engaged a poet's fancy, became a fairly numerous species, which, with some debts to the pastoral tradition, may trace its ancestry to the *Georgics* of Virgil. But, as is notably true of James Thomson's *The Seasons*, which, despite all its descriptions, hardly belongs within the topographical tradition at all, these poems are often even more concerned with moral and philosophical reflections than with portraying landscapes, which serve only to suggest the reflections. Although, according to Joseph Warton, Pope considered a descriptive poem "as absurd as a feast made up of sauses,"[1] and not much reading of his poetry reveals that his superb talent did not lie in describing the world of external nature; nevertheless as a youth he composed *Windsor Forest*,[2] in which, however, he is primarily interested not so much in a topographical description of Windsor Forest, with which, from living there, he was well acquainted, as in using the description as a vehicle for a meditation on a life of retirement, on court life, on peace and plenty, on the blessings of the peace of Utrecht, and other themes. Although the poem has its felicities and Popean elegance—with some lapses—it is not likely to suggest that its author could produce such a masterpiece as *The*

[1] *An Essay on the Genius and Writings of Pope* (London, 1806), I. 49.
[2] Part of the poem, Pope said, was wriiten in 1704, when he was sixteen, in imitation of Denham's *Cooper's Hill*. In 1712, at the suggestion of Lord Lansdown, it was revised, and lines 291 to the end were added to honor the peace of Utrecht. It was published in 1713. See George Sherburn, *The Early Career of Alexander Pope* (Oxford, 1934), p. 101.

Rape of the Lock; for Pope is not wholly in sympathy with his subject, and the result is something of a hodge-podge.

After a generalized description of Windsor Forest, its groves comparable in beauty—if less renowned than those of Eden—and once frequented by Diana and her nymphs, its peace and plenty, and the sports and pastimes there pursued, all of which might equally well describe any one of many other scenes in England, Pope, at line 171, introduces the following episode of Lodona, one of the nymphs of Diana, who of old "in early dawn . . . traced the dewy lawn":

171   Above the rest a rural nymph was famed
        Thy offspring, Thames! the fair Lodona named
        (Lodona's fate, in long oblivion cast,
        The Muse shall sing, and what she sings shall last),
175   Scarce could the Goddess from her nymph be known
        But by the crescent and the golden zone.
        She scorn'd the praise of beauty, and the care;
        A belt her waist, a fillet binds her hair;
        A painted quiver on her shoulder sounds,
180   And with her dart the flying deer she wounds.
        It chanced as, eager of the chase, the maid
        Beyond the forest's verdant limits stray'd,
        Pan saw and lov'd, and, burning with desire,
        Pursued her flight; her flight increas'd his fire.
185   Not half so swift the trembling doves can fly,
        When the fierce eagle cleaves the liquid sky;
        Not half so swiftly the fierce eagle moves,
        When thro' the clouds he drives the trembling doves;
        As from the God she flew with furious pace,
190   Or as the God, more furious, urged the chase.
        Now fainting, sinking, pale, the Nymph appears:
        Now close behind, his sounding steps she hears;
        And now his shadow reach'd her as she run,
        His shadow lengthen'd by the setting sun;
195   And now his shorter breath, with sultry air,
        Pants on her neck, and fans her parting hair.
        In vain on Father Thames she calls for aid,
        Nor could Diana help her injur'd maid.

Faint, breathless, thus she pray'd, nor pray'd in vain:
200   "Ah, Cynthia! ah—tho' banish'd from thy train,
Let me, O let me, to the shades repair,
My native shades—there weep, and murmur there!"
She said, and melting as in tears she lay,
In a soft silver stream dissolv'd away.
205   The silver stream her virgin coldness keeps,
For ever murmurs, and for ever weeps;
Still bears the name the hapless virgin bore,
And bathes the forest where she ranged before.
In her chaste current oft the Goddess laves,
210   And with celestial tears augments the waves.
Oft in her glass the musing shepherd spies
The headlong mountains and the downward skies;
The wat'ry landscape of the pendent woods,
And absent trees that tremble in the floods;
215   In the clear azure gleam the flocks are seen,
And floating forests paint the waves with green;
Thro' the fair scene roll slow the ling'ring streams,
Then foaming pour along, and rush into the Thames.

This is Pope's fanciful account of the origin of the little river Loddon, and in introducing it as a narrative episode, he is diversifying his poem and adding action to otherwise static material. The device of introducing narratives in long poems on large general subjects was anything but new. Ovid, one of those from whom Pope may have learned it,[3] often effectively uses it in the *Ars Amatoria*, in which all the narrative episodes are *exempla* of the themes which he treats. The same is true of such episodes as the man lost in the snow in James Thomson's *Winter* (276-321) and that of Celadon and Amelia in *Summer* (1169-1282), with all their sentimental and moral appeal. And it is generally true that episodes of this kind are most fitting and effective when they are

---

[3] "When I was young," Pope said, "I was a vast admirer of Ovid. ... I translated above a quarter of the *Metamorphoses*" (Joseph Spence, *Observations, Anecdotes, and Characters*, ed. Edmund Malone [London, 1820], pp. 29, 49). His only published translations of Ovid, however, are *Sappho to Phaon* (*Her.* 15), *The Fable of Dryope* (*Met.* 9. 324-393), and *Vertumnus and Pomona* (*Met.* 14. 623-772).

clearly *exempla*, and thus integral parts of the poems which they are intended to embellish, and not merely excrescences. But the story of Lodona in not an *exemplum* of any of Pope's themes mentioned above, nor of anything else, unless it be chastity under attack. And unlike Thomson's characters, who are natives of the British countryside which he describes, Lodona, Diana and her nymphs, and Pan belong in Arcadia, not in any English landscape.

"The story of Lodona," writes Joseph Warton, "is prettily Ovidian; but there is scarcely an incident in it, but what is borrowed from some transformation of Ovid."[4] Dr. Johnson, who admitted that there are "variety and elegance" in *Windsor Forest*, also observed that "the desire of diversity may be too much indulged; the parts of *Windsor Forest* which deserve least praise are those which are added to enliven the stillness of the scene, the appearance of Father Thames and the transformation of Lodona. . . . The story of Lodona is told with sweetness; but a new metamorphosis is a ready and puerile expedient; nothing is easier than to tell how a flower was once a blooming virgin, and a rock an obdurate tyrant."[5] The best that Warton and Johnson can say for the story is very faint praise. Johnson is not objecting to a tale in a descriptive poem, but only to the undeniable triteness and perfunctoriness of this particular tale. And truly chaste maidens preserving their chastity at all costs are a much worn theme. Leslie Stephen, not always one of Pope's gentler critics, summarily dismisses the tale as "a silly episode,"[6] a judgment with which even an admirer of Pope can hardly disagree.

Pope's account of Lodona's adventure is clearly an adaptation of two of Ovid's stories in the *Metamorphoses*, both much too long to be quoted here, that of Daphne and Apollo (*Met.* 1. 452-567)[7] and that of Arethusa and Alpheus (*Met.* 5. 572-641), as Arethusa herself tells it to Ceres, in each of which, as in certain other of

[4] *Op. cit.* 1. 23.

[5] *Lives of the English Poets*, ed. G. B. Hill (Oxford, 1905), 3. 225.

[6] *Pope* (London, 1880), p. 31.

[7] Did Pope know the tradition that Daphne was the daughter of Ladon (Pausanias 9. 20. 1; Servius, *ad Aen.* 2. 513), not of Peneus (Ovid, *Met.* 1. 472; Hyginus, *Fab.* 203), and did the similarity of the names Ladon and Loddon suggest the imitation of Daphne's story?

Ovid's tales, a terrified nymph is pursued by a violently amorous god, from whose clutches she escapes only by being transformed, Daphne into a laurel tree, and Arethusa, like Lodona, into a stream of water. Pope's story closely follows the same pattern, and, as Warton remarks, adopts even incidental details from Ovid, and from Virgil he might have added.[8] But when Pope reaches the

[8] In the details of Pope's story there are the following debts to Ovid and Virgil:

175-176.   Scarce could the Goddess from her nymph be known.
Met. 1. 695-698.   ritu quoque cincta Dianae
          falleret, ut posset credi Latonia, si non
          corneus huic arcus, si non foret aureus illi;
          sic quoque fallebat.

178.   A belt her waist, a fillet binds her hair.
Met. 1. 477.   vitta coercebat positos sine lege capillos.
Met. 1. 497.   spectat inornatos collo pendere capillos.

179.   A painted quiver on her shoulder sounds.
Aen. 1. 500-501.   illa pharetram
          fert umero gradiensque deas supereminet omnis.
Aen. 9. 659-660.   agnovere deum proceres divinaque tela
          Dardanidae pharetramque fuga sensere sonantem.
Aen. 11. 652.   aureus ex umero sonat arcus et arma Dianae.

185-188.   Not half so swift the trembling doves can fly,
          When the fierce eagle cleaves the sky;
          Not half so swiftly the fierce eagle moves,
          When thro' the clouds he drives the trembling doves.
Met. 1. 506.   sic aquilam penna fugiunt trepidante columbae,
Met. 5. 605-606.   ut fugere accipitrem penna trepidante columbae
          ut solet accipiter trepidas urguere columbas.

192-194.   Now close behind, his sounding steps she hears;
          And now his shadow reach'd her as she run,
          His shadow lengthen'd by the setting sun.
Met. 5. 614-617.   sol erat a tergo; vidi praecedere longam
          ante pedes umbram, nisi si timor illa videbat;
          sed certe sonitusque pedum perrebat et ingens
          crinales vittas adflabat anhelitus oris.

199-202.   Faint, breathless, thus she pray'd, nor pray'd in vain:
          "Ah, Cynthia! ah—tho' banished from thy train,
          Let me, O let me, to the shades repair,
          My native shades—there weep and murmur there."
Met. 1. 543-547.   viribus absumptis expalluit illa citaeque
          victa labore fugae spectans Peneidas undas;
          "fer, pater," inquit, "opem! si flumina numen habetis,
          qua nimium placui, mutando perge figuram."

transformation of Lodona, he abandons his models. Daphne's change of form is thus depicted:

vix prece finita torpor gravis occupat artus,
mollia cinguntur tenui praecordia libro,
in frondem crines, in ramos bracchia crescunt,
pes modo tam velox pigris radicibus haeret,
ora cacumen habet; remanet nitor unus in illa.   [*Met.* 1. 548-552]

and thus Arethusa's:

occupat obsessos sudor mihi frigidus artus,
caeruleaeque cadunt toto de corpore guttae,
quaque pedem movi, manat lacus, eque capillis
ros cadit, et citius, quam nunc tibi facta renarro,
in latices mutor.   [*Met.* 5. 632-636]

These are not static but moving pictures of experiences horribly moving to Daphne and Arethusa, but moving also to the reader whose pity and fear for the hapless nymphs have already been aroused by the breathless urgency of Ovid's narrative, effected by the rapid tempo of his verse and his use of vivid historical present tenses.[9] And nothing could better convey a sense of Daphne's fate than the pathetic words, *remanet nitor unus in illa.* As Rolfe Humphries once said in a lecture, "Ovid does not tell us, he shows us." He knew that seeing a marvel taking place before one's eyes is always far more effective than merely hearing about it at second hand. Compared with Daphne and Arethusa, Lodona, by what at least for the reader is an instantaneous and unmoving change,

---

209-210.   In her chaste current oft the Goddess laves,
             And with celestial tears augments the waves.
Met. 1. 583-584.   Inachus unus abest imoque reconditus antro
             fletibus auget aquas.
   [9] Ovid merely reports metamorphoses when the preceding action is the more significant element of his narrative, but Brooks Otis is surely right in saying that he "delights in the detailed process of transformation" (*Ovid as an Epic Poet* [Cambridge, 1966], p. 261). Apuleius, possibly inspired by Ovid, evidently felt the same delight, for three times in *The Golden Ass* (3. 21, 24; 11. 13) he describes the process of transformation with even greater detail than is usual with Ovid.

dissolves into a river in the following commonplace couplet—
which is followed by fourteen other commonplace, otiose lines:

> She said, and melting as in tears she lay,
> In a soft silver stream dissolv'd away.

Pope is telling us, he is not showing us. Usually sensitive as he was
and skillful in creating poetic effects, he here misses the opportunity to be impressive.

Finally, of one of the prime qualities of Ovid's tales, namely
pathos, there is little if any in the tale of Lodona, which is almost
wholly lacking in Ovid's breathless urgency of the flight and
pursuit. Within the space which he allowed himself for the tale,
and he could not allow more without an imbalance in the poem,
the action cannot be sufficiently developed to achieve a pathetic
effect, if that were his intention. But since pathetic love affairs do
not seem to have strongly appealed to his poetical genius, he was
unfortunate in attempting to follow Ovid, to whose genius they
unquestionably did appeal, Ovid who could aptly say of himself:
Tiphys et Automedon dicar Amoris ego. (*A. A.* 1. 8)

As Ovid's stories bear witness, in telling them he is actuated by
and appeals to a love of the marvelous and the picturesque aspects
of life and the outer world, and using these elements he is a skillful
artist; but he lacks ethical and religious feeling, and his stories
accordingly are lacking in ethos and reverence; they are told for
their own sake, not with any of Virgil's and Horace's intention to
impart a lesson.[10] To impart a lesson, however, is the whole
purpose of the metamorphosis which Milton ever memorably
recounts in the tenth book of *Paradise Lost* (504-577).

Satan, after successfully tempting Adam and Eve to sin, and
dismissing Sin and Death to begin their deadly work on earth,
returns to hell to report his success. "Unmark't / In shew Plebeian
Angel militant" he passes through the midst of the fallen angels,
and making himself invisible sits a while on his throne in
Pandemonium; then with theatrical effect, to the amazement of
all beholders, he reveals himself in such tarnished glory as since

[10] See W. Y. Sellar, *Roman Poets of the Augustan Age: Horace and the Elegiac
Poets* (Oxford, 1899), pp. 350-351.

his fall is yet left to him. When the "Stygian throng" and the "great consulting Peers" have acclaimed him on his return, he delivers the report of his successful mission to earth, the dangers and difficulties of which he is careful not to minimize. His speech is a long rhetorical performance designed to enhance himself in the minds of his fellow rebels, and to cheer them in the desperate plight into which he has led them with the assurance that by his "adventure hard / With peril great achiev'd" they may escape from "this infernal Pit / Abominable" and "Now possess, / As Lords, a spacious World, to our native Heaven / Little inferiour." But all that he is boasting and exulting about is nothing but an act of spite, like his final, desperate attempt against Christ in *Paradise Regained*. God, as he well knows, is not to be reached by his madly desired revenge; but great romantic that he is, he refuses to accept what he knows to be fact; and so, powerless to injure God, he vents his malice and jealousy upon innocent, frail man who has not in the slightest way wronged him.

His long speech, discreditable to him like all the others that have preceded it, is a compound of gloating, boasting, false promises, and sneering. Especially does he sneer at the curse, mentioned almost as an unimportant afterthought, which God has pronounced upon him that Eve's "Seed shall bruise thy head, thou bruise his heel"; but in his literalmindedness, which can never penetrate the meaning of a metaphor, he completely fails to understand its tremendous significance.

His speech ended, he stands a while expecting a "universal shout and high applause," when "contrary he hears / On all sides from innumerable tongues / A dismal universal hiss, the sound / Of public scorn." At this he wondered

<blockquote>
but not long
Had leasure, wondring at himself now more;
His Visage drawn he felt to sharp and spare,
His Armes clung to his Ribs, his Leggs entwining
Each other, till supplanted down he fell
A monstrous Serpent on his Belly prone,
Reluctant, but in vaine; a greater power
Now rul'd him, punisht in the shape he sin'd,
</blockquote>

> According to his doom; he would have spoke,
> But hiss for hiss returnd with forked tongue
> To forked tongue, for now were all transform'd
> Alike, to Serpents all as accessories
> To his bold Riot; dreadful was the din
> Of hissing through the Hall, thick swarming now
> With complicated monsters.   [10. 509-523]

This description of Satan's transformation into a serpent is clearly reminiscent of that of Cadmus as Ovid gives it in *Met.* 4. 576-580, 586-589:

> dixit, et ut serpens in longam tenditur alvum
> durataeque cuti squamas increscere sentit
> nigraque caeruleis variari corpora guttis
> in pectusque cadit pronus, commissaque in unum
> paullatim tereti tenuantur acumine crura. . .
> ille quidem vult plura loqui, sed lingua repente
> in partes est fissa duas, nec verba volenti
> sufficiunt, quotiensque aliquos parat edere questus,
> sibilat.

The difference between these two transformations, however, is that Ovid's, though pathetic, has no meaning that points beyond itself, whereas Milton's is symbolic and bitterly ironic. Satan deliberately chose the form of a serpent for the temptation of Eve, but now against his will, ruled by a greater power, at the very moment when he expects a triumph, he, proud Satan, in the sight of his audience, ignominiously falls to the ground a writhing serpent; and once loquacious he now can only hiss. Thus outwardly he manifests his inward degradation, as do all his followers. In representing them as thus punished, Milton probably remembered the punishments of sinners in the *Inferno* of Dante, which are symbolic of the sins which they have committed.[11]

The meaning of the hissing of the serpents, or devils as they may now be called, and of Satan himself, except as it is antithetical to the music of the angels at the creation of the world in *Paradise*

---

[11] See, e.g., *Inf.* 24-25 where sinners are tormented by serpents.

Lost 7. 558-574, was not noticed until James Hutton pointed out[12] that it is the negation of all music, that is, music in the sense of the harmony of the soul, as Lorenzo uses it in *The Merchant of Venice* 5. 1. 83-88. The souls of Satan and the fallen angels, we are then to understand, are great discords in which passion rules and turns all morality upside down.

The following chaotic scene in the hall of hissing "complicated monsters" owes something to Lucan's account (9. 700-733) of the African serpents engendered by the blood that dropped from the Gorgon's head as Perseus carried it over Libya. But Merritt Hughes[13] is doubtless correct in observing that the representation of the fallen angels as transformed into serpents rests upon a belief which Jakob Boehme "interpreted religiously when he wrote that after 'the divine light went out of the Devils, they lost their beauteous form and Image and became like Serpents, Dragons, Wormes, and evill Beasts.' "[14]

After this scene Satan, "now Dragon grown," leads his audience of devils forth to "th' open field," where those who had not been in the hall were awaiting the triumphal appearance of "thir glorious Chief." But all they see is "a crowd / Of ugly Serpents," and to their horror into serpents they are themselves transformed; and their intended applause is turned to "exploding hiss, triumph to shame / Cast on themselves from thir own mouths." The symbolism here is too obvious to need explanation.

Nearby on the field stood a grove, which God, "to aggravate / Thir penance," has caused to spring up as they are being transformed. On the trees grows fair fruit like that which tempted Eve. The multitude of hungry and thirsty serpents climb the trees, eagerly pick the fruit and begin to eat; but the fair-seeming fruit is Dead Sea apples, often mentioned in Renaissance encyclopedias of science and traceable to Josephus, *B. J.* 4. 8. 4, and they chewed "bitter Ashes," which in disgust they spat from their mouths. But

---

[12] "Some English Poems in Praise of Music," *English Miscellany*, ed. M. Praz (Rome, 1957), 2. 59.

[13] *John Milton: Complete Poetry and Major Prose* (New York, 1957), p. 418.

[14] *A Description of the Three Principles of the Divine Essences*, tr. John Sparrow (London, 1648), p. 64.

Satan at the end of his speech had assured the devils—he called them Gods—that they were to "enter now into full bliss." The moral meaning of the symbolism is again transparently clear. Satan and his deluded followers have won only "joyless triumphals." And when last we see him, ages later, in *Paradise Regained*, in all his evil doing he has found no satisfaction, no moment of peace, no slightest happiness, but is still "rackt with deep despair," the fate of the self-damned.

Esoteric Symbolism

D. P. WALKER

This essay deals with symbols having a hidden meaning or meanings which can be grasped only by interpreters who have some special skill or fitness. I shall confine myself largely to verbal symbols, to ordinary language. My examples will mostly be taken from the sixteenth century, a period when esoteric language was much in favour, but when the principles behind its use were not often discussed. Among the many fields in which esoteric language was and is used, I shall concentrate on one where it has always been prevalent: religion. But I want first to mention some of these other fields, which may turn out to be relevant to religious esoteric language.

In military and diplomatic life one often conveys a hidden meaning by means of a code or cipher. This brings us to one basic distinction by which all esoteric language can be divided into two classes. A cipher may be so devised that either, as in most present-day ones, the enciphered text presents an apparently unintelligible series of letters, Class I, or, as in most of the methods proposed by Trithemius in the early sixteenth century,[1] the enciphered text reads like an ordinary message, but the clear is a quite different message, Class II. In more general terms: a meaning may be hidden, either by using obscure, difficult, apparently unintelligible language, but susceptible of only one correct interpretation, or by using language that conveys two or more meanings, the less evident of which is usually the more important. As examples of

---

[1] Joannes Trithemius, *Polygraphiae Libri Sex* (n.p., 1518); *Steganographia, hoc est, ars per occultam scripturam animi sui voluntatem absentibus aperiendi certa ...* (Darmstadt, 1606). Cf. D. P. Walker, *Spiritual and Demonic Magic* (London, 1958), pp. 86-90.

this distinction we could take Plato and Aristotle, as presented in Leone Ebreo's discussion of the question in his *Dialoghi d'Amore*.[2] Plato (Class II) conceals his secret truths by his myths (e.g. the cave in the *Republic*), whereas Aristotle (Class I) equally effectually conceals his by the extreme brevity and profundity of his language, which can be understood only by those intellectually fitted to do so. Ficino makes a similar contrast.[3] Plotinus was the first to unveil the religious truths which the Ancient Theologians had hidden by their mathematical symbols and poetic fables, but he did so with such "incredible brevity of words, richness of opinions and profundity of sense" that he needs Ficino's commentaries to be comprehensible. Or we could take our examples from the Bible: any parable is in Class II, and the beginning of the Gospel of St. John is in Class I.

A vast field of esoteric language of Class I is that of technical jargons, ranging from medicine to music, from logic to law. Here I want to make another distinction, applying also to Class II, which seems to me fundamental. Either the jargon may be used, or even devised, in order to be incomprehensible to all but the initiate, Class A; or it may just happen to be so, Class B. This distinction rests, of course, primarily on the intention of the

[2] Leone Ebreo, *Dialoghi d'Amore*, ed. S. Caramella (Bari, 1929), pp. 101-102 (the most ancient sages shut up the truth in both verse and fable): "Platone divino, volendo ampliare la scienza, levò da quella una serratura, quella del verso; ma non levò l'altra de la fabula: si ch'egli fu il primo che ruppe parte de la legge de la conservazione de la scienza; ma in tal modo la lassò chiusa col stile fabuloso, che bastò per la conservazione di quella. Aristotile, più audace e cupido d'ampliazione, con nuovo e proprio modo e stile nel dire, volse ancor levar la serratura de la fabula e rompere del tutto la legge conservativa, e parlò in stile scientifico in prosa le cose de la filosofia. E ben vero che usò si mirabil artificio nel dir tanto breve, tanto comprensivo e tanto di profonda significazione, che quel bastò per la conservazione de le scienze in luogo di verso e di fabula."

[3] Ficino, *Opera Omnia* (Basel, 1576), p. 1537 (*Prooemium* to his commentary on, and edition of Plotinus): "Veterum autem Theologorum mos erat, divina mysteria cum mathematicis numeris & figuris, tum poeticis figmentis obtegere: ne temerè cuilibet communia forent. Plotinus tandem his Theologiam velaminibus enudavit: primusque & solus, ut Porphyrius Proculusque testantur, arcana veterum divinitus penetravit. Sed ob incredibilem cum verborum brevitatem, tum sententiarum copiam, sensusque profunditatem, non translatione tantum linguae, sed commentariis indiget."

user, so that the same jargon might come into both classes. A doctor, as the pagan speaker in Bodin's *Heptaplomeres*[4] suggests, may use strange signs and abbreviations in his prescriptions merely to impress ignorant patients or to avoid being laughed at ("neque enim facilè carpimus, quae non capimus"), Class A; or, Class B, the doctor could reply that he uses them because they are the shortest and clearest way of conveying his instructions to the apothecary. But in many cases jargons or other forms of esoteric language belong fairly clearly to one or other class: most religious prophecies or oracles were not meant to be comprehensible to everybody, whereas most philosophers of the last two hundred years have tried to write as clearly as possible, however difficult many of their readers may find them.

Finally, before I come to religion, there is an important field of esoteric language, Class IA or IIA: various kinds of games— guessing games, in which players invent deliberately obscure symbolic expressions of which their opponents must guess the meaning (charades, riddles, anagrams, picture-messages), or games which involve expressing two meanings with one set of symbols (acrostics, enigmas, puns). I have called these important because I want to suggest that these games are closely allied to certain kinds of verse, music, and picture, and, more generally, that the delight in sheer ingenuity of expression, in difficulties overcome, which appears in a pure form in such games, is an important element in many forms of art, perhaps in all art (both from the artist's and the recipient's point of view), though its importance varies, I think, considerably at different periods.

There is a striking example of the connexion between games and verse in the dominant school of French poetry of the early Renaissance, the *Grands Rhétoriqueurs*, as they have been called,[5]

---

[4] Jean Bodin, *Colloquium Heptaplomeres*, ed. L. Noack (1857; repr., Stuttgart, 1966), p. 72: " . . . plerosque verborum obscuritatem sic affectare videmus, ut admirabilitatem sui efficiant, sic enim seplasiarii notis Graecis, Arabicis verbis et Gothicis litteris utuntur, ut medicinam faciant confusiorem, aut ne intelligentibus sui irridendi praebeant argumentum, neque enim facilè carpimus, quae non capimus."

[5] Cf. Henry Guy, *Histoire de la poésie française au XVIe siècle*, I, *L'Ecole des Rhétoriqueurs* (Paris, 1910).

First, there is the obvious connexion: they are very fond of acrostics, puzzle-poems, complicated puns, etc. Secondly, their attention is often concentrated on feats of technical ingenuity, especially on difficult rhyme schemes. Here poetry has plainly become a game of skill, both for the poet and his public. One can see similar tendencies in the music of this period, the vogue for contrapuntal patterns imperceptible even to the most attentive listener, and for ingenious canons, often written down in the form of puzzles.[6] Such poetry and music began to disappear by the middle of the sixteenth century, perhaps because, even as games, they defeated their own ends. It is a fine exercise of skill to write an acrostic which is also a good poem; but the game is too easy to be worth playing, if the poem need not even make sense.

If these suggestions about the connexion between games and some forms of art in the Renaissance are well founded, we have one simple, underlying motive for the widespread use of esoteric symbols and the wish to find them wherever possible, that is, the delight in skill, difficulty-value—but there are certainly many other motives as well.

Before leaving the subject of games, I want to give one more example of a poetic game involving hidden meanings, one which will take us into the field of religion. The last chapter of Rabelais' *Gargantua* consists of a longish poem, entitled *Enigme en Prophétie,*[7] and of comments on it by Gargantua and Frère Jean. This poem, probably by a contemporary of Rabelais', Mellin de Saint-Gelais, belongs to a recognized genre of poetic puzzles, described in Sebillet's *Art Poétique françoys* (1548),[8] in which something trivial is alluded to in mysterious, solemn language. In this case a game of tennis is described in the language of an apocalyptic prophecy of world-shaking catastrophes, followed by a blissful peace for those predestined to enjoy it. This was certainly the original poet's

---

[6] See, e.g., A. T. Davison and W. Apel, *Historical Anthology of Music* (Cambridge, Mass., 1947), pp. 72, 92.

[7] François Rabelais, *Gargantua*, ed. R. Calder and M. A. Screech (Geneva, 1970), Ch. LVI, pp. 306-314; cf. M. A. Screech, "The Sense of the 'Enigme en Prophétie'," *Bibliothèque d'Humanisme et Renaissance*, XVIII (1956), pp. 392-404.

[8] See Screech, p. 399.

intention.[9] Gargantua, however, interprets it as describing the
persecution of evangelical reformers and urging them to hold fast
to their faith. Frère Jean, a good-natured but far from intellectual
character, thinks it *is* about a game of tennis and is able to quote
many hints in the poem in favour of this interpretation. Here the
novel ends. What Rabelais is doing is to use the surface-meaning
of a text designed to convey a hidden meaning in order to make
evangelical propaganda.[10] His motives for using this ingenious
procedure were probably complex. First, he would have enjoyed
the ingenuity for itself—as a poet he belonged to the school of the
Rhétoriqueurs. Secondly, since he was writing probably just after
the great wave of persecutions in France, which began in the
autumn of 1534, he probably wanted to avoid his book or himself
being burnt as heretical—the harmless hidden meaning provided
quite a good escape-hole. Finally, I think he wished his message to
reach only those fitted to receive it, the elect, those predestined to
the kingdom of God. This use of double-meaning symbols as a
means of sorting out the sheep from the goats is an important and
ancient one in Christianity, and I shall return to it.

In terms of the distinctions I have suggested, Rabelais' enigma
belongs to Class IIA, i.e., it has more than one meaning, and the
important meaning (in this case, exceptionally, the surface-
meaning) is intended to reach only a restricted group of recipients.
I shall mostly be dealing with this class of esoteric religious
language. My main reason for concentrating on deliberately
veiling language is that in the Renaissance it was, I think, generally assumed that all language containing a hidden meaning was

---

[9] Rabelais has reinforced the apocalyptic tone of the original by adding two
lines at the beginning and ten at the end.

[10] There is a similar prophecy, in prose, by Cornelius Agrippa, published
by Paola Zambelli in "Umanesimo magico-astrologico e raggruppimenti
segreti nei platonici della preriforma," in *V Convegno Internazionale di Studi
Umanistici* (Padova, 1960), pp. 168-172. Agrippa gives two interpretations of
it: one as predicting apocalyptic disasters, one as describing people playing
cards and chess all night. Agrippa's prefatory epistle would lead one to suppose
that he is satirizing astrological predictions; but Rabelais also published
satirical almanachs against these.

If I am right, Trithemius was playing a similar double game in his *Steganographia* (see Walker, pp. 86-90).

intentionally obscure, designed to exclude the majority of hearers or readers.

There are some important exceptions to this statement. The tradition, for example, of negative theology, deriving from Pseudo-Dionysius, does suppose that all discourse about God, who is wholly transcendent, is necessarily always metaphorical and can only be a starting point for the meditations of the elect.[11] Or there is Cabalistic exegesis, which rests on the assumption that the words, and the letters in the words, of the Old Testament contain many meanings because they are of divine origin and have magical powers and affinities.[12] But what you do not find at this period, I think, is anything like the various modern theories which explain the multiplicity of more or less hidden meanings in some kinds of language, especially poetic and religious, not by the author's intentional obscurity, but by some aesthetic principle, such as the value of ambiguity in Empson, or the creative nature of language in Croce or Cassirer, or by the action of a Freudian or Jungian subconscious. Renaissance discussions of esoteric language, then, usually suppose that the hidden meaning could have been expressed quite clearly and adequately, and that the writer deliberately concealed it; the discussion sometimes, though not often, goes on to the obvious questions: why, for what reason, with what motives?

Ronsard, for example, states repeatedly that religious and philosophical truths must be veiled by a cloak of fable or myth—one must "bien déguiser la vérité des choses / D'un fabuleux manteau dont elles sont encloses,"[13] or again "envelopper la chose veritable . . . du voile d'une fable."[14] The mythical or allegorical symbol is plainly considered as something detachable from the hidden meaning—one could remove the fabulous veil and see the naked truth beneath. The main answer Ronsard gives, not very

[11] Cf. E. H. Gombrich, "*Icones Symbolicae*," *Journal of the Warburg and Courtauld Institutes*, XI (1948), 167-168.

[12] Cf. D. P. Walker, "The *Prisca Theologia* in France," *Journal of the Warburg and Courtauld Institutes*, XVII (1954), 229-232.

[13] Ronsard, *Hymne de l'Automne* (*Œuvres Complètes*, ed. Vaganay [Paris, 1923-1924], VI, 159).

[14] Ronsard, *Discours à Monsieur de Cheverny* (ed. Vaganay, IV, 444).

clearly, to the question Why? is that ignorant people would despise the naked truth, and that the half-transparent veil will entice such people to search out the truth beneath it.[15] What he means is, I think, that people tend to despise anything easily acquired, and that by making them work hard to discover the truth he will lead them to value it. We find the same idea in Bodin's discussion of esoteric language. After asserting that precious things lose their value if too easily obtained, the Jewish speaker in Bodin's dialogue justifies the obscurity of much of the Old Testament by recounting the fable of the father who bequeathed to his sons a treasure buried in his vineyard, but without telling them where; so, with great profit to our moral and religious development, we spend our lives hunting diligently for the treasures of truth buried in the Scriptures.[16] Of course the point of the fable is that the treasure is not really there—which may perhaps be what Bodin meant. This is probably at all times one of the most widespread motives for using esoteric language, namely, because one has nothing to say or something which, if clearly expressed, would be recognized as

---

[15] Ronsard, *Hymne de l'Hyver* (ed. Vaganay, VI, 171-172):

Puis afin que le peuple ignorant ne mesprise
La vérité precieuse apres l'avoir apprise,
D'un voile bien subtil (comme les peintres font
Aux tableaux animez) luy couvre [sc. la philosophie] tout le front,
Et laisse seulement tout au travers du voile
Paroistre ses rayons, comme une belle estoile,
Afin que le vulgaire ait desir de chercher
La couverte beauté dont il n'ose approcher.

Cf. Ronsard, *Abbregé de l'Art Poétique Françoys*, (ed. Vaganay, IV, 471): "Car la Poesie n'estoit au premier âge qu'une Theologie allegorique, pour faire entrer au cerveau des hommes grossiers par fables plaisantes et colorées les secrets qu'ils ne pouvoient comprendre, quand trop ouvertment on descouvroit la verité."

[16] Bodin, *Heptaplomeres*, p. 74: " . . . legistis eleganter fictam Aesopi fabulam, qua paterfamilias jam moriturus liberos consolatur, qui tametsi non magnas opes ac latifundia legaret, thesaurum tamen in vinea sua latere affirmabat, quo suam inopiam cumulate sublevarent. Mortuo patre liberi summo studio ac labore conquirentes, cum nusquam thesaurum reperirent, vineam paternam aliud agentes cultissimam ac noxiarum herbarum purgatissimam reddiderunt, unde proventus uberrimos collegerunt. Ita quoque si divina scripta studiose legamus ac lecta saepius meditemur, thesauros studioso incredibiles eruere licebit."

trivial or ridiculous—a motive which the pagan speaker in Bodin suggests as universal by the example of doctor's prescriptions, which I mentioned earlier.

One finds more convincing answers to the question: why veil the truth? in Leone Ebreo's discussion.[17] He begins by listing the layers of meaning which ancient poets expressed by their myths: literal (an historical event, by euhemerist interpretation), moral, allegorical (natural, celestial, theological), i.e. the traditional mediaeval scheme, and gives as an example a fivefold interpretation of the myth of Perseus and the Gorgon.

His justifications of fabulous veiling start with the familiar assertion that important truths ("la vera e profonda scienza") must be concealed from the vulgar; but he gives as a reason for this, not that the vulgar would despise them, but that they would corrupt and distort them, and thus eventually produce a universal corruption of the truth in all men—for the true doctrine "is constantly corrupted more and more by passing from one inept mind to another." And this Leone thinks has happened in his own day.[18] The ancients, by wrapping the kernel of truth in a husk of fable, enabled it to pass unchanged through many minds of various quality. The ignorant could enjoy merely the outer layer, the literal story, the more intelligent and virtuous the moral meaning as well, and the few sages could add to these the allegorical meanings.[19] Thus these fables became known to all kinds of

[17] Leone Ebreo, *Dialoghi d'Amore*, pp. 98 seq. Mersenne quotes the whole of this discussion in his *Observationes, et Emendationes ad Francisci Georgii Veneti Problemata*, cols. 3-6 (at the end of his *Quaestiones celeberrimae in Genesim* [Paris, 1623]).

[18] Leone Ebreo, pp. 99-100: " . . . perché stimavano essere odioso a la natura e a la divinità manifestare li suoi eccellenti segreti ad ogni uomo; e in questo hanno certamente avuto ragione, perché dichiarare troppo la vera e profonda scienza è commutare gli inabili di quella, nella cui mente ella si guasta e adultera, come fa il buon vino in tristo vaso. Del quale adulterio séguita universal corruzione de le dottrine appresso tutti gli uomini, e ognora si corrompe più, andando d'ingegno inabile in ingegno inabile. La qual infermità deriva da troppo manifestare le cose scientifiche; e al tempo nostro è fatta ...."

[19] Ibid., p. 101: " . . . perché con un medesimo cibo potessero dar mangiare a diversi convitati cose di diversi sapori: perché le menti basse possono solamente pigliare degli poemi l'istoria con l'ornamento del verso e la sua melodia; l'altre più elevate mangiano, oltr'a questo, del senso morale; e altre poi più

men, and when a nation passed through a period of cultural decline and intellectual traditions died out, as has happened with the Greeks, the fables, still containing their hidden though forgotten truths, would be preserved by the ignorant common people for posterity.[20]

Leone also gives some other purely rational motives for using this kind of esoteric language: brevity and compendiousness, mnemonic virtues, the power of fables to attract children and childlike people towards abstract truths.[21] These reasons for veiling religious and philosophical truths seem to me valid, but I doubt whether they have in fact been as important as less purely rational motives, those which derive first, from sheer expediency, and secondly, from the religion itself.

Motives of expediency will operate when members of a persecuted religious minority wish to communicate with each other or to proselytize. Plato, for example, according to some Church Fathers and Renaissance Platonists, disguised his true monotheistic, even trinitarian views, because he had learnt from the example of Socrates' death, due to imprudently unveiled talk about religious truth.[22] I have already cited Rabelais' use of a poetic enigma in *Gargantua*. The whole book is full of evangelical propaganda, as well as unorthodox opinions on other matters of practical importance—education, war, monasticism—and it is in the form of a popular prose romance about giants. In his

---

elevate posson mangiare, oltr'a questo, del cibo allegorico, non sol di filosofia naturale, come ancora d'astrologia e di teologia."

[20] Ibid.: " . . . essendo questi poemi così cibo comune ad ogni sorte d'uomini, è cagione d'essere perpetuato ne la mente de la multitudine che le cose molto difficili pochi son quegli che le gustino, e de li pochi presto si può perdere la memoria, occorrendo una età che facesse deviare gli uomini da la dottrina: secondo abbiamo veduto in alcune nazioni e religioni, come negli greci e negli arabi, i quali, essendo stati dottissimi, hanno quasi del tutto perso la scienza. . . . Il rimedio di questo pericolo è l'artifizio di mettere le scienze sotto li cantici fabulosi e istoriografi, che per la sua dilettazione e suavità del verso vanno e si conservano sempre in bocca del vulgo, d'uomini, di donne e di fanciulli."

[21] Ibid., pp. 100-101.

[22] See Walker (above, n. 12), pp. 242-243.

prologue[23] Rabelais very carefully *both* prepares suitable readers to look for hidden, serious meanings, *and* puts off unsuitable ones from looking for anything but a funny tale. He recalls Alcibiades' comparison of Socrates to the statues of Silenus which, when opened, showed within images of gods;[24] he asks his readers to break the bone of his book and suck out its "sustantificque mouelle"; and then, immediately, laughs at the idea that Homer or Ovid ever intended to put into their poems any of the allegorical meanings that commentators have found there. A simpler example of veiling for expediency is the correspondence between Saint-Cyran and Jansen, in which they used the mysterious code-word Pilmot to refer to a projected religious movement that was to be based on the latter's as yet unwritten book, the *Augustinus*[25]—a movement which succeeded in splitting the French Church in two for about a century.

There are several more properly religious motives for using esoteric language. Certain religious objects or names may be thought to have magical power, which must be kept secret because otherwise it might be misused. This is one reason for saying Adonai or Elohim instead of the tetragrammaton; Bodin and others complain of sorcerers' using this powerful name to evil ends.[26] Here should come two subjects which I am too ignorant to treat: alchemy and hieroglyphs. Finally, I want to discuss a specifically Christian reason for veiling the truth.

When discussing religious esoteric language, Renaissance thinkers often refer to Christ's teaching in parables, for example, Guy Lefèvre de la Boderie when describing the transmission of the Cabala,[27] or Valeriano in the dedication of his book on hieroglyphics.[28] Now when, after preaching the parable of the sower to

[23] Rabelais, *Gargantua*, pp. 9-18.

[24] Plato, *Symposium*, 215 A–B; Rabelais turns the statues into apothecary's boxes and paraphrases Erasmus' eulogy of Socrates (*Adagia*, III. III. 1).

[25] See N. Abercrombie, *The Origins of Jansenism* (Oxford, 1936), p. 163.

[26] See Walker (above, n. 12), pp. 232-233.

[27] Ibid., p. 222.

[28] Ioannes Pierius Valerianus, *Hieroglyphica, sive de sacris Aegyptiorum* (Basel, 1575), sig. a 4v: "In nova verò lege novoque instrumento cùm Assertor noster ait, Aperiam in parabolis os meum, & in aenigmate antiqua loquor, quid

a great multitude, Christ was asked by his disciples, "What might this parable be?", he answered, in Luke: "Unto you it is given to know the mysteries of the kingdom of God, but to others in parables; that seeing they might not see, and hearing they might not understand."[29] In Mark, He adds: "lest at any time they should be converted, and their sins should be forgiven them."[30] And in Matthew, He quotes openly from Isaiah: (the Lord) "Make the heart of this people fat, and make their ears heavy, and shut their eyes; lest they see with their eyes, and hear with their ears, and understand with their hearts, and convert, and be healed."[31] Then, in all three versions, Christ explains the parable to His disciples. These answers of Christ, coupled with the parable itself and St. Paul's references to the Isaiah passage,[32] indicate that the purpose of preaching in parables is to communicate a secret to a few and to keep it from a majority, to sift out the wheat from the chaff, the elect from the reprobate, and in particular to blind the carnally-minded Jews by means of the "letter that killeth."[33]

I have suggested that this was one of Rabelais' motives in using the apocalyptic enigma. It is a motive which Pascal applies as a general principle to the whole Christian revelation:

The prophecies, the miracles even and the proofs of our religion are not of such a nature that one can say that they are absolutely convincing. But they are also convincing in such a way that one cannot say that it is unreasonable to believe them. Thus there is both evidence and obscurity, in order to enlighten some men and darken others. But the evidence is such that it surpasses, or at least equals, the contrary evidence; so that it cannot be reason that leads one not

---

aliud sibi vult, quàm hieroglyphicè sermonem faciam, & allegoricè vetusta rerum proferam monumenta? Et illud, Iesus in Parabolis loquebatur ad turbas, nonne sermones suos arcano quasi velamine quodam contegebat?" Cf. Boccaccio, *Genealogie Deorum Gentilium Libri*, XIV, xviii (ed. V. Romano [Bari, 1951], p. 737).

[29] Luke, VIII, 10.
[30] Mark, IV, 11-12.
[31] Matthew, XIII, 11-15; Isaiah, VI, 10.
[32] Acts, XXVIII, 26-27; Romans, XI, 8.
[33] II Corinthians, III, 6.

to follow it; and therefore it can only be concupiscence and evilness of heart. And by this means there is enough evidence to condemn, and not enough to convince.[34]

That is to say, the revealed truth is hidden to a nicely adjusted degree, so that its acceptance or rejection may be determined, not by the reasoning or the intelligence, but by the moral state of the recipient. In Pascal's theology, of course, the acceptance of the revelation can only be brought about by Grace, not by any good moral condition; but its rejection *is* caused by moral corruption, at least as a secondary cause, the primary cause being God's reprobation.

God could have manifested Himself so clearly that even the most corrupt would have been converted;[35] but His justice demanded that the revelation be half hidden by a veil that would blind the reprobate but not the elect. Not only the Scripture, but the whole world "shows neither a total absence, nor a manifest presence of divinity, but the presence of a God who is hiding Himself. Everything bears this character."[36] Pascal does not directly mention the parables, and he is thinking primarily of Old Testament messianic prophecies. He compares the Old Testament to a letter written in a Trithemian cipher with two meanings:

an important letter in which one can find a clear meaning, and in which it is said nevertheless that its meaning is veiled and obscured,

[34] Pascal, *Pensées* (ed. Léon Brunschvicg), No. 564: "Les prophéties, les miracles mêmes et les preuves de notre religion ne sont pas de telle nature qu'on puisse dire qu'ils sont absolument convaincants. Mais ils le sont aussi de telle sorte qu'on ne peut dire que ce soit être sans raison que de les croire. Ainsi il y a de l'évidence et de l'obscurité, pour éclairer les uns et obscurcir les autres. Mais l'évidence est telle qu'elle surpasse, ou égale pour le moins, l'évidence du contraire; de sorte que ce n'est pas la raison qui puisse déterminer à ne la pas suivre; et ainsi ce ne peut être que la concupiscence et la malice du cœur. Et par ce moyen il y a assez d'évidence pour condamner, et non assez pour convaincre." (Translations from Pascal are my own.)

[35] *Pensées*, No. 430, near the end: "S'il [sc. Dieu] eût voulu surmonter l'obstination des plus endurcis, il l'eût pu, en se découvrant si manifestement à eux qu'ils n'eussent pu douter de la vérité de son essence."

[36] Ibid., No. 556, near the end: "Ce qui y [sc. le monde] parait ne marque ni une exclusion totale, ni une présence manifeste de divinité, mais la présence d'un Dieu qui se cache. Tout porte ce caractère."

that it is hidden in such a way that one will see this letter without seeing it and understand it without understanding it.[37]

—a clear reference to the Isaiah passage quoted by Christ to explain His reasons for preaching in parables.

One of God's purposes in using this kind of cipher is similar to one of Leone's reasons for veiling truth with fables: in order that the prophecies might be faithfully transmitted by unsuspect witnesses, namely, the Jews, who misunderstood them and therefore would not accept Christ as Messiah—"If the Jews had all been converted by Jesus Christ, we should have been left with only suspect witnesses."[38]

In the same Augustinian tradition of unmitigated predestinationism as Pascal, there were some theologians who did interpret Christ's words about the parable of the Sower as I have done. Calvin, in his commentaries on the synoptic Gospels, accepts without hesitation that Christ is in this case using parables mainly in order that the reprobate may *not* understand Him:

Since Christ deliberately gave out his teaching in such a way that it profited only a few, being firmly implanted in their minds, but kept others uncertain and perplexed, it follows that the doctrine of salvation is presented by God to men not for one purpose only, but is adjusted with admirable skill so that it is no less a savour of death unto death for the reprobate than a savour of life unto life for the elect.[39]

Calvin assumes, I think, that all present, except the disciples, were reprobate. Some other, more liberal Protestant commentators,

[37] Ibid., No. 678: "une lettre importante où l'on trouve un sens clair, et où il est dit néanmoins que le sens en est voilé et obscurci, qu'il est caché en sorte qu'on verra cette lettre sans la voir et qu'on l'entendra sans l'entendre."

[38] Ibid., No. 750: "Si les Juifs eussent été tous convertis par Jésus-Christ, nous n'aurions plus que des témoins suspects."

[39] Calvin, *In Novum Testamentum Commentarii* (Braunschweig, 1891), pp. 524-525 (on Matthew, XIII, 1-17): "Iam quum suam doctrinam consulto ita dispensaverit Christus, ut paucis tantum prodesset solide eorum animis infixa, alios vero suspensos teneret ac perplexos, sequitur non unum in finem divinitus hominibus proferri salutis doctrinam, sed admirabili consilio sic temperari, ut non minus odor sit mortis in mortem reprobis quam electis odor vivificus (II Corinthians, II, 16)."

Pellicanus,[40] for example, suppose there were also "not a few elect among the crowd," who were stimulated by the obscurity of the parables to further investigation and eventual salvation; the reprobate would have rejected the plain truth anyway. And most Catholic commentators, from the Fathers onwards, go to great lengths to avoid supposing that Christ's main purpose in using parables was to blind the reprobate.[41] The Jesuit theologian Maldonat, following Chrysostom, suggests that Christ knew the Jews would reject the plain truth, as they had rejected His miracles, and wished therefore to excite their curiosity by presenting them with things "which they did not understand, but which they realized, however, had some portentous meaning."[42] Lefèvre D'Etaples, with characteristic kindliness, supposes that, since the Jews would have rejected, and later did reject, the clear statement of Christ's being the Son of God, He announced the kingdom of heaven enigmatically so that their guilt might be less.[43]

[40] Conrad Pellicanus, *Commentaria Bibliorum*, VI (Zurich [Tiguri], 1546), f. 42 (on Matthew, XIII): "Non omnia autem locutus est eis in parabolis, sed multa. . . . Perspicua ergo miscet obscuris, ut per ea quae intelligunt provocentur ad eorum notitiam quae non intelligunt. . . . Illi quae sunt manifestissima nolunt intelligere; ego [sc. Jesus] tenebris involvo sermonem, ut vel sic provocem ad discendi vestigandique studium. . . . Aderant sanè in turbis illis quidam reprobi, nullas ad audiendum aures habentes, quibus ad convincendam ipsorum impietatem, veritatem praedicari quidem oportebat, quam licet agnoscant, non tamen per eam persuadeantur. Non tamen deerant nec pauci in turba electi, qui per parabolas illas saltem aliquid erudiebantur, ac omnino ad hoc apparabantur, ut scilicet suo tempore etiam ipsi mysterium dei agnoscerent."

[41] For example, Thomas Aquinas, *Expositio continua super quatuor Evangelistas*, ed. J. Nicolai (Würzburg [Herbiboli], 1704), pp. 151-154 (on Matthew, XIII, quoting Chrysostom, Jerome and Augustine).

[42] Joannes Maldonatus, *Commentarii in quatuor Evangelistas* (Pont-à-Mousson [Mussiponti], 1596), cols. 306-309 (on Matthew, XIII: Christ, referring to His miracles): "In poenam ergo incredulitatis obscurè illis loquitur. . . . Excitatur enim auditorum studium, & inquirendi diligentia, cum ea audiunt, quae non intelligunt, & habere tamen magnarum rerum significationem animadvertunt. Ita fit, ut poena illis in emendationem evadat, nisi poena ipsi abutantur. Huius loci si qua erat difficultas, explanata est." (On Mark IV, 12: Christ): "non in perpetuum, sed ad tempus clausit illis salutis januam, ut pulsarent, qui, cum aperta esset, ingredi noluerunt. Nitimur enim in vetitum. Noluit tunc malè converti, ut, cum se derelictos viderent, meliùs converterentur."

[43] Jacobus Faber Stapulensis, *Commentarii in quatuor Evangelia* (Basel, 1523),

Finally I would like to suggest that in the history of any revealed religion the question of esoteric, disguised language is likely to be of cardinal importance, for this reason: if the revelation were utterly clear and convincing, then there would be only one religion and everybody would be bound to believe in it; since there have always been several competing religions and at least some unbelievers, the revelation must in every case be supposed to be to some degree obscure, in order to account for this fact. If, as with some kinds of Christianity, such as Pascal's, the reasons for this obscurity can be built into the religion's theology, this is a great advantage when trying to convert intellectual, sophisticated unbelievers, as Pascal was.

f. 6ov, (on Matthew, xiii): " . . . nam si aperte eis dixisset: ego sum filius dei. . . id multo minus audire voluissent, quam parabolam. . . . Expediebat ergo populo, Scribis, & Phariseis ad ipsorum minorem damnationem, & ad electorum illuminationem, ut dominus loqueretur eis in parabolis."

Index

Poetry and Poetics from
Ancient Greece to the Renaissance

Designed by R. E. Rosenbaum.
Composed by The St. Catherine Press, Ltd.
in 11 point Baskerville monotype, 2 points leaded,
with display lines in Baskerville monotype.
Printed offset by Thomson-Shore, Inc.
Bound by John Dekker and Sons, Inc.
in Joanna Linen Finish book cloth
and stamped in All Purpose gold foil.